P9-CCI-700

# A LOVE IN SHADOW

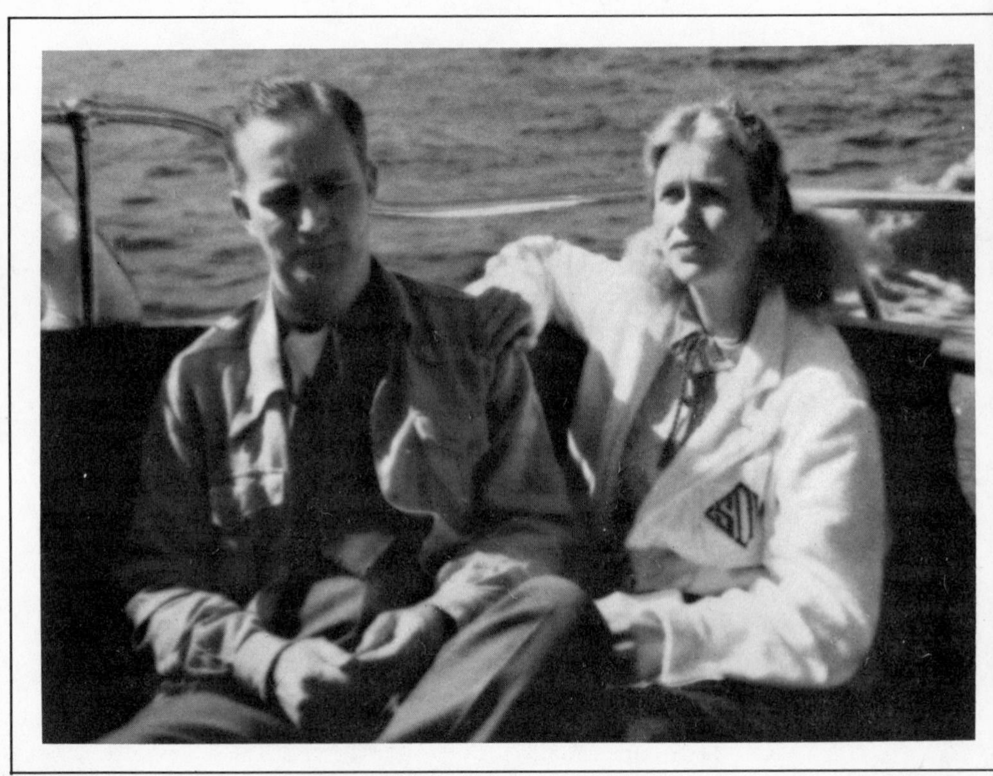

NEW YOR

# *A Love in Shadow*

*By* JOHN R. BOETTIGER

· W · NORTON & COMPANY · INC ·

 Published simultaneously in Canada by George J. McLeod Limited, Toronto. Printed in the United States of America.

This book is typeset in photocomposition Caledonia with Garamond display. Manufacturing is by The Maple-Vail Book Manufacturing Group. Book design is by Marjorie J. Flock.



Library of Congress Cataloging in Publication Data
Boettiger, John R
A love in shadow.
1. Roosevelt family. 2. Roosevelt, Anna Eleanor, 1906–1975. 3. Boettiger, John, 1900–1950. I. Title.
E807.1.R33B63 1978 973.917'092'2 [B] 78-6106

ISBN 0-393-07530-3

2 3 4 5 6 7 8 9 0

*For my children*

*Adam and Sara*

*Joshua and Paul*

*with love*

# Contents

*Contents*

# *Illustrations*

## *Illustrations*

# *Foreword*

I SET out, in these pages, to portray my parents' marriage. In doing so, I was drawn inevitably to the stories of their families—their parents and grandparents, their own experiences of childhood. For those are the stories of the enduring patterns in their lives, a prelude without which an account of their marriage could not be clearly told.

Since a good deal of Part I—on the Roosevelts and my mother Anna's life among them—is offered in and drawn from her own words, I want to convey my sense of her reliability. Many who knew her in other contexts have confirmed my experience of her honesty and careful observation, and her reflectiveness. Her lifelong difficulty and reticence in writing publicly of her parents and family, her constraining sense of responsibility to historical truth, her anger with those within and without the family who played faster and looser with the facts (in haste or in their own interests), were well known to those close to her. Of course, her perceptions, like all of ours, were shaped by her wishes and fears; but her fundamental inclination to the truth helps to locate more reliably the edges and limits of her vision. And when that is said, the fact is that she characteristically saw with unusual sensitivity and clarity.

The Roosevelts are a family about whom a great deal has been written, and a family replete for generations with a sense of its own historical significance. My mother herself, in fragmentary and largely unpublished form, left many notes of her experience of her parents and the events of her childhood and youth. My task in researching and writing about my father's life and family history was of a substantially different order, and the style and content of the story told necessarily reflects those differences. There is, among my father's family, no comparable tradition of historical significance, no biographies or autobiographies, no great repositories of papers and memorabilia; indeed, no single instance of self-reflectiveness of the kind so revealingly found in my mother's and her mother's writing. My father died when I was eleven, and I saw in the following years little of his family, so I had virtually no access to an oral tradition or even occasional stories. When I wrote the first preliminary draft of Part II in the summer of 1976, I did not even know the name nor had I seen a picture of my father's mother, much less anything of her life or his with her.

So I have traveled and corresponded at some length in search of John Boettiger and his family, and considering where I began it has been a remarkably rewarding forage. All but one of his siblings are still alive and vigorous, all had the grace to retire within a short distance of one another in southern California (eloquent testimony to the family's cohesiveness), and all were wonderfully responsive to my inquiries. I spent several rewarding days with them and their children, and with the family's indubitable champion storyteller and historian, my father's eighty-six-year-old cousin, Dorothy Partington. I tape-recorded nearly everything, asked a great many questions, pored with them over old photographs and scrapbooks, and there gradually emerged, in the unique and rather consistent style of that family, a composite self-portrait and a set of recollections of my father's childhood, his parents, and, more briefly, his grandparents. Among the Boettigers of my father's generation, memory—or the wish to share with the son of a beloved and self-destructive brother—leans to the lighter side of life. For example, my father's closest friend, his brother Bill, had saved a collection of letters between my parents in the wake of their separation. A loving man, Uncle Bill finally gave them to me, still concerned that my reading them would make me sad.

I corresponded with many of my father's former newspaper colleagues, and interviewed several whose memories were unusually helpful. On two successive trips to Florida in 1975 and 1976, I obtained from his third wife Virginia eight packing cartons full of my father's personal papers, papers he had asked be saved for me, and for which my readiness was twenty-five years in the making.

Part III, the story of the marriage itself, is grounded in my parents' substantial volume of correspondence, in the records of their newspaper ventures in Seattle and Phoenix, in a considerable collection of family photographs and films, and in the writings and recollections of others who knew them. Most notable in that last category are my mother's other two children, my half brother and half sister Curtis Roosevelt and Eleanor Seagraves, who were enormously helpful in responding to early drafts and in sharing their memories with me. They are nine and twelve years older than I, and thus bring another and valuable order of memory to these chapters of the story. That is also to say that had either of them told this tale rather than I it would no doubt have emerged with differences in tone and emphasis, just as sisters and brothers—so recognizably kin—are also such different souls.

I would like to acknowledge the generous support and assistance of a number of persons who at various points of the writing were particularly helpful:

Dr. William R. Emerson, director of the Franklin D. Roosevelt Library, and his able staff, including Raymond Teichman, supervisory archivist, and Paul J. McLaughlin and William F. Stickle, who provided guidance and technical assistance through a vast collection of photographs; and Frances Seeber and Raymond Geselbracht, who so ably prepared the collection of my mother's papers.

Joseph P. Lash, whose *Eleanor and Franklin* and *Eleanor: The Years Alone* are such fine models of careful and sympathetic biography, and who generously shared with me his notes on several long conversations he had with my mother between 1966 and 1970.

Several of my father's former colleagues and friends in the newspaper world, whose recollections in interview and correspondence allowed me to recover a richly textured picture of his professional life in the 1920s and early 1930s: Stanley H. Armstrong, Levering Cartwright, Willard Edwards, Thomas Furlong, Ernest K. Lindley, J. Loy Maloney, Manley S. Mumford, Edward J. Roddan, Francis M. Stephenson, and Walter Trohan.

*Foreword*

Marie Donogh, who welcomed me back to my birthplace of Seattle, Washington, arranged for several rewarding visits there, and offered me again the kind of warm and gracious hospitality for which I had so long and vividly remembered her and her husband Stanley. The frontispiece photograph of my parents, which so strikingly captures their spirits, was given to me by Marie.

Bernard Asbell, whose illuminating interview of my mother in 1967 helped me further to understand her relationship with her parents and grandmother.

Theodor Swanson, who first in the early 1960s and again more recently offered to share his memory and the records he had preserved of the last months and days of my father's life.

Virginia de la Plante, who saved my father's papers for me, and shared with my wife and me her experience and her love of him.

Dr. James A. Halsted, my mother's husband for the last twenty-three years of her life, who loaned me a significant collection of notes, interview transcripts, correspondence, and other material she had begun to collect for a writing project of her own, a project interrupted by her last illness.

Robert Lescher, my friend and agent, who has had from the beginning a sensitive understanding of the personal significance of this work, and who read the manuscript with critical care.

George P. Brockway, chairman of W. W. Norton & Company, whose immediate and continuing interest in this book has been a sustaining pleasure.

Behind this portrait of a marriage there exists another marriage whose continuity and change are at the center of my life. Time after time, in the whole course of the work, my wife Janet has offered a key question, a fresh and wise perspective, a confirming presence. She heard it all, read it all, and has been far and away my best editor. To have shared this venture with her has been an extraordinary gift.

JOHN R. BOETTIGER

*January, 1978*

# A LOVE IN SHADOW

# *January 18, 1935*

IT WAS clear and cold in New York City on the morning of the wedding. A light snow had fallen the day before, but little trace of it remained on the streets. The front page of that morning's newspapers bore accounts of President Franklin D. Roosevelt's presentation to Congress of his new social security program, considered by many to be the very heart of the New Deal. Much ingenuity and effort had been expended at the White House and in New York to assure that the press did not learn in advance of another, more personal event in the president's life: his daughter Anna's marriage to a young reporter turned publicist, John Boettiger.

Eleanor Roosevelt, the bride's mother, had appeared with her husband at a reception for the Supreme Court the evening before, and then caught the midnight train from Washington to New York. Sara Delano Roosevelt, Anna's grandmother, was on hand, as were two of Anna's four brothers, Elliott and John. The president chose to stay in Washington, but called his congratulations by telephone at the end of the ceremony.

A few minutes before nine o'clock that morning, then, a small group of Roosevelt family and friends gathered in the second-floor library of the Roosevelts' home at 49 East Sixty-fifth Street. The room was unadorned, and appeared somewhat bare, since most of the president's books and ship models that had filled its shelves had been removed to the White House.

The simple civil ceremony was conducted by Judge Frederick Kernochan, a friend and fishing companion of FDR. Immediately afterward, just as Stephen Early, the presidential press secretary, made known the news in Washington, Anna and John left by car for a weekend in the country with friends. Eleanor stayed at the house to meet with the reporters who soon arrived. She said she had no more idea where they went "than the man in the moon." She was asked what her daughter wore at the wedding. "A suit," she replied. "Yes, it was a suit, because I remember she wore a skirt and a blouse. I couldn't tell you what color."

There was, of course, another family for whom this marriage was a special event. All of the Boettigers were then living on the West Coast. John had told his father and his brother Bill of his plans when he was in California earlier that month. But somehow the absence of Boettigers at the wedding suggests the extent to which the Roosevelt presence overshadowed this marriage from the start.

The day before the ceremony, Franklin Roosevelt wrote letters to his daughter and to John.

My own dearest Anna—

Oh, I so wish I could be with you tomorrow morning—and I shall await your voice. I know all is well with you and that you are going to be happy—you deserve all happiness. And John is a real man and will take very good care of you. All my love and be sure to get here in a week! Call me on the phone Monday if it is safe!

Your devoted
Pa

It must have been important to Anna that her father recognized John as "a real man"—and to John as well, for he was not without anxiety on that issue, nor was he secure in relationship to his powerful and self-confident father-in-law. The president wrote to him:

Dear John—
My love and blessings over you both—you know I have faith in you, and I am very confident you will make my Anna happy, and that the two of you can face the future with confidence in each other—I shall be with you in spirit at nine tomorrow—I so wish I could be there in person—But in a week it will be grand to see you here.

Affectionately,
Franklin D. Roosevelt

Eleanor evidently talked to her daughter before the ceremony, but wrote this letter to my father—warmer, more giving, and more personally engaged than either of her husband's notes, and reflective of her own most cherished and unfulfilled hopes. It stands, at the beginning of this story of a marriage, both as a dark hint of peril to come and as a statement of enduring truth and hope from one who had so movingly drawn care and wisdom from the adversity of her own experience of intimacy.

John dear,

I won't get a chance to talk tomorrow so this is a last word of motherly advice. You know I shall always want to help you both to be happy but never let me interfere and remember that Anna is, I think, rather like me. She'd always rather have the truth even if it is painful and never let a doubt or a suspicion grow up between you two which honest facing can dispel. I love Anna so dearly that I don't need to tell you that my willingness to let her go to you speaks much for my trust and love of you. Bless you both, live so you keep the precious thing you now have, have patience in the daily rubs of life with each other and enjoy life together and with those you love.

My love to you
L.L.*

*L.L.—the initials stand for "Lovely Lady"—was my father's private name for Eleanor Roosevelt. In good humor and no doubt with some pleasure, she occasionally used the initials in writing to him.

PART ONE

# *Anna and the Roosevelts*

ONE

# *A Secure and Tranquil State*

MY MOTHER'S parents, Eleanor and Franklin Roosevelt, were distant cousins, members of a wealthy and socially prominent Roosevelt clan that traced its American heritage back eight generations to Claes Martenszen van Rosenvelt and his wife Jannetje, who came to New Amsterdam from Holland in the 1640s. My grandfather jokingly said that he had never been able to discover what that first American Roosevelt had done for a living in Holland before emigrating, and had been forced to the conclusion that he must have been a horse thief or some other fugitive from justice. However obscure its Dutch origins, the family evolved in two distinct lines which came to be identified by their respective New York geographies—Oyster Bay and Hyde Park—and later by the qualities of the two Roosevelt men who served as president of the United States.

Three of my mother's four grandparents had died before she was born, but the fourth—her father's mother Sara Delano Roosevelt—was a vivid and influential presence in her life for thirty-five years. In fact, Eleanor Roosevelt once said, "As it turned out, Franklin's children were more my mother-in-law's children than they were mine."

Sara Delano was born in 1854, the seventh of eleven children. The Delanos were part of a comfortably landed Hudson River aristocracy. Phillipe de la Noye, the first family member to arrive in America, came to the Massachusetts Bay Colony in 1621. The family mansion, Algonac, overlooked the Hudson River at Newburgh. It was a beautiful place, my mother recalled, "with lovely old trees and wide sloping lawns." Sara was raised there with love and security, firmly rooted in a vigorous and narrow class consciousness; and that combination was to nurture a woman of vitality, assurance, and powerful will. She married James Roosevelt in October, 1880, and thus came to be mistress of Springwood, the Roosevelt estate across the river.

James, FDR's father and my great-grandfather, was a quintessential gentleman and country squire: huntsman, manager of his Hyde Park estate, horse and cattle breeder, member of the Volunteer Fire Department, warden and vestryman of St. James Episcopal Church, and devoted husband. He was also a businessman with substantial transportation and coal holdings, and was active in three large-scale but unsuccessful monopoly ventures in coal production, railroads, and a Nicaraguan interocean canal project. But James's principal interest was his family and estate on the Hudson. As a businessman he sought first and without fail to assure the comfort and security of his home and those he loved.

Springwood, James's one-thousand-acre estate, was to become—and remain—a powerful reality in my mother's life, and it was certainly that for James and his bride. Its character reflected the security and stability that was their heritage. It would have fitted well, writes historian Frank Freidel, "into the landscape of southern England. Its walls and lanes divided fields where Aldernay and Jersey cattle grazed, and its spacious home commanded a sweeping view of the Hudson. Among these serene meadows and groves, along these rural bluffs the master moved commandingly and at ease in his role of country squire. In this aspect his son Franklin best knew him and eventually came to emulate him." That landscape—its refuge, its compelling presence evoked in memory or visit, the poignance of its loss and the problematic search for some partial or symbolic restoration of its form and meaning—has been of very real importance to those in the family, including my mother and her children, whose early lives were vividly touched by it.

James was quiet, dignified, and warm, fifty-two years old and a widower. Sara was beautiful, spirited, and confident, and at twenty-six just half his age. Her father, Warren Delano, made his fortune in the China trade, lost it in the depression of 1857, and made it again on a return venture to Hong Kong. He was a benevolent and dominant patriarch in his large family, and Sara loved and respected him deeply and wholeheartedly. Her marriage to a man of similar qualities, twenty-six years her senior, continued that pattern of faith and devotion. James responded with a love and solicitous care which must have been deeply familiar to her.

Their twenty years of married life at Hyde Park were ordered, secure, and, by Sara's testimony in diary and letter, wholly and mutually satisfying. "They worshiped the same household gods," wrote Joseph P. Lash; "they had the same convictions about education and manners, *noblesse oblige,* and honor. They shared a love for the tranquil, secluded life of Hudson Valley and agreed that its old families, to most of whom they were related, embodied and defended the precious old standards in which they had been bred." In my mother's words, "Everything they did, their lives at home, their traveling, their entertaining, and their work were all done in the same quiet, orderly, dignified fashion."

James Roosevelt died when his son was eighteen, but Sara lived until 1941, and it was largely through her influence that Franklin and his children were imbued with a strong class consciousness. Sara's grandson James begins his recent book, *My Parents,* with these remarks: "Contrary to popular belief, the Roosevelts never were rich as the Rockefellers, but we were born blue bloods, or so Sara Roosevelt kept telling us. Granny, or Mama, as my father called her, never let us forget for a moment that we were special people, inheritors of a grand name and proud tradition, and a part of high society. We were expected to act accordingly."

By family heritage, then, and in his immediate family environment, my grandfather Franklin—James's and Sara's only child—was born into a secure and tranquil state. In light of the insecurities and overshadowings he and his wife bequeathed to his children and grandchildren, it is especially interesting to note a biographer's comment: "Roosevelt enjoyed as his birthright the self-assurance as well as the sense of responsibility that came from membership in a well-rooted aristocracy. He suffered nothing like the introspective feeling of Henry Adams and his brothers that they were overshadowed by the brilliant achievement of their ancestors."

Franklin Delano Roosevelt was born on January 30, 1882. The birth occurred at the Hyde Park home, and the baby weighed ten pounds. (Both mother and son were very nearly extinguished by an overdose of chloroform, used as an anaesthetic.) The accounts of Franklin's boyhood at Hyde Park sound like a romantic idyll. Sara breast fed her child for nearly a year. Franklin had a nurse, a devoted woman named Ellen or "Mamie" who stayed with the family for nine years, but Sara enjoyed and did many of the daily tasks of mothering. This pattern of infant care—Sara's own happiness and comfort in mothering, her undistracted and extensive time with her child, the added companionship of a devoted nurse who remained for so long, the loving mutuality between Sara and James, and the pastoral surrounding of Hyde Park—may go far to explain some of the differences in basic security and confidence between Franklin, on the one hand, and his wife and the children he fathered, on the other.

While Sara took major responsibility for her son's upbringing, Franklin spent a good deal of time with his equally adoring father as he grew out of babyhood and into boyhood. James was almost fifty-four when his son was born, but his paternal companionship during the fourteen years before Franklin went off to boarding school must have been an extraordinarily important gift, one which his own sons were to have as well, but in a much more complex and interrupted way. He and his father sledded together, ice boated, rode horseback, fished, and sailed; and James took Franklin along on tours of the estate and farther ventures to inspect his railway and steamboat holdings. Sara later wrote that Franklin's father "never laughed at him. With him, yes—often. They were such a gay pair when they went off on long rides together." Franklin often called his father "Pops" and "Popsy," the names I used as a child for my own father—without, of course, knowing their origin.

If it was an ordered life, it nonetheless left room for mischief, and James's disinclination to discipline in such matters was both relief and model for his son. Franklin's own son Elliott recalled:

"Father used to tell how he once filched two Seidlitz [effervescent] powders from Grandfather's medicine cabinet and hid them in the china chamber pot under the bed of his staid German governess. In the middle of the night, when the chinaware had been put to use, the terrified woman ran screaming for Granny with a tale of effervescent woes. Grandfather had no trouble in guessing the cause of the eruption. He summoned his son into the little octagonal room which had been added off the dining room at Hyde Park; he used it as his study. 'Consider yourself spanked,' he said. According to Father, Granny was never told what happened."

It was, as many have remarked, a sheltered and overprotected boyhood, but one that must have bequeathed to him a profound legacy of well-being. "All that is in me," he said, "goes back to the Hudson." Sara's goal for him was "that he grow to be a fine, upright man like his father and like her own father, a beloved member of his family and a useful and respected citizen of his community just as they were, living quietly and happily along the Hudson as they had." If that goal seems cloistered and modest in light of his later life, it was an image and a gift still central to his achievement. And it is an image for which more than one of his grandchildren now feel a strong affection.

Is there—to pursue a preoccupying metaphor—a shadow in the corner of this bright, formative boyhood space? Where were the costs, for Franklin's development, in this pattern of secure heritage and harmonious, loving family? At least in part, the costs are imbedded in the words of his mother's biographer (writing, in substance, what Sara herself said): "He never saw ugly moods or emotions. He was never the inwardly shrinking victim of conflicting interests, envenomed jealousies or ill-tempered words." Sara had little reason to appreciate (despite her and her son's overdose of chloroform) that pain killing can itself be a lethal act. I am reminded of the story of the Buddha's father, who, out of love, tried to shield his son from the world of illness, aging, and death, not knowing that such protection was also a shield from life. If there remained in Franklin Roosevelt throughout his life a certain detachment in important relationships, an insensitivity toward and discomfort with profound and vividly

Sara Delano Roosevelt and her infant son Franklin.

James Roosevelt with sixteen-month-old Franklin on his shoulder, June, 1883.
*Franklin D. Roosevelt Library photos*

Sara and Franklin in 1893.

A family portrait taken in May, 1899, when Franklin was seventeen.

*Franklin D. Roosevelt Library photos*

expressed feelings, it may have been in part the lengthened shadow of his early sheltering from ugliness and jealousy and conflicting interests.

My mother felt that her father was a lonely man despite his omnipresent retinue of advisors during his adult life, wanting terribly to be "one of the boys," but never achieving it with secure success. As a boy he had grown up at Hyde Park mostly in the company of adults, without much companionship of his own age. "His nearest friend," she said, "was about a mile and a half away. . . . When he went to Groton at fourteen, he no more knew how to get along with the boys his own age than the man in the moon. He was much more at ease with older people." Somehow, she felt, this had greatly to do with his need for, and success in, reaching out to the public as president. Sara's and James's love had given him a profound security and self-assurance; his isolation and loneliness as a growing boy left a legacy of self-containment and a hunger for and mistrust of intimacy. He never, she felt, fully gave himself to—or allowed himself to be fully known by—anyone.

Missy LeHand, his long-time personal secretary, agreed: he "was really incapable of a personal friendship with anyone." That personal isolativeness was no doubt strengthened by the often-remarked loneliness of the presidential office. The historian Christopher Lasch has written: "Roosevelt's life gives strong support to the view that a certain emotional impoverishment is either a precondition or a consequence of public eminence. Men who find the demands of strong friendship too exacting easily develop a taste for public life, where personal feelings necessarily take second place to policy. But even those who enter public life reluctantly, clinging to their privacy, soon find that the machinery of mass publicity and promotion obliterates every vestige of personal life."

Finally, and likely of first importance in any catalogue of shadows having their origin in Franklin Roosevelt's childhood, there is evidence that he never fully succeeded in completing a process of separation from his devoted and imposing mother. She probably remained the central figure in his household and in his heart for virtually the remainder of both of their lives (and they died within four years of one another). It may be within this context of attachment to his mother that we may best understand that which my mother ascribed to his loneliness as a child: his need throughout his life for wholehearted devotion from those closest to him, and his failure to offer wholeheartedly of himself in return. In the realm of personal relationships, FDR remained pre-eminently his mother's son, a man of great charm and fun who deeply touched the lives of others but who fundamentally found it much easier to receive than to give.

The unfolding of Franklin Roosevelt's public life has been much chronicled: the years of schooling at Groton and Harvard, Columbia Law School, the New York State Senate, the years as assistant secretary of the navy, the campaign for the vice-presidency in 1920, the governorship of New York, and the unprecedented twelve years as president of the United States. I will touch upon these events only as they may have affected the growth of his only daughter—my mother—Anna.

TWO

# *A Solemn Heritage*

"MY MOTHER was one of the most beautiful women I have ever seen." So begins the first and most revealing volume of Eleanor Roosevelt's autobiography, *This Is My Story*. Anna Hall, Eleanor's mother, was born in 1863, the eldest of six children. Her father, Valentine Hall, Jr., was a stiff, austere man, authoritarian in his family and much preoccupied with theological doctrine. He treated his wife, Mary Livingston Ludlow, like a child, and it was largely his constrained spirit that pervaded the house at Tivoli on the Hudson. The Hall children were taught (with remarkably varied success) to observe a strict standard of life's duties and responsibilities. That moral heritage passed, with significantly altered direction but little diminished in power, to Valentine Hall's granddaughter Eleanor, and through her to her daughter Anna. But it was Eleanor's mother who clearly bore the stamp of Valentine Hall's stringency of personality. After her beauty, Eleanor recalled most vividly her mother's reserve and discipline, her "strength of character, with very definite ideas of right and wrong, and a certain rigidity in conforming to a conventional pattern which had been put before [her] as the only proper existence for a lady."

One of Anna Hall's close friends remembered her as severe in self-judgment and "peculiarly sensitive; sometimes during early childhood almost painfully so. . . . She was quick to feel the slightest change in voice or manner. . . . Anna's love of the approbation of those dear to her was remarkable. Many times I noticed that the least failure to please was a disappointment to her; and, on the other hand, words of approval made her face glow with delight." It is a description strikingly similar to Eleanor Roosevelt's recollections of her own childhood.

The Halls of my great-grandmother Anna's generation, while secure members of what her daughter Eleanor later referred to as "society with a capital S," were only two generations removed from an Irish immigrant grandfather, Valentine Hall, Sr., who settled in Brooklyn and quickly and skillfully amassed a considerable fortune in commerce and real estate. Through her mother's family, Anna was a member of two older American clans, the Ludlows and the Livingstons. The first Ludlow had come to New York in 1640. The house Anna Hall's father built near the village of Tivoli was on land that had been part of the estate of Chancellor Robert Livingston, who was one of the three drafters of the Declaration of Independence and administered the presidential oath of office to George Washington.

At age nineteen Anna Hall was married to Elliott Roosevelt, a man who could have reminded her of her dour father only by contrast. "My father," wrote Eleanor, "charming, good looking, loved by all who came in contact with him, high or low, had a background and upbringing which were a bit alien to her [Anna's] pattern." More spontaneous and outgoing than Anna, and the third of four children, in contrast to Anna as the responsible eldest, Elliott had been lovingly raised in a large, vigorous, and demonstratively affectionate family.

Elliott's father, the senior Theodore Roosevelt, was a successful businessman, heading the plate-glass division of the established family firm, Roosevelt and Son. But his preoccupying interests were his family and his pioneering work for civic betterment and social welfare. Elliott's mother, Martha Bulloch Roosevelt, was a graceful and vivid southern belle, adored and protected by her husband and children. Elliott had two sisters, Anna (or Bamie) and Corinne, and an elder brother Theodore, who would become the first Roosevelt to be president of the United States.

Elliott was much loved by his parents and his sisters and brother and had an especially strong attachment to his father, who returned his love with tenderness and warmth. Elliott's sister Corinne recalled, "My father was the most intimate friend of each of his children, and in some unique way seemed to have the power of responding to the needs of each, and we all craved him as our most desired companion."

The principal shadow in Elliott's childhood remains somewhat obscure. "He had," his daughter Eleanor later wrote, "a physical weakness which he himself probably never quite understood." When he was eight or nine he began to have periods of severe dizziness, headaches, fainting, and attendant nervousness. While these symptoms were never clearly diagnosed, there remains some suspicion of organic disorder underlying his later alcoholic deterioration. The prescription in those days for such elusive problems was travel and physical discipline, and Elliott was sent on several trips abroad, to the South and out West to Fort McKavett, Texas. While he came to love the outdoor life of riding and hunting, he was often intensely homesick and particularly missed his father.

Shortly after Elliott's return from his second stay at Fort McKavett in 1877, his father developed an intestinal cancer, and during the increasingly painful progress of the disease Elliott stayed close by his father's bedside. Corinne later wrote: "Elliott gave unstintingly a devotion which was so tender that it was more like that of a woman and his young strength was poured out to help his father's condition." On February 10, 1878, his father died at age forty-six. Elliott was seventeen. The impact must have been enormous, and Elliott may have assumed, as surviving children often do, that his own inadequacy was in part responsible for his father's death. If so, the consequent burden of impotence and guilt must have powerfully shaped his later life. Sensitive, handsome, and athletic, a boy of great charm and warmth, he increasingly pursued the sporting and social life at which he shone, and saw himself in more serious matters a failure in contrast to his brother Theodore, "a far better man . . . Father's son and namesake." In response to pain of obscure and undoubtedly complex origin, he soon began to drink heavily.

Elliott Roosevelt and Anna Hall were married on December 1, 1883. "He adored my mother," wrote Eleanor, "and she was devoted to him, but always in a more reserved and less spontaneous way." They were absorbed and highly successful in the New York social scene, but shadowed by Elliott's drinking and recurrent periods of depression. Anna was soon pregnant, and their daughter Eleanor was born on October 11, 1884. Elliott's mother and his brother Theodore's young wife both died shortly before his daughter was born. Feeling those losses grievously, he may have experienced the birth of his daughter as an act of virtually divine compensation: "To him," Eleanor wrote, "I was a miracle from heaven."

Eleanor Roosevelt's childhood was a striking contrast to the pastoral security of her husband Franklin's early years. "I was a shy, solemn child even at the age of two, and I am sure that even when I danced, which I did frequently, I never smiled." She emerges, in her own later portrayal, as a sensitive child, full of fears, hungering for affection and praise, secure only in the presence of her loving but undependable and increasingly absent father. "He dominated my life as long as he lived, and was the love of my life for many years after he died. With my father I was perfectly happy."

Pervasive fearfulness in young children is often grounded in an absence or inconsistency of maternal love and care, and such was very likely true for Eleanor. She recalled an "inordinate" admiration for her mother as a beautiful vision, dressing to leave the house (and, therefore, her daughter) for the evening. But Eleanor remembered her mother's attitude as one of stern judgment, duty to the minimal requisite tasks of mothering, absence of empathy or understanding, and disappointment in her child's shyness, solemnity, and lack of physical beauty. "One is tempted to wonder," writes Joan Erikson, "how much of the onus of this mother's disappointment in her 'uncontrolled' husband was projected onto the little daughter who looked so much like him. . . . Be that as it may, the daughter could not learn from this mother how to become the loving and caring mother of her own children."

Nurses must have had principal responsibility for Eleanor's care, but there is no mention of anyone who would have offered her the sense of security and continuity provided Franklin by his mother and his nurse Mamie. Not yet three, just after a terrifying experience of a collision between two ships as she and her parents were starting a European trip, Eleanor refused to board another ship and was left with relatives for several months while her parents were in Europe seeking redress or respite from Elliott's increasingly serious drinking. It was a profoundly disturbing experience: the terror of the accident itself, which left her with an enduring fear of the water; the guilt that accompanied her refusal to board ship so soon again; and the distress of her parents' desertion.

It was the first desertion of many. In 1890, when Eleanor was six, the battle with Elliott's disintegration had reached critical proportions. The family—there was now a second child, Elliott, Jr., and the third, Hall, was born the following year—spent over a year in Europe, and Eleanor spent many unhappy months sequestered in a convent in Paris.

By this time she had already begun to develop a protective, compensatory tendency to self-control and self-sustenance, a tendency reinforced by some of her nurses' and governesses' ways of teaching. Near the end of her life she wrote of this theme: "Thanks to my childhood, I was very disciplined by the time I grew up. I remember the method by which a nurse taught me to sew, when I was only six. After I had darned a sock, she would take the scissors and cut out all I had done, telling me to try again. This was very discouraging, but it was good training. . . . When people have asked how I was able to get through some of the very bad periods in my later life, I have been able to tell them honestly that, because of all this early discipline I had, I inevitably grew into a really tough person."

Back in New York, and at her grandparents' house at Tivoli, Eleanor remained a solemn child, hungry for love, feeling herself outside the circle composed of her mother and two young brothers. "I felt a curious barrier between myself and these three," she wrote, ". . . and still I can remember standing in the door, very often with my finger in my mouth—which was, of course, forbidden—and I can see the look in [my mother's] eyes and hear the tone of her voice as she said: 'Come in, Granny.' If a visitor was there she might turn and say: 'She is such a funny child, so old-fashioned, that we always call her "Granny."' I wanted to sink through the floor in shame, and

I felt I was apart from the boys." Her mother adopted the custom of a "Children's hour," when she would play or read with them between six and seven o'clock each evening. "I often felt so tired," she told a friend, "I can scarcely do it, but I feel it is *so* important to see my children regularly every day, and this is the only hour I can command."

Eleanor passionately missed her father, who, whether drinking or in search of cure, was seldom at home. When she overheard whispered conversations about him, they provided "a strange and garbled idea of the troubles which were going on around me," and no one told her anything directly. She knew only that her father was the sole source of joy in her life, that there *could* be nothing wrong with him, and that he had gone away. (Elliott wanted to be with his family, but his behavior was so erratic that his wife refused to have him and—after another "cure" for alcoholism—he went to work on some family properties in southwest Virginia.)

Anna Hall Roosevelt died of diphtheria on December 7, 1892. Eleanor's own description of her experience of her mother's death is a graphic and poignant statement of the distance between them and her contrasting love for her father: "I can remember standing by a window when Cousin Susie (Mrs. Parish) told me that my mother was dead. She was very sweet to me, and I must have known that something terrible had happened. Death meant nothing to me, and one fact wiped out everything else—my father was back and I would see him very soon." Eleanor was eight.

Elliott did come for a visit, but not as soon as she had hoped. "Later I knew what a tragedy of utter defeat this meant for him. No hope now of ever wiping out the sorrowful years he had brought upon my mother—and she had left her mother as guardian for her children. My grandmother did not feel that she could trust my father to take care of us. He had no wife, no children, no hope!"

The power of Eleanor's vision of her father—and of their relationship—was great. Indeed, in the midst of so much desertion and emotional deprivation, that vision amounted to a central, sustaining, and life-long myth, and an extraordinary testimony to the self-healing potency of fantasy.

"After we were installed [at Grandma Hall's house] my father came to see me, and I remember going down into the high ceilinged dim library of the first floor of the house on West 37th Street. He sat in a big chair. He was dressed all in black, looking very sad. He held out his arms and gathered me to him. In a little while he began to talk, to explain to me that my mother was gone, that she had been all the world to him, and now he had only my brothers and myself, that my brothers were very young, and that he and I must keep close together. Some day I would make a home for him again; we would travel together and do many things which he painted as interesting and pleasant, to be looked forward to in the future together.

"Somehow it was always he and I. I did not understand whether my brothers were to be our children or whether he felt that they would be at school and college and later independent.

"There started that day a feeling which never left me—that he and I were very close together, and some day, would have a life of our own together. He told me to write to him often, to be a good girl, not to give any trouble, to study hard, to grow up into a woman he could be proud of, and he would come to see me whenever it was possible.

"When he left, I was all alone to keep our secret of mutual understanding and to adjust myself to my new existence."

"I knew a child once who adored her father," she wrote on another occasion.

"She was an ugly little thing, keenly conscious of her deficiencies, and her father, the only person who really cared for her, was away much of the time; but he never criticized her or blamed her, instead he wrote her letters and stories, telling her how he dreamed of her growing up and what they would do together in the future, but she must be truthful, loyal, brave, well-educated, or the woman he dreamed of would not be there when the wonderful day came for them to fare forth together. The child was full of fears and because of them lying was easy; she had no intellectual stimulus at that time and yet she made herself as the years went on into a fairly good copy of the picture he had painted."

Anna Hall Roosevelt in February, 1890, when Eleanor was five years old.

*Franklin D. Roosevelt Library photos*

Elliott Roosevelt with his three children, Elliott, Jr., Hall, and Eleanor, in 1892, the year of their mother's death.

It seems likely that such a guiding and sustaining fantasy had a shadow side, too. Eleanor was never to know—even in her early years with Franklin—the sort of intimacy she dreamed of finding with her father, nor did she have a deeply intimate relationship with her own children, and she keenly felt the pain of that absence in both instances. Her fantasy father, having acquired such potency in her early years, free from tempering and complication in the world of real relationship, may have remained the great love of her life.

The impact of this loving and undependable man upon his daughter's later development must in fact have been very complex. He was, as she wrote, inspiration for a remarkable and resilient integrity and strength of purpose. At the same time the power of his continuing presence in her heart may have enhanced her reticence, limited her inclination or access to other deep loves, and occasionally impaired her vision of others around her. As her friend and biographer Joseph Lash remarks, she sometimes "tended to overestimate and misjudge people, especially those who seemed to need her and who satisfied her need for self-sacrifice and affection and gave her the admiration and loyalty she craved. Just as her response to being disappointed by her father had been silence and depression because she did not dare see him as he really was, so in later life she would become closed, withdrawn, and moody when people she cared about disappointed her."

Unlike in so much of their experience of childhood, Eleanor and Franklin Roosevelt had this in common: a powerful and enduring attachment to a parent of the opposite sex. It may have been an element drawing them to one another, but it proved ultimately estranging, and may well have affected in somewhat similar ways the scope and quality of their relationships with others.

Eleanor's little brother Ellie died, also of diphtheria, the year after her mother's death. And the following year, again drinking heavily and living in New York under an assumed name—"Mr. Elliott"—her father fell, was knocked unconscious, and died. "On August 14, 1894, just before I was ten years old, word came that my father had died. My aunts told me, but I simply refused to believe it, and while I wept long and went to bed still weeping, I finally went to sleep and began the next day living in my dream world as usual."

In the years following her parents' deaths Eleanor was raised by her grandmother, Mary Ludlow Hall, in New York and at Tivoli. Mrs. Hall was a sympathetic but strict guardian. Her confining sense of propriety and Eleanor's natural shyness and solemnity were compensated to some degree by the vitality of her aunts Maude and Pussie (her mother's sisters) and the companionship of her brother Hall. And, living largely in her own world of fantasy, she became "an omnivorous reader."

Valentine Hall, her grandfather, had died when Eleanor's mother was seventeen. He left no will, and his wife Mary had virtually no preparation for managing either a household or a brood of six energetic children. Her intentions were kindly, but assuming full responsibility for two more children twelve years later must have refueled a significant resentment. "She was determined," Eleanor wrote, "that the grandchildren who were now under her care should have the discipline that her own children had lacked, and we were brought up on the principle that 'no' was easier to say than 'yes.' "

Eleanor was raised, then, by two unhappy women—her mother and then her grandmother—both of whom experienced themselves as deserted by their husbands and left with taxing, if not unacceptable, responsibilities for children. While in her writings she reveals no love for either, she does speak of an example that centrally and poignantly affected her own—and her children's—lives: "My grandmother's life had a considerable effect on me, for even when I was young I determined that I would never be dependent on my children by allowing all my interests to center in them. The conviction has grown through the years. In watching the lives of those around her [Grandma Hall's own children] I have felt that it might have been well in their youth if they had not been able to count on her devotion and her presence whenever they needed her."

Perhaps the greatest gift to Eleanor's growing up began as she was turning fifteen, when Grandmother Hall decided that she should be sent to Allenswood, a boarding school in England run by a remarkable Frenchwoman, Mlle. Marie Souvestre. Eleanor's three years at Allenswood, and particularly her relationship with Mlle. Souvestre, nurtured a vitality and independence of mind, an inclination to know and speak the truth, and a new confidence in relationships with her peers. Mlle. Souvestre also stimulated Eleanor's social and political consciousness, and reinforced that which remained, from her profoundly insecure childhood, a centrally guiding principle: to be useful to others.

Returning to New York in the summer of 1902, Eleanor soon began settlement-house teaching, reluctantly and painfully agreed to the Halls's insistence that she endure her debut into the society world at age eighteen, and began to find some new friends. Among them was her debonair cousin, Franklin D. Roosevelt, then a junior at Harvard. Eleanor and Franklin saw one another increasingly over the following months, and in November, 1903, they became secretly engaged. Having eluded the considerable obstructions of his mother Sara, Eleanor and Franklin were married on March 17, 1905. The bride's uncle, President Theodore Roosevelt, gave her away and incidentally stole the show at the reception following the ceremony.

Apart from their common social class and distant family tie, there seemed little resemblance between Franklin and Eleanor Roosevelt. One can hardly imagine emotionally more antithetical childhoods. But Franklin offered to Eleanor a handsomeness and vitality that may have been reminiscent of her father, and his family had a security and stability she had never known. "Franklin, for his part," writes Frank Freidel, "must have been strongly drawn to this shy, highly feminine girl who shared his interests in people and perhaps even surpassed him in the keenness and quickness of her perception." He may have found in her some premonitory echo of his own as yet latent serious purpose. Her close friend Isabella Greenway recalled, "Even at that age life had, through her orphanage, touched her and made its mark in a certain aloofness from the careless ways of youth. The world had come to her as a field of responsibility rather than as a playground."

THREE

# *Anna's Early Years*

FIVE months after their marriage Eleanor was pregnant, and on May 3, 1906, at 1:15 P.M., my mother was born. She weighed ten pounds, one ounce. Eleanor's experience of pregnancy had been trying: the last three months were a time of considerable pain and nausea. When the birth was over, however, Eleanor regarded her first child as "just a helpless bundle but by its mere helplessness winding itself inextricably around my heart." On July 1, 1906, aged nearly two months, my mother was christened Anna Eleanor—after her mother and maternal grandmother—at St. James Episcopal Church in Hyde Park.

Anna was born at home, 125 East Thirty-sixth Street, a house Sara had rented for the newlyweds on their return from a European honeymoon. (Sara also furnished the house and provided three servants. Her own home was three blocks away.) Eleanor was helped by a trained nurse, Miss Blanche Spring, whom she liked a great deal and who was to become a regular presence around the time of her subsequent births. The baby was delivered by Dr. Albert H. Ely, and Sara was, of course, on hand.

The example provided by Eleanor's own mother had been neither inspiring nor instructive, and she faced motherhood in a spirit of anxious responsibility. She felt helpless, dependent, and perhaps unconsciously somewhat resentful. Miss Spring, she said, "took care of me and of the baby single-handed. She adored babies, and she tried to teach me something about their care. I had never had any interest in dolls or in little children, and I knew absolutely nothing about handling or feeding a baby." The young nurse Sara hired to take over from Miss Spring was, in Eleanor's eyes, not very satisfactory: "She knew a considerable amount about babies' diseases, but her inexperience made this knowledge almost a menance, for she was constantly looking for obscure illnesses and never expected that a well fed and well cared for baby would move along in a normal manner."

For Anna, it was the first of a frequently changing and often problematic collection of nurses and governesses. In the fall of 1906 the young nurse was replaced by "a friendly old Irish woman who had brought up babies for many years"; but Eleanor found her "too old for the job." Of the next few years Anna's brother Jimmy recalls: "One of the hazards of life during this period for Anna, Elliott, Franklin Jr., and me—Johnny escaped it by virtue of his tender years—was the procession of proper English nannies foisted on our household by well-meaning Granny. Mother, though she disliked some of the early martinets as much as we did, had not yet developed gumption to stand up to Granny on such things." "I was not allowed to take care of the children," Eleanor recalled, "nor had I any sense of how to do it. Actually, as I was terribly inexperienced about taking responsibility of any kind whatever, I was frightened to death of the nurses, and I always obeyed every rule they made."

How distressingly and truly her coming into motherhood reawakened her experience as a child, and how closely she came to recapitulating her own mother's and grandmother's experiences and basic postures toward her. As Joan Erikson remarks, "Motherhood seems to have happened to her as an inexorable fate, before she could grasp its meaning. In her story she emphasizes how strongly she felt her responsibility for her children's welfare, how dutifully she cared for them when ill or injured, but little joy or even satisfaction in mothering shines through."

Apart from their manner of child care, the fact of nurse succeeding nurse at frequent intervals must have confused and inhibited the children and stimulated their mistrust. My mother had at least four successive nurses in her first five years. With one notable exception—a woman Jimmy calls "Old Battleaxe"—the nurses were not so much cruel as conventionally stiff sorts who lived by rules and pun-

Eleanor and Franklin at Hyde Park, awaiting the birth of their first child.

*Franklin D. Roosevelt Library photos*

The first photographs of my mother with her parents, in the summer of 1906.

ishments and offered little humor, empathy, or physical comfort. My mother, fortunately for her, was older—about nine or ten—when "Old Battleaxe" reigned. That sadistic woman—"our English torturess," says Jimmy—on successive occasions knelt on Anna's chest and "cuffed her around a bit," locked Elliott in a closet for three hours, locked Franklin Jr. in a closet, forced Jimmy to eat a whole pot of hot English mustard, and made Jimmy walk up and down the sidewalk outside the house, dressed in his sister's clothes, with a sign on his back reading "I am a liar." She was finally fired only when Eleanor found a drawer of her dresser full of empty liquor bottles.

Eleanor, in retrospect, bore a heavy burden of self-blame and guilt for her failure to take a more active, informed, and humane hand in the raising of her children. "If I had it all to do over again," she wrote, "I know now that what we should have done was to have no servants those first few years; I should have acquired knowledge and self-confidence so that other people could not fool me either as to the housework or as to the children. . . . Had I done this, . . . my children would have had far happier childhoods." Her location of the source of her difficulties as a mother in so derivative an issue as the presence or absence of servants may seem naïve. But her history of being "fooled" by other people—betrayed by those who should have given more fully and consistently of their love—was in fact central to her struggle with mothering. Having learned as a child to depend heavily upon self-control and withdrawal into fantasy for her emotional survival, she often seemed stern and withdrawn to her small daughter. How like the image Eleanor's own mother had left so painfully and indelibly in her mind.

If there was in my mother's infancy a pattern of impersonal constraint and inadequate warmth, its symbolic focus may have been "the cage," for it certainly remained vividly in her mind in later years. Accounts of the cage had been so often told to her, she recalled, "that it almost became a memory. . . . The story was told most often by Granny who (I am now sure) delighted in her preamble to the effect that Eleanor was foolishly following a newfangled idea of bringing up children: foolishly, because she should have been taking only the advice of her mother-in-law!" In Eleanor's words: "I had a curious arrangement out of one of my back windows for airing the children, a kind of box with wire on the sides and top. Anna was put out there for her morning nap. On several occasions she wept loudly, and finally one of my neighbors called up and said I was treating my children inhumanly and that she would report me to the S.P.C.C. if I did not take her in at once! This was rather a shock to me, for I thought I was being a most modern mother. I knew you should not pick up a baby when it cried, that fresh air was very necessary."

From the moment of my mother's birth, her grandmother Sara was a continuous and very significant presence. Anna's early memories of Granny were of an imposing woman ("a *grand dame* of the old school," she was later to write), wholly self-assured and a little awe-inspiring, but warm and affectionate, with a large motherly bosom that could be both comforting and confining. Anna recalled with notable ambivalence: "Granny loomed large in my young life, at least until we moved to Washington when I was six, which meant she only visited us during the winter months and I felt she was a guest. She was very affectionate, spoiled me, I'm sure, as her first grandchild, but she could be very firm and demanding. It was the custom to have tea served at five o'clock every afternoon. I was to be dressed up and on hand when she asked for me, which seemed to me to be quite often. I had long, fine blond hair which tangled easily and I don't remember any nurse who didn't delight in making me cry as she pulled through those strands. [Granny] would show me off to her lady guests, calling me 'dear little Anna,' and how I hated it!" It was to Granny that my mother wrote her first letter at age six:

Dear Grandmama,

My love and I hope you will soon see us. Again love and kisses from Baby James and Anna.

Anna and Eleanor agreed in later years that Sara had a larger hand in her grandchildren's raising than did their mother, and until her adolescent years Anna felt closer to Granny than to her mother. Eleanor often chafed at Sara's matriarchal power. "What she wanted," Eleanor wrote bluntly much later, "was to hold onto Franklin and his children; she wanted them to grow up as she wished." But Sara's confident assumption of responsibility was also a relief to Eleanor, and the impact on the very young children was mostly beneficial. Granny offered to them the same sort of confident devotion she had provided her son, and in doing so may have served as an antidote to the relative severity of Eleanor and the nurses. So Sara's diary often suggests: "I told Nurse Watson she *must* get up and turn her [Anna] over and soothe her."

Franklin evidently spent as little time with his infant children as was conventional in those circles and those days. As his son Jimmy noted, "Father's attitude on nurses and other household affairs was strictly hands off." But the descriptions of his times with the infant Anna evoke images of his own father playing with him at an early age. He clearly enjoyed her in a more physically and emotionally relaxed way than Eleanor could. When Anna was eight months old, "She kept her eyes fixed on the door and said 'pa pa pa' all the time." And Eleanor wrote Sara of her pleasure at Franklin carrying his little daughter piggyback up the hill. Franklin was twenty-four and in his last year at Columbia Law School when Anna was born. The following spring, having passed his bar exams, he joined the New York law firm of Carter, Ledyard and Milburn. I suspect one considerable benefit in my mother's earliest years, in contrast to her younger brothers, was the absence of preoccupying seriousness in Franklin's schooling or work and, therefore, his relative accessibility as a father.

Whatever the mixed blessings of being the only child recipient of the family's attentions, they were brought to a close on December 23, 1907, with the birth of brother James. Eleanor wrote significantly of her own responses to James's birth: "he will never know with what relief and joy I welcomed him into the world, for fear I would never have a son, knowing that both my mother-in-law and my husband wanted a boy to name after my husband's father. Many a time since I have wished that two girls had started our family, so that Anna might have had a sister." The effect of Anna's displacement was heightened, no doubt, by James's general sickliness,

*Above left*: Franklin with Anna on horseback. *Right*: Sara and Anna with baby James in 1908.

Anna, Miss Spring, and the first Franklin, Jr., 1909.

*Franklin D. Roosevelt Library photos*

which developed into pneumonia in the spring of 1908. Those months were trying ones, one of the times, Eleanor wrote, she "would rather not live over again." Anna's natural hostility to James, under the circumstances, is suggested in Eleanor's account of Anna's pushing the baby in his carriage off the porch of the summer house they were renting on the New Jersey shore. Jimmy and carriage landed in the sand and were unhurt. "I got even," Jimmy later recalled, "by stabbing her in the palm of her hand with a pencil. She carried the scar all her life."

For a very young child especially, there must have been some confusion and anxiety, as well as some excitement, in the pattern of moves undertaken by the family each year: winters largely in New York, holidays and summer visits to Hyde Park, and, beginning with my mother's first summer in 1906, a long summer stay on Campobello Island. And there were to be other moves as well. Sara gave Eleanor and Franklin a Christmas present of a new town house (with several connecting doors to one she built for herself next door), and the family moved in the autumn of 1908 to 49 East Sixty-fifth Street. (It was to remain the family's house in New York until after Sara's death in 1941, and was the house in which my parents were married).

Eleanor was again pregnant at the time of the move, and on March 18, 1909, the first Franklin Jr. was born. He grew ill the following autumn, and died on November 8. Anna, at age three, must have felt the emotional impact of that family tragedy, for her mother was devastated: "I was young and morbid and reproached myself very bitterly for having done so little about the care of this baby. I felt he had been left too much to the nurse and I knew too little about him, and that in some way I must be to blame. I even felt that I had not cared enough about him, and I made myself and all those around me most unhappy during that winter."

Eleanor's apprehension, distress, and self-reproach were chronic feelings made acute in this crisis of premature death, a crisis which must at least unconsciously have revived her responses to the deaths she suffered as a child. Those feelings persisted into the following year, shadowing the bearing and birth of her next child, Elliott, who arrived on September 23, 1910. Named for her beloved father, Elliott "suffered for a great many years," she said, with "a rather unhappy disposition," and she blamed herself.

The attitudes of Anna's mother and nurses toward sexual expression no doubt reflected the prevailing repressiveness of that culture and time, but one wonders about its relation, also, to Eleanor's own emotional and sexual constraint. (Years later she was to tell her daughter that "sex was an ordeal to be borne.") In a brief unpublished memoir of her early years, after recalling the story of "the cage," my mother wrote:

"There was another traumatic experience for me in those earlier years . . . which I relate because it is indicative of the taboos and inhibitions of that time within the social structure in which I was brought up. It was an experience which haunted me through various types of persecution dreams for many years. Finally, in my latish teens I asked my mother why, at the age of three or four I had my hands tied, above my head, to the top bars of my crib whenever I went to bed. Her answer was simply that I masturbated and this was the prescribed cure. Later (I have no idea how much later but it can't have been long because I was still sleeping in the 'big' nursery at Hyde Park), I remember graduating to 'bells': aluminum-type contraptions which covered my hands and had air holes in them. Cloth pieces were attached which were made firm around my wrists. These were 'heaven' to me because I made up marvelous stories: the holes were windows in castles; people lived behind those windows and had wonderful adventures. The answer from Mother was given in a tone which precluded any further questions—if I had any. The indication was clearly that I had had a bad habit which had to be cured and about which one didn't talk!"

When I shared this story with my brother, he recalled "the wire cages for my thumbs Mummy imposed at night." How slowly, when at all, do we succeed as parents in reversing or redressing our sufferings as little children. I am nine years my brother's junior, and by then, as I remember, while masturbation was still regarded as anathema and thumb-sucking discouraged, my hands were left free.

Among the notes my mother wrote and filed away for a writing

My mother at age five. *Franklin D. Roosevelt Library*

project that never materialized, there is a short and revealing account of her memory of daily life as a very young child. It offers a remarkable summary of the themes that have begun to emerge in this narrative, and some insight into the manner of her looking back, as an adult, on her earliest years. "What happens to a child's security and development," she asks, "when his first learning pattern is that he is required to pay allegiance to two separate hierarchies?"

"The first hierarchy is that of the Nanny or nurse, and a governess is in the picture too if there are older siblings. This hierarchy bathes, teaches the unwelcome task of washing behind the ears, brushing the teeth night and morning, toilet training, dressing and undressing, and the rule of hand-washing before meals and before presenting oneself to the second hierarchy. The second hierarchy is that of the parents and, in my case, the only grandparent alive when I came into the world and the most solidly* important individual in this category in my earliest childhood.

"At about the age of four I had learned that the nurse group did not have to command my respect because they came and went, always replaced by someone else—with the usual human differences in training emphasis, severity and kind of punishment, empathy or the opposite toward the 'charges.' At an early age I learned to judge, sometimes fairly sometimes not, and to try wiles and my own brand of cunning in making life as easy as I thought possible for myself.

"The same age brought the realization that the second group did remain constant, and quite obviously had power over the first group, as well as ultimate power over me. Also, this second group were surrounded by surrogate 'nurses' who catered to their individual needs: a personal maid for my grandmother, and male and female people who cleaned the house, cooked and served the meals, and washed and ironed. At Hyde Park, the only place I really thought of as home, there was an additional surrogate group who took care of another aspect of the lives of the permanent hierarchy: the farmer and his helpers, the coachman and his helpers (in my earliest years) and later the chauffeur, and the gardeners.

*In place of "solidly" my mother had first written "puzzlingly," and though rejected I think we may take her first word seriously too, for she was no doubt confused, in this panoply of appearing and disappearing caretakers, as to just who was who.

"Obviously the permanent group provided an important segment of childhood security. To varying degrees, depending on the personal characteristics of the parents and grandparent, affection and love could be counted on. But childhood dependence on a consistent, warm and spontaneous love was muted to accommodate to circumstances: emotional display was abhorrent in company; a good-bye or hello kiss was an off-hand, perfunctory affair; a squeeze from Granny in public meant she was talking about you in adult fashion to another adult and I felt only [her] condescension and [my] embarrassment because I couldn't understand and suspected 'double-talk'; a pat on the head from an 'outsider' adult had the same effect on me.

"On the other hand, when I was sent down to say Good Morning to Granny as she finished her breakfast in bed, her kiss and hug were indeed warm—almost suffocating as my own daughter complained when she was very young and going thru much the same childhood routine as I had, and to whom I explained that Granny's bosom was a bit too ample and therefore somewhat like a pillow held against your face against your will. I don't remember much about Mother's and Father's greetings in the early mornings except for perfunctory kisses from each of them on our cheeks as we or they arrived at the breakfast table. But Mother made quite a ritual out of evening prayers and tucking the chicks into bed. I think Father joined in once in a while. Mother came to the nursery for this ritual. We knelt at her knee for prayers, and at our bedsides if we were alone with the nurse. If nurse complained of our behavior, Mother's disapproval was quite evident, usually expressed by dampening down the warmth of her goodnight hug and kiss."

Themes thus formed in her childhood were to echo significantly throughout Anna's adult life, and find their ways thereby into the lives of her children: the inhibiting power of public "circumstances" on family relationships; the mistrust of "double-talk," a suspicion that people did not reliably mean what they said and, therefore, could not be counted on; and the potent, if muted, vision of "a consistent, warm and spontaneous love."

The ambivalence toward Granny that pervades these memories no doubt reflects in part Anna's later identification with her mother.

It may be, too, that since Granny was the most reliably loving and available parenting figure, she was the safest one to whom a child could consciously attach negative feelings. And apart from all this, her embrace *was* ardent and her bosom *was* ample.

# FOUR

# *The Hero Father*

PICTURES of my mother in her early years show a beautiful, golden-haired child. Like her mother, and indeed in her mother's eyes, Anna was distinctively her father's child: "fair-skinned like her father, with good features, blue eyes and straight hair which was bleached almost white by the sun." Nurses, as she has written, and then increasingly her brother Jimmy, were her principal companions. Eleanor adopted a ritual remarkably like that of her own mother: "I was home every afternoon, and had tea with the children. I read with them or played with them till they went to bed. I tried having little Anna to lunch with us, but after spending a solid hour over the meal on our first attempt, I returned her to the nursery."

Eleanor later had a custom "of reading to the children after lunch and after tea each day, in order to keep them quiet." It was a custom, I remember, that she continued many years afterward with her grandchildren, gathered around her chair in the living room of her own Val-Kill cottage at Hyde Park. Anna remembered, as a small child, liking her mother's reading, "because she had a most expressive voice and intonations." And Eleanor may have found herself more comfortable with her children when she had a familiar book to share.

In the autumn of Anna's fifth year her father was elected to the New York State Senate from Dutchess County, and there began a political career that was profoundly to affect his children's lives. It was in the Albany house to which the family moved on January 1, 1911, that Anna located, in later years, her earliest memory of her father. "It seemed to me that on many too many occasions Father would come home from work and shut himself up in a room with a lot of other men. I was forbidden to interrupt. But curiosity got the best of me and one day I sneaked into the room, *with* Father and his political cohorts. I had sense enough not to utter a sound, so no one bothered me. But pretty soon I noticed that the air began to smell and was filled, right up to the ceiling, with smoke. It wasn't long before I began to cough, rub my smarting eyes and wish I could get away. Of course, I was discovered. I still associate cigar smoke with politics."

The earliest memories that remain vivid in the minds of grown children often hint at or gather central personal themes. One such theme, in this event, is surely my mother's deep-seated love for her father, and ambivalence toward the political world that was his greatest preoccupation: her wish to be included, the enormous pleasure of being close to him, and awareness that the price of inclusion was self-control and discomfort. Her brother Jimmy's account of Anna's memory of the incident portrays a stronger reaction: "Suddenly Sis [Anna] had to run from the parlor to avoid being asphyxiated." If there was ambivalence in her experience of her father's world, there was also this pre-eminent truth: Franklin was a magically attractive figure to his children, and Anna, like the others, was deeply drawn to him and repeatedly was to return to his side. He was, she said, "my childhood hero."

In the first volume of Frank Freidel's biography of my grandfather, there is a brief discussion of the early years of Franklin's and Eleanor's marriage: "They did not talk over analytically what they expected of it and of each other. She expected much; so did Franklin, but he seemed to get what he wanted effortlessly, and apparently took for granted that now in addition to a doting mother, he should have a devoted wife and a growing number of adoring children. In return he gave his unquestioning affection, and until politics claimed him, much of his time. Yet that sensitivity of his which became razor-sharp in political affairs never seemed to extend to domestic matters."

My mother, looking back upon her childhood, evidently agreed.

She remarked, in the margin of her copy of Freidel's book, on her father's "lack of desire to face what might prove disagreeable" in relationships with his wife and children. Remembering a later period, she once recalled, "Nothing could bother him more than to have one of the close females [she had been talking of herself, her mother, and Missy LeHand] burst into tears . . . even in his secretarial staff, if they took to becoming the emotional type, this he couldn't stand." That parental intolerance, particularly when compounded by Eleanor's extraordinary self-control and reserve, was very powerful. My mother was to become, like her father—and, later in life, her mother—an unusually vivid, energetic person, possessed of liveliness, humor, and warmth. And, like both parents, she was very self-controlled. She did not have easy access to her emotions, and did not share her more profound feelings easily with others. She very seldom cried. And her negative feelings in general—anger, sadness, fear—tended to work within her rather than to find expression without.

Like his father before him, my mother wrote, FDR was not "a disciplinarian by temperament. Nor was he ever fond of long, solitary talks with his children about troubles they might have. These parental duties he seemed to feel lay entirely in the feminine realm and should rightfully be tackled by Mother and Granny. . . . But as we were perfectly normal children from the standpoint of getting into mischief, there were times when we definitely annoyed Father. And *then* there was nothing uncertain or gentle about his wrath. He would often be sarcastic in his chastising remarks and end up by sending us coldly from the room or to our beds."

For all of that, she experienced her father as a much more openly affectionate person, more playful, less serious and preoccupied, than her mother. In the years after Franklin's entry into politics—the two years of his service as a state senator and the family's early years in Washington—she must have had some of her most vivid experiences with him. It seems likely that he was, for her as for her brother Jimmy, "the handsomest, strongest, most glamorous, vigorous, physical father in the world." When Franklin was ill once, his ten-year-old daughter wrote him:

Three portraits of Anna in about 1913. In the photograph at the left she is with her younger brothers Elliott and James. *Franklin D. Roosevelt Library photos*

Dear Father,

I am sending you these little pictures [cutouts] of indians and boy scouts. You can make a very nice little picture if you put them together. Ask Mother to put them together for you, and stand them up against something. I hope you feel better, and will be all right again very soon. Goodly Father I wish I could kiss you. Mother will kiss you for me.

Love from Anna

"Father was fun," Anna said, "because he would sometimes romp with me on the floor or carry me around atop his shoulders." Once, she added, "when I was six, this last was disastrous for me. We were picnicing by a rushing stream outside of Washington. He set me up top and started jumping with me from stone to stone. I was delighted until he slipped and we crashed into the water. I was bruised and started choking on water with the result that to this day I'm a scare-cat about jumping from stone to stone in a rushing stream!"

The overriding theme of life with her father was excitement. And an underlying theme of stress or risk weaves its way through Anna's and Jimmy's accounts. When he was with them—which, both make clear, was not often enough for them—"he inundated us with fun and activity—and with love, too—but in his special way, which was both detached and overpowering. Sometimes we felt we didn't have him at all, but, when we did have him, life was as lively and exciting as any kid could want it to be." His attention to his children during the whole period before my mother's adolescence was vividly active and affectionate, but even in Jimmy's positive images there is indication of a shadow side.

Jimmy gives the impression that his father was an energetic man who swept his children up into his orbit, but not an empathetic man who would take the time to be with his children on their ground, to listen to their stories and respond to their spoken and unspoken wishes, fears, and pleas. He elicited great devotion in his children—he was, Jimmy says, "a wonderful father, the most loyal and understanding parent a son or daughter could want"—but he must, by his absences, his "detached and overpowering" presences, have also elicited some loneliness and fear and anger. It was as if, sometimes, he was simultaneously absent and inescapable. And he was to become so very much more so.

Something of Anna's experience and the quality of Franklin's vivid companionship with his children, especially on vacation at Hyde Park and Campobello, is suggested in Jimmy's recollections: "In the wintertime at Hyde Park, there was ice skating and hockey on the pond, and coasting behind the South Porch down the long hill leading to the river. Father was like a kid himself on these sledding expeditions. He would chase us back up the steep road at a pace so fast our lungs would ache with the hurt of the cold air and hard breathing. Spills were frequent but it was our code to treat them with great hilarity."

"In spots where there were sudden bumps," my mother recalled, "the toboggan would take off into the air, landing with a big bump several feet below and beyond. It was always a question as to whether the toboggan would land right side up or spill us all into the snow. As children and grown-ups alike crowded into the same toboggan, I remember that at one such upsidedown landing a rather heavy-set cousin of mine, Theodore Douglas Robinson, came to rest squarely on my stomach, knocking me out. I can remember the uncomfortable feeling of struggling to get a little breath into my lungs. But, here again, there was no sympathy, and loud laughter was the first sound that greeted my ears as I came to. Of course, being a sturdy child, I made the very next toboggan run down the hill."

My mother was taught to swim in a similarly rough way, "with a laundry rope tied around my middle, by being dumped in the Rogers' pond at Hyde Park while a grown-up, standing on the float, alternately gave me enough rope so that I "swallowed the pond," as we used to call it, and hauled me to the surface long enough to exhort me to keep kicking my arms and legs. That pond is bottomless except at the extreme edges."

Her father also taught her and her brothers to sail during the summer at Campobello. Leaving detailed and basic instruction to a local captain, he delighted in demonstrating his mastery of seamanship to his children by navigating narrow and treacherous passages. He "loved adventure and excitement. . . . I learned at an early age to hold my breath in excitement, and to be Johnny on the spot when it came to obeying orders from the skipper, for a second's delay might mean disaster. Very young, I learned that delay in doing something of this sort for Father annoyed him and brought forth reproachful remarks, which often made me cry."

"We also rode at Hyde Park," Jimmy recalled, and it was there, as he said, that "Anna took the honors. . . . Thanks to Granny and affluent Delano relatives, Sis had a succession of ponies and horses, and she rode them skillfully and daringly—sidesaddle, astride, and even bareback—with her long blonde hair streaming behind her like a pennant." Anna's father encouraged her to ride sidesaddle, claiming that the traditional lady's riding method happened also to make high-jumping easier and safer. She taught herself to ride astride and bareback. It was when she was eleven years old that she was given a small Norwegian horse by her father's uncle, Warren Delano. Her own determination to master that horse and its recalcitrant ways reflected her parents'—especially her father's—admonition and example: "The horse was stubborn, and when he and I disagreed as to which direction was to be followed, he would frequently knock me out of the saddle by backing fast under a low limb of a tree. He would buck me off and drag me along the ground because I insisted on hanging on to the reins. Father was never one to offer sympathy if he felt you could do something better. So I carefully kept these little incidents to myself."

"Even when Sis was a tiny little girl," Jimmy wrote, "Father would place her in front of him on his favorite horse, Bobby, and they would canter over the Hyde Park countryside." My mother recalled, "He would ride horseback with me, and point out varieties of birds as they darted by. His favorite rides were to wood plantations he had put in. Some were close to wood roads and some were in the most unexpected spots in peaceful, deserted glens deep in the woods. I loved those rides and the companionship. Here again Mother didn't fit into my childhood picture. She rode but didn't care for it much, saying that Father had trained Bobby to charge at a dead gallop up all small hills. She was never sure when he'd take off and was therefore unrelaxed. And of course, though I don't remember being aware of it, she was often pregnant with one of my five brothers."

Such was the early character of a deep-seated, early attachment to her father, an attachment strengthened—as was her mother's before her—by a lack of identification with her mother. Although balanced by a growth of such identification in Anna's late adolescence, she—again, like her mother—was to remain throughout her life overwhelmingly her father's daughter. And as Eleanor's attachment to her father was to shadow and burden her adult relationships with other men, so too were Anna's adult relationships with men overshadowed by the presence of her father, her first love.

# FIVE

# *Conformist and Rebel*

FAMILY moves continued. In the winter of 1911–1912 they lived in another house in Albany, and the following winter Anna, aged six and presumably living in the house on Sixty-fifth Street, was taken by her mother to begin school. She remained at Miss Davidge's school in New York only for one term, though, for that spring her father was appointed assistant secretary of the navy by President Wilson. In the autumn of 1913 the family rented Auntie Bye's* house at 1733 N Street in Washington, where they remained for the next three years.

Eleanor described the house on N Street as comfortable and old-fashioned. Her son Elliott added his own recollections: "Number 1733 was one of a red-brick row, indistinguishable from its neighbors, with an unfenced, handkerchief-sized lawn in front and a miniature garden in the rear, where we occasionally ate breakfast if the weather turned hot and humid, with the dishes served on a wrought-iron table in the little rose arbor. The street's massive shade trees made the rooms gloomy, even with the sliding double doors between them on the main floor pulled open to give us children more space to roam in. The house had never been wired for electricity. Gas sconces stood out from the walls and chandeliers from the ceilings, lit by a servant with a taper at dusk. One of the first of my admonitions I remember is Mother's 'You must never, *never* play with the gas.' " The house now, unfortunately, no longer exists, nor do the massive shade trees on N Street.

Anna was sent to school that autumn with "the Misses Eastman"

*Eleanor's father's elder sister, Anna Roosevelt Cowles, or "Bamie."

in Washington, where she continued for the next seven years. There is no evidence of Anna's enjoying her school work, nor of the Misses Eastman offering much stimulus to learning. Eleanor was belatedly—at the end of Anna's years there—to recognize the school as "stuffy."

Franklin's professional responsibilities in the Navy Department, the copious social life expected of both him and Eleanor, the inspection trips to naval installations on which she often accompanied him, and as the country joined World War I, her own heavy work schedule with the Red Cross and other agencies—all this meant that the children saw even less of their parents. Sara was frequently at the house and with the children. Eleanor continued her custom of being home by teatime and staying with the children until their bedtime. Anna was anxious at her parents' leavetakings. She once asked her mother what would happen if she and the other children had to buy anything "or got lost or put in prison."

The two youngest boys were born during this period: the second Franklin Jr. on August 17, 1914, and John on March 13, 1916. If they had less access to their parents when very young (by virtue of the acceleration of Franklin's, and now Eleanor's, public activities and the growth in the family's size), there was compensation in Eleanor's growing self-confidence and active leadership in mothering (as well as in other realms). It is in that context that we should probably understand Lash's impression, "of all her children the two youngest . . . were the ones Eleanor seemed to enjoy most." She later felt that those two boys "had far better childhoods than the first three children, whose lives were run almost entirely by their nurses." She surely must have felt better about her own more assertive role in child rearing, but it is not clear that such a change implied a markedly different pattern of experience for the children.

The family having grown so, Auntie Bye's house was too small, and a move was made in the autumn of 1916 to a larger house at 2131 R Street. Anna loved the regular morning ritual of walking to school with her father, who would then walk on to his office at the Navy Department. "Those walks I remember because we talked about all sorts of things I liked to hear about—books I was reading, a cruise

A portrait of four generations: Anna with Grandma Hall, Eleanor (standing), and Aunt Tissie (Mrs. Stanley Mortimer). *Franklin D. Roosevelt Library*

Anna on her pony at Campobello, about 1916. *Franklin D. Roosevelt Library*

we might be going to take down the Potomac River the following weekend, the historic old Virginia houses Father planned to show us."

Weekends in Washington, particularly during the four years before the United States entered World War I, "were filled with joys which were primarily instigated by Father." He organized baseball games in Rock Creek Park, the teams "made up evenly of young adults his age, and Jimmy and me and our friends; and paper chases, or 'Hare and Hounds,' " through the woods of the same park. "Some of these chases were on foot and some on horseback, and as with the baseball games, they included all ages. The team of hares would get a ten-to-fifteen-minute head start and leave a faint trail of finely cut-up newspapers. To befuddle the following team of hounds, false trails would be occasionally laid by one of the hares. It was always a fast and furious chase across country, with a destination known only to the hares. And usually reached by them in safety."

Eleanor's efforts, during those Washington years—Anna's years between seven and fourteen—to redress her early subordination to Sara and the nurses bore some fruit. During a time when her husband was less available, she took more of a hand in play with the children; and she became more involved in efforts to compensate and supplement the dull and unimaginative aspects of their schooling. But it was hard to overcome the patterns of her own deep-seated experience. The really intimate parts of their lives, my mother recalled, were still "run by nurses and governesses." Of her mother Anna said later in life, "She felt a tremendous sense of duty to us. It was part of that duty to read to us and to hear our prayers before we went to bed, but she did not understand or satisfy the need of a child for primary closeness to a parent." Eleanor herself wrote with perception and poignance: "It did not come naturally to me to understand little children or to enjoy them. Playing with children was difficult for me because play had not been an important part of my own childhood."

Eleanor's mother was said by a friend to have approached her children with "almost an heroic conscientiousness," and her daughter followed suit. "Mother was a terribly conscientious person,"

Anna said. "She tried, you always felt she was doing her darndest to do the right thing by her children, or to get across to them the things that she felt were right and the things that she felt were wrong. She didn't have too much sense of humor about it during those years of developing." My grandmother herself wrote in retrospect: "Instead of enjoying [my children], most of the time I was disciplining them or worrying about their health or trying to give them pleasure that their father's illness prevented them from enjoying with him. I never was really carefree. It is a pity that we cannot have the experience that comes with age in our younger days, when we really need it."

Eleanor's own unsureness about right and wrong behavior, and her growing sense of moral complexity and ambiguity, may have reinforced her natural tendency to treat such matters rather solemnly. She and Granny, she recalled, "had opposite views on a number of moral issues; to her black was black, and white was white. She would sometimes ask me, 'Eleanor, why don't you tell the children what's right and what's wrong?' Then I would reply, 'Because I don't know myself.' "

"Father, Mother, and my grandmother were not demonstrative with sympathy or even affection . . . in case of illness or injury, the emphasis was on courage and keeping quiet about whatever pain we felt." My mother remembered her brother Jimmy as a child having a bad case of poison ivy. She led her mother into Jimmy's bedroom explaining how much he was suffering. "I'll never forget my surprise when Mother calmly said, 'You silly boy, you ought to know better than to get near poison ivy.' " Brother and sister burst into tears, and Anna left the room.

That which Eleanor was taught as a child sometimes appeared identically in her treatment of her daughter. "Mother patiently taught me to knit and to embroider. She had one of the maids teach me how to darn; and how I hated that process because the lessons consisted of cutting a hole out of a piece of cloth and telling me to fill it in. Impatient and rebellious, I would darn so loosely that the hole was not really filled. The scissors would be applied and I would be handed back the same cloth with a hole that was even larger. I *must* have learned that the fastest way to escape was to do a good job the first time!"

Like her mother, Anna had some tendency in looking back on such experiences to view them as useful lessons in self-discipline and doing one's best. But, of an adult generation less impressed with the sufficiency of self-discipline and hard work, Anna's recollections retained much of the childhood spirit of resentment and rebellion. Her memory of the darning as a lesson in effective concentration is followed immediately by a long passage in which she recalls how shut out she felt by the "concentration" of the three most significant adults in her life: her parents and her grandmother. "All three had great powers of concentration, and they concentrated on practically everything they did. I learned at an early age that certain 'concentrations' were not to be interrupted by small fry. This was good discipline, but I fear that it made me resent concentration as such—until I achieved adulthood and understood the necessity and satisfactions of this attribute."

In that formal last phrase, the parental voice—her mother's voice—still dutifully salvages useful learning, but her heart is hardly in it.

"If Granny was writing at her desk or talking to the gardener in the garden (the same Rose Garden where Father and Mother are buried) I learned that interruption would not be welcomed; though Granny was indeed more indulgent of child interruptions than my parents. But she would manage with a pat on the head or shoulder and a remark that she'd talk to me later, to make me know that my question and I were not as important at the moment as I would undoubtedly have liked!

"When Mother was concentrating—talking to someone, reading or working at her desk—she had a far more chilling way of putting me in my place. This way persisted with her throughout her life so I remember very well the sound of the low but cold voice which said, 'What do you want, dear.' It was not a question; just an unmistakable announcement that she was busy and preoccupied.

"Father was more outspoken: he'd talk about that later; or he would respond with a bit of sarcasm to the question which made it apparent that he considered the question to be trivial, perhaps rather dumb, certainly unnecessary, and probably something I should have thought through for myself. Now, I believe that this was good therapy. It did force me to think for myself. But it also (as well as my mother's method) made me increasingly reticent about talking to my parents about any and all types of difficulties as they arose in my life."

"It has always seemed to me," she wrote at another time, "that the greatest contradiction in my parents was, on the one hand, their supreme ability to 'relate' to either groups of people or individuals who had problems, and on the other hand, their apparent lack of ability to 'relate' with the same consistent warmth and interest to an individual who was their child." Later, as she observed her parents' remarkable public life, the paradox seemed all the more striking and no less painful: "To the farmer in the area to the east of our house at Hyde Park, Father related with obvious warmth and sincere interest. On the radio his voice radiated this same warmth and personal interest to the extent that people have often told me they felt his words were specifically directed to them as individuals. To the many groups Mother addressed, or welcomed to a meeting in the White House, she radiated a knowledge of their problems and a sincere and personal desire to help them solve these problems. In the same way she gave her undivided and reassuring . . . attention to whomever she was talking to. Whereas I felt, throughout her life, that I should (though I did not always do so) find the appropriate time for approaching her with a subject I felt a need to or wanted to discuss."

On the whole, my mother remembered herself as "a social conformist" as a child. She respected, at least outwardly, Granny's admonitions that "children have their place" and that "Father was a special person and an important person entitled to special thoughtfulness and respect." She waited for "the appropriate time" with her mother, adhering to the "very structured life" she and her brothers were led. But increasingly she found two notable outlets for her resentment and rebelliousness. She was a healthy, robust child, full of physical vitality, and found herself joining her brothers in playful—and sometimes warlike—opposition to the regime of nurses, governesses, and parental preoccupation.

"To act out Indian raids with my brothers, on horseback, galloping and dodging between the long rows of tall fodder corn, whooping and hollering in what Granny so frequently called unlady-like behavior; running pony-cart races down narrow country lanes, with hay piled high in the cart making one's driving perch both precarious and dangerous; dropping paper sacks filled with water from the third story window of our house in Washington, with the hope of hitting the large, beflowered hats of Mother's formally dressed callers on her official day at home; secreting foul-smelling stink bombs in the hallway and dining room immediately before a formal dinner party was to start; acting out sea adventures, ship wrecks and all, in a high and dry fishing dory safely moored among the wild blueberries and scrub brush well below our Campobello house, where our shrieks and nautical commands could not be heard; playing ghost after dark in the big Hyde Park house when some fortunate circumstance took our parents and grandmother away simultaneously—a most unpopular game with our elders because all closets and nooks and crannies took a beating—all of these and many more activities provided us with healthy outlets. Not that we didn't get roundly punished for pranks, but not so roundly that we gave them up or didn't put our imaginations to work on new ones."

At another time she remembered of this same period "sliding down the roof of our Campobello house, thereby loosening the shingles; . . . filling guests' pajama pockets with crushed onions we picked up in Virigina fields on one of our cruises down the Potomac." One evening in Washington—around 1916—she left a note, presumably in the downstairs hall, addressed to "Hon. F. D. Roosevelt":

Dear Father,

Will you please come and say good-night to James and [me] if it is not too late. I am going up now to put something in James' bed and you may hear some shrieks when you come in.

Anna

And there was more: sliding down the bannisters in Auntie Bye's Washington house, "not turning up when I was supposed to, or listening to them yelling for me . . . being at the top of a great fir tree and just sort of hah-hahing to myself."

And there, in that last wonderful image, is a perfect instance of her second mode of escape: the kind of isolation and immersion in reading and fantasy her mother knew so well as a child. In later years she remembered vividly her love of her time alone, and the Hyde Park estate was a home for that aloneness. Indeed, Hyde Park was the center of her child world: the home her beloved father loved so deeply and where father and daughter shared their closest moments in the pre-polio years; the books in the library she began to consume hungrily around age twelve; and the land, the woods, and stables in which she treasured her time alone.

The big house at Hyde Park was Sara's and Franklin's home. Eleanor was never to feel that it was hers. "For over forty years," she wrote at the end of her life, "I was only a visitor there." But for the children it was the place to which they always returned, the place identified with the security of family, the fun of adventure with their father, the reliable excitement of Christmases, the solid social world epitomized by Sara, who knew without doubt who she was, where she belonged, and what was right. "Hyde Park," my mother once told an interviewer, "was very definitely my most favorite place in life. . . . Hyde Park was home, and the only place I ever thought was completely home. . . . I felt that that was *the* one place that I could be completely myself."

While reading through my mother's papers at the FDR Library in the early winter of 1976, I came upon several drafts of a story called "The Place." It was written in the third person, but was clearly an account of her experience of Hyde Park; and it was extraordinary in several respects. Most striking is its flowing, romantic narrative form, unique in her published and unpublished writings. Though clearly and articulately self-reflective, she was not, in general, a storyteller. It is likely that the story was written (and revised with the thought of publication) during the last years of her marriage to my father; that is, during a time of stress and unhappiness when it might have been natural to return, in a kind of dreamlike consciousness, to the memories and the most potent symbols of whatever security she had known. And written when it was, in the midst of a ruining marriage that had begun as such a high romance, it is perhaps kin to the story of that relationship; of its shadowing parallel, her life and the death of her life with her father; and even of the central pattern she then saw in her life: a warmth grown cold.

SIX

# "The Place," by Anna Roosevelt Boettiger

YES, The Place, and the rambling big house, meant more to her than anything that had ever come into her young life.

In her earliest memories she felt she was a part of The Place, just like a branch of the tall hemlock which stood in front of the house.

She loved that hemlock and the other tall and spreading trees on the rolling lawn surrounding the house. There was reason for her attachment to the hemlock. She would make trips up that tree, to the very top, from whence she could see over the roof of the big house, to the purple hills on the other side of the broad Hudson river. What a sense of triumph over "things"! And that hemlock had a very special branch, a big "comfy" one about twenty feet above the ground, on which she would sit leaning against the huge trunk, and read to herself by the hour.

Reading was a very favorite pastime during the long summer months. The family's big library offered row on row of classics—histories, biographies and her beloved Dickens' novels. Here a deep chair was fine for rainy days.

But there was a more exciting way of "absorbing" the library. This was on the days when she and "Oscar" her Norwegian pony, and "Chief," her own tawny police dog, set out together of an early morning with a picnic lunch and a book strapped to the saddle. The trio would roam the woods, never sticking to wood roads or trails, but busting through swamps, tangled woods and stands of fast grow-

*On the facing page, above*: Springwood, the Hyde Park home that was my mother's "favorite place in life." *Below*: A Hyde Park woods road on the Roosevelt land.

*Franklin D. Roosevelt Library photos*

Anna at fourteen, with her beloved Chief.

ing pines, where pine needles hushed every pony footfall. She knew by heart the spots where the pony could be given rein to run at full tilt while the wind pulled her hair straight back from its roots. She gradually learned by experience the swampy spots where venturing meant getting mired, climbing off and pulling with all her might to help her pony struggle free from half mud, half quicksand.

But when the sun neared the center of the sky she always knew it would find her in some peaceful spot—a cool one for the hotter days and a sunfilled one for the cooler days—where she and "Chief" could share the picnic lunch while "Oscar" contentedly munched the grass and leaves.

Then, with tummy full and hours stretching ahead, she would reach for the book. Only a change in the shadows cast across the pages would remind her that it was time to be starting homeward.

And to her, The Place meant other things: it meant house parties; her brothers' friends and her friends all gathered together for long and glorious weekends; lights out at night but not quiet in the household because adolescent figures would steal out into the long corridors and start firing pillows; there would be squeals, muffled giggles and then outright, uncontrolled shouts of laughter as mattresses were overturned; then the inevitable appearance of Grandma or Mother or Father, with stern admonitions to get back to bed.

It meant Christmas, with candle-lighted tree, and carols sung as family and friends gathered around the piano. It meant the freedom to be alone with the horses and dogs she loved; the humor of knowing that Grandma did not like the brown knickers her granddaughter wore, protesting almost daily with such remarks as: "A divided skirt would be so much more ladylike," and "My dear, you have a decided stable odor. A bath, of course, will cure it. And, don't forget now, you must wear a dress for lunch!"

She remembered how close to the surface in those young years was laughter and song, and tears.

During the years of adolescence she became aware of other things which made The Place important to her. Her family and the varied assortment of people they gathered around them provided her with a new stimulation. She listened avidly to the stories told by visitors from other lands; to political discussions ranging from the selection of a town supervisor through the state of the nation and on to the current troubles of the world.

She never tired either of stories told by Grandma, Father and Mother, of their own personal experiences: Grandma's memories of childhood days in China, France and Germany. Mother's recollections of her famous uncle's ways of "toughening" the younger generation by such methods as teaching them to swim by throwing them into a pond with a slack rope around their middles and shouting "Now swim!" Father's stories of his boyhood bicycle trips through Europe, the lack of red tape involved in crossing the borders in those days from one country to another, and his ability to tie in historical facts of years ago with events of the present day.

All of this the daughter absorbed, asked questions on her own and learned to love the lively and often controversial discussions where one member of the family took issue with another.

Over it all was an atmosphere of warmth and genuine family cohesiveness. The family might and would argue with each other to the point of high pitched and even angry voices—but let an outsider criticize one of them to another and the fur would fly!

Then there came the time when Father became an important public figure. The girl had become a woman, but she was still wangling every possible way to be at The Place. And she brought her children back there, filling them full of her own love for it.

True, she knew that these children were never to know it as she had. Public life inevitably meant that days were full of people arriving or leaving, from morning to night. Public life had to bring public curiosity, and these grandchildren were not to know the same carefree privacy of home life at The Place as their mother had enjoyed.

But still they could love the trees and the selfmade adventures in the woods. And this they did, because children have the happy knack of taking life as they find it, and because the exactions of being a part of a family with one member in public life had crept up rather gradually through the years.

As the years slipped by, guards' pillboxes sprang up. They were taken for granted by her children. But she couldn't quite kill a guilty feeling of resentment when she couldn't walk the lawn overlooking the Hudson without crossing the mooncast shadow of a guard on duty!

The years passed—and for the first time in her memory, death caused a break in the strong family unit. She knew she had lost a baby brother many years before; could remember her Mother telling her about it, but she could not remember having any feeling about it. So, when Grandma passed quietly on in her sleep, it made her suddenly aware of the inevitable slipping away of time and the changes which were bound to come with it.

Grandma was far more than a grandparent. She was inextricably interwoven with The Place. There she had come as a bride, sixty-one years before. And for the forty-one years since her husband's death, she had been the mainspring of The Place. Her code of life was consistent, strong and continuous, throughout her long life. She saw to it that it extended to her grandchildren and great-grandchildren, and when they deviated she accepted only because family loyalty was the core of her life philosophy.

Without Grandma, The Place could never be quite the same, but her influence had been so strong that her long-established family habits and traditions were carried on with almost no changes. And so The Place lived on.

The years following brought ever increasing burdens to Father; the worries and pressures of war; the planning for the years which would follow it, in a world left with human suffering, with hopes and prayers for permanent peace, and with inevitable distrust and greed.

The daughter joined in family discussions of the hoped-for days when Father would once more be a private citizen, with time in which to quietly pursue his many personal interests.

It became very clear to her and to the others that The Place could never again go back to the quiet and privacy of earlier days. The old house had been the home of a man who had become a world figure. And so The Place would have to be shared with people of the outside world who would want to see it.

But it didn't occur to her to resent or challenge this sharing of The Place. She still felt that all she loved about The Place would always remain vibrantly alive.

Then, without warning, fate struck down the man about whom all of The Place revolved, and who loved it as it seemed to love him. In those grief-stricken days she was too numbed to take in fully the significance of all the changes this meant. And almost immediately she went away—thousands of miles away—and from that distance she could be objective about The Place, and she could face the fact that for historical reasons The Place should, from then on, belong exclusively to the people of the country.

Then one day she returned to The Place. It was a chilly dusk. The solid gray skies seemed gloomily immovable. There was no sunset to cast colorful shadows.

She went first to the garden, inside the tall thick hemlock hedge. She stood silently in front of the grave—now covered with a warm blanket of evergreen myrtle. She gazed at the simple and impressive white marble monument. It was lonely, but blessedly peaceful and quiet—which seemed so right. She knew Father would always live in her heart.

Then she turned and walked over to the big old house. Suddenly an overwhelming sense of depression came over her. The same trees were still there, the same lawns and fields sloping towards woods and river, the same walls, doors and windows.

But it was all dead to her.

There was no life behind those dark windows; the front door would not suddenly open and frame laughter and welcome.

In her mind she could picture each room: the dining room with its high and heavily carved dark sideboards, and chairs whose leather seats were far too well worn for comfort; her own bedroom with the chintz patterned wallpaper, the old fashioned double bed and so-hard mattress which Grandma always insisted was too new to be changed, and the bureau-dressing table with its marble top; Grandma's formal drawing room with its impossibly uncomfortable furniture and its Dresden chandoliers and figurines; the big library with Father's tall chair on the north side of the fireplace. All of these rooms would be just as she remembered them; just as Grandma and Father lived in them—and they would be spotlessly neat and clean, kept so by loving caretakers whose lives had also been a part of The Place.

But there would be no fire in that fireplace; Father's chair would be too correctly placed, and no cigarette ashes on the floor beside it, dropped because of his too great interest in the conversation at hand.

These rooms would be cold—cold because the people who had kept them warm with love and laughter and tears were no longer there.

A shutter banged and she jumped. The house looked dismally gray, forlorn and uninviting. "No thanks," she said in answer to a quiet question from a caretaker-guard. She couldn't go into the house and "have a look around." Not then, anyway.

She slipped away. The Place, as she had known it and loved it, had died. . . .

S E V E N

# *Two Family Crises*

CHIEF, the police-dog friend of whom my mother wrote, was the first and most cherished of a life-long line of dogs upon whom she lavished great attention and affection. She won Chief in a Red Cross raffle when she was twelve. "The dog became my closest companion and lived until after my own second child was born." He is buried alongside her father's dog Fala in the Rose Garden at Hyde Park. I remember noting with some jealousy, well into my adulthood, the attention and unconflicted devotion my mother shared with her dogs. They offered, unlike her human companions, a consistent, unfailing affection, and while they occasionally ran off or got into trouble, there was no doubt as to who was boss.

My mother once described her inclination to aloneness during her preadolescent and teenage years—her pleasure in long, solitary horseback rides and long hours of reading at Hyde Park—as a way of escaping the tensions of her family and "the feeling that I was bossed all the time": by nurses and governesses, and also by her mother and grandmother. She took pride in her "unladylike," tomboy behavior, and competed with her brothers for her father's attention—becoming, as she said, "a better woodsman and rider than they." The most visible family tension, in Anna's eyes, was that between Eleanor and Sara; and her awareness of that tension must have served as a convenient mask for her less conscious—and probably more frightening—experience of serious tension between her parents.

The years of Anna's transition into adolescence unhappily coincided with a major crisis in her parents' relationship, a crisis which nearly brought them to divorce: Eleanor's discovery of Franklin's

Franklin and Anna at Campobello in 1920, a year before polio paralyzed his legs. *Below*: The family at Campobello that same summer.
*Franklin D. Roosevelt Library photos*

love affair with Lucy Mercer. Her discovery came in September, 1918, when Anna was twelve, and must—for all its secrecy from the children—have profoundly affected the family for many months after. It brought Eleanor "to almost total despair," and the following year was often virtually unbearable for her. Gradually she emerged more independent, more securely grounded in her own purposes, more determined to be of active and significant service to others; but the wound, opening as it must have such deep, older wounds, was lasting. She wrote Joe Lash twenty-five years later: "The bottom dropped out of my own particular world, and I faced myself, my surroundings, my world, honestly for the first time. I really grew up that year."

It was not until 1925 that Eleanor told her daughter about Franklin's affair with Lucy Mercer, but the impact must still have been considerable at the time. Both parents' tendencies to preoccupation—in Anna's eyes, their unavailability—may have been heightened. It may be, too, that Anna's romantic attachment to her father was strengthened by her mother's more pronounced withdrawal. Eleanor wrote of a later crisis in her relationship with Anna some lines that may bear relevance to this time as well: "[Anna] was an adolescent girl and I still treated her like a child and thought of her as a child. . . . I have always had a very bad tendency to shut up like a clam, particularly when things are going badly; and that attitude was accentuated, I think, as regards my children."

In 1920 Franklin was nominated for vice-president by the Democratic party, and Anna went along with her parents on one campaign visit to the Dayton, Ohio, home of the presidential nominee, James M. Cox. She was fourteen, it was her first such appearance, and, according to Eleanor, she enjoyed it enormously. "She was pretty, her light golden hair, which at that time was long, attracted a good deal of attention, and everyone was as kind to her as could be. For her the day was over far too quickly." Thirty-eight years later Anna recalled: "I haven't the slightest memory of being much made over. What I do remember is that I was made to wear a Navy blue alpaca dress, which the family thought was simply beautiful but which I hated because it scratched, and that I had a private bathroom at the Cox's place, which I thought was really something."

With Franklin's resignation as assistant secretary of the navy, the family's first Washington years were over, and Eleanor took Anna and Elliott to Hyde Park for the winter of 1920–1921, where they were tutored by Miss Jean Sherwood, a Vassar student. Eleanor divided her time between Hyde Park and Sara's New York house. With the overwhelming defeat of the Democratic ticket in the 1920 election Franklin returned to his law practice in New York.

If that transitional winter and spring of 1920–1921 held any promise of some quieter, less public, and less crisis-filled years for the Roosevelt family, that prospect was cruelly cut off by Franklin's contracting polio the following summer. For the children it was a huge and frightening experience. Franklin Jr. was seven, and years later he recalled for his brother Jimmy his first memory of his father, a scene that Jimmy says, "I too never shall forget—that of standing on the porch at Campobello, watching Father being carried out on a stretcher, and recalling how he tried to wipe away the scare of it by smiling wonderfully at us and cheerily singing out, 'I'll be seeing you chicks soon!' "

Jimmy himself was thirteen, but he says he felt "as young and scared as little Johnny," who was five. Jimmy remembers his thought as four men carried his father from the house: "Just the month before he came to Campobello, I thought, this big, wonderful father of mine had taken me to see the Dempsey-Carpentier world's heavyweight championship fight in Jersey City, and on the way out I got pulled away from him in the crowd and was scared to death until he found me. Would he ever, I wondered, take me anywhere again?"

Anna, then fifteen, must have shared her brothers' fears that they were losing their father. When the doctors met in her bedroom to discuss their diagnosis, she hid in a closet to listen; "I heard the word 'polio' for the first time." Franklin's ways of being with his children had been so physical, so full of movement; the prospect of his paralysis struck to the heart of their life with him. And his illness, the absences it was to bring and the other people it brought between them, came at a time in Anna's life when she felt most keenly her bond with him. The image of the hero father grew, but at the expense of real intimacy, for which she must have hungered greatly.

My mother's own public recollections, written in 1949, emphasized her admiration for her father's struggle, and the spiritedness he succeeded in impressing upon his children:

"This was the beginning of a period of adjustment to an entirely new life for the whole family. Mother became more and more busy. . . . I gradually grew accustomed to a new relationship with Father—a relationship where I had to go to his room and sit on a chair or at the foot of his bed when I wanted to talk to him. For some months my knowledge that he was suffering made me shy with him. But gradually his gayety, his ability to poke fun at himself as he learned to move himself around through the use of his arms, broke down the tension we had been feeling. . . .

"Every time I saw him walking, with great effort, on his crutches, for as long a distance as he possibly could, I couldn't help but feel a wrench in my heart. I would see him walk out our Hyde Park driveway, oh so slowly, and see the beads of perspiration on his forehead after he'd gone a short distance.

"But then his own spirit was transmitted to all of us. He apparently knew it would be a shock for us to realize that the useless muscles in his legs would cause atrophy. . . . So Father removed the sadness by showing us his legs. He gave us the names of each of the muscles in them, then told us which ones he was working hardest on at that moment. He would shout with glee over a little movement of a muscle that had been dormant. So, gradually, I almost forgot that he had once had well-developed muscles. The battle Father was making became a spirited game."

Her brother Jimmy's recollections of his father during the polio period—the onset of the illness and the struggle for recovery during the early and mid-1920s—are notably ambivalent. On the one hand, he too was moved and impressed by his father's gallantry in fighting to recover from "the cruelest blow that could have afflicted such an active man." On the other hand grew the corresponding—already well rooted—themes of detachment and absence. Jimmy writes: "These were the lonely years; for a long while during this time of illness and recovery we had no tangible father, no father-in-being, whom we could touch and talk to at will—only an abstract symbol, a cheery letter writer, off somewhere on a houseboat or at Warm Springs, fighting by himself to do what had to be done."

The confusion of those years, the renewed need for a father and the wish to be *his* parent, the difficulty in coping with conflicting feelings, and particularly the constraint attending negative feelings, is vividly indicated in Jimmy's next paragraph: "Only now do I realize how sorely we missed him during that period. But when we saw him, he was so—well, so damned gallant that he made you want to cry and laugh and cling to him and carry him in your arms and lean on him for support all at the same time." Franklin's example of gallantry, striving in the midst of his pain "to pass it all off as a nothing, a nuisance, to ease the shock of the five scared kids who watched him," had great precedent-setting impact on the children, who had already been taught by both parents "to face illness and injury without tears or complaint; pain was to be borne silently."

Further, Eleanor's growing political activity, and the renewal—albeit on a less intimate familial plane—of the relationship between Eleanor and Franklin as she performed more and more public functions on his behalf, amounted in Anna's eyes to a partnership that too largely excluded the children. "I always felt that the polio was very instrumental in bringing them much closer, into a very real partnership. . . ." While Anna may have resented her exclusion from this partnership, she must have also experienced some reassurance in the renewal of her parents' bond. My mother spoke, for example, of the "real discussions" between her parents during this period, and added, "I think this was good for all of us growing up. We could join in at times." Still, this was principally a time of loneliness for Anna, a loneliness deepened by the absence of brotherly companionship: Jimmy and Elliott were both away at Groton, and Franklin Jr. and Johnny were too young for satisfying confidence or conspiracy.

Anna turned sixteen in that dark spring of 1921. The strain and anxiety of the next months and years is revealed in accounts of some particular moments in her life. By the following fall the family was back in the house on East Sixty-fifth Street, and Anna was put into Miss Chapin's School, where she felt rejected as an outsider, shy, desperately lonely without friends, unhappy, and bewildered: all echoes of her feelings about matters closer to home. And those at the school, for all of Eleanor's hope that Miss Chapin might be for Anna something like Mlle. Souvestre had been for her, responded with little understanding or sympathy, indeed little constructive attention of any sort.

It seems likely that some of Anna's strong, complex feelings toward her father, which must have included an element of anger at his desertion, were in part displaced onto Louis Howe, Franklin's political lieutenant, who was now living in the house and had become a real friend to Eleanor in her distress and a guide in her emergence as a public person. For some years before that time Anna, following the earlier example of both Sara and Eleanor, had disliked Louis Howe. So he was a natural—and relatively safe—alternative target for her resentment of both parents. My mother later remembered her jealousy of Louis's new closeness to her mother, and of all those—Louis, her mother, nurses—whom she experienced as separating her from her father.

Anna recalled in conversation with Joe Lash: "Granny, with a good insight into my adolescent nature, started telling me that it was inexcusable that I, the only daughter of the family, should have a tiny bedroom in the back of the house, while Louis enjoyed a large, sunny front bedroom with his own private bath. Granny's needling finally took root; at her instigation, I went to Mother one evening and demanded a switch in rooms. A sorely tried and harassed mother was naturally anything but sympathetic; in fact, she was very stern with her recalcitrant daughter."

Eleanor wrote discreetly in her autobiography, "Because of constant outside influences the situation grew in her mind to a point where she felt that I did not care for her and was not giving her any consideration. . . . There were times at the dinner table when she would annoy her father so much that he would be severe with her and a scene would ensue, then she would burst into tears and retire sobbing to her room."

It was in recalling this time that Eleanor mentioned her own "very bad tendency tò shut up like a clam," and her conviction that had she shared more of her own experience with her daughter they would have understood one another a great deal better and saved them both "several years of real unhappiness"—years in which Anna particularly resented the preoccupation and relative inaccessibility of both her parents; years, finally, from which she was to seek escape through marriage.

Eleanor broke into uncontrolled tears twice that winter and spring, once while reading to Franklin Jr. and John, and once with Anna. The children were frightened: "to my horror," my mother said in recalling the moment. For if the children needed more comfort and understanding than Eleanor was offering, they also depended on her, especially at that time, for continuity and stability, and the free expression of strong feelings of pain or fear or anguish was not in the family canon.

EIGHT

# *Conflict and Reconciliation*

BUT IN the wake of those tearful occasions Eleanor did begin to open up more with Anna, and their relationship became a little less strained. Anna "began to straighten out," wrote Eleanor later, "and at last she poured some of her troubles out and told me she knew she had been wrong and that I did love her, and from that day to this our mutual understanding has constantly improved." Eleanor does not say whether she confessed to Anna any regret for her own distance and sternness.

Anna's own tendencies to withdrawal and the tension in her relationship with her mother were somewhat moderated in adolescence by the growth of significant new awareness of Eleanor and identification with her. She learned for the first time the stories of her mother's childhood, and struggled with the differences and underlying similarities to her own: "By the time I reached my teen years, and through them, I had withdrawn within myself insofar as my questions about life and daily living were concerned. Mother did tell me about menstruation, saying that no one had told her ahead of time and she had been a very frightened child. This brought out the different circumstances in our childhoods. Hers was unbelievably lonely, introverted into a dream world made up of recollections of her father, surrounded by young aunts and a grandmother who were far too busy with their own lives to give consistent personal attention and affection to a quiet, serious little girl who was, seemingly, satisfactorily engrossed with her books and her own thoughts. On the other hand, I had all the outward trappings to make a child happy, school-girl friends and young girl cousins with whom I exchanged whatever biological information (and rumors) were available to us. I, too, however, lacked that consistency of love and personal attention but in a totally different way."

Anna's tendencies to identify with her mother developed particularly between her sixteenth and eighteenth years, the years of her coming into womanhood. The feelings of identification were rooted in the more candid talks the two began to have at that time, and—as is indicated in the above passage—in Anna's growing appreciation and respect for her mother's personal growth in the face of great difficulties: "It was a real struggle for her too, to really exploit the potentials that she had." The single most memorable event between them, in this spirit, was Eleanor's telling her daughter of Franklin's affair with Lucy Mercer. My mother had, in fact, already been told a year before, when she was seventeen, by Cousin Susie Parish; but her mother's confiding in her strengthened the bond between them. "I felt very strongly on Mother's side. . . . I think that was an emotional thing . . . a woman thing. Sort of, here I was growing up, and probably going to get married and have a family, and was this something that I was going to have to face? . . . I think I was probably putting myself a little fearfully into Mother's shoes." And she felt angry with her father for the deep hurt he had caused her mother.

Another incident in the late spring of 1922—Anna was sixteen—illustrates the complex pattern of continuing tension and rapprochement between my mother and both her parents. She and her father were in the library of the Hyde Park house.

"I was on a ladder moving some of the books to make room for others. Father was in his wheel chair giving me directions. Suddenly an armful of books slipped from my grasp and crashed to the floor. I saw Father start, and an expression of pain passed swiftly over his face. My apologies were interrupted by his voice, very sternly accusing me of being too careless for words and no help at all.

"As a child I admired Father for so many things that I took his criticism and his praise very much to heart, and if his criticism was severe I would burst into tears. This time I felt so acutely ashamed of myself that I would cheerfully have disappeared into the floor if that would have undone my carelessness. I had been so proud of being able to help him—as I always had been if I felt he was talking to me about something I thought of as important in the adult world, and he was asking me to help him with it.

"On this occasion I fled from the room—in tears, of course. I fled to a room at the other end of the house, where I ran into Mother. To her I sobbed out my story and my grief. But, typically adolescent, I added that I didn't see why Father had to be so mad at me for making a mistake.

"Mother talked of the battle Father was fighting against great odds; of the naturalness of his nervous reaction; how lucky we were to have him alive and to be able to help him get well; how much more patience and grit he had to have than we."

In retrospect, Anna understood her mother's words as an act of comfort and explanation, addressed to her less as a child than as the adult she was becoming. Eleanor's reasonableness and concern for her husband left little room in that encounter for sympathy. No wonder that Anna emerged "very sheepish and even more ashamed." The appeal to her own incipient maturity was both distressing and beguiling. She experienced her sheepishness and shame, she recalled, "in a different way, a more adult, understanding way. Back I went to the library where, of course, I not only found forgiveness but also a sincere and smilingly given invitation to resume my place on the library ladder."

Granny's mischievous role in Anna's conflict with her mother over which bedroom she deserved was evidently indicative of a growing pattern: as Eleanor became more confident in making her own decisions as a parent, Sara sought to strengthen her influence by direct appeals and gifts to the children. "She continually spoiled the children," Eleanor wrote much later, "overriding my belief in a certain amount of discipline for character-building."

Indicative of the singular power of her devotion to her son, Sara clearly thought of the children as her own. And since she was, in this time, usually more available and more sympathetic to them than was either parent, they in some real measure were inclined to agree. Granny's manipulativeness in playing family members off against one another for the sake of her own security and satisfaction—

however much motivated and compensated by her love—bred anxiety, anger, and mistrust, and set a problematic example for her grandchildren. (My mother, later in life, succumbed to the same temptation from time to time, though—being more conscious—never with Granny's wholeheartedness.) By 1922, when Anna was sixteen, she recalls having begun "to get on to the fact that, unless I chose differently I could be used as a football by Granny."

The tension between daughter and mother was refueled as Eleanor supported Sara in her insistence that Anna follow traditional social conventions. Anna's anger toward both her mother and grandmother was strong, but under protest she remained the social conformist. "When I got to the age of seventeen, I was informed that I had to come out in society, and I died. And I wasn't going to come out. And Granny said, 'You are.' And I went to Mother, and she said, 'Yes, you must.' . . . She *made* me . . . go to Newport for what they call 'Tennis Week' . . . to stay with her cousin, Susie Parish, who was the really old [guard]. . . . She made me go there, and I completely abhorred this stuff to such an extent that Cousin Susie had to procure two young men to go to the dances with me. But Mother made me do this. It was Granny who took me to get the clothes for this business."

Her father, she knew, would be no help, and he did not avoid her anger by his characteristic refusal to get involved in domestic conflict. "I couldn't go to Father on this, because he'd just say, 'That's up to Granny and Mother. You settle all this with them.' And he would never—he wouldn't give me the time of day."

My mother, at least in retrospect, experienced her parents' behavior in this social realm as painfully contradictory. "I grew up," she said, "in a most inconsistent . . . very difficult atmosphere to think through. Because on the one hand, here were my parents with [their] political and social views, and the people I was listening to at meals and conversations; and on the other hand, here I was being *forced.* I couldn't go out without a chaperone with a young man." Nor, she told Joe Lash, was she allowed to go to a movie without a chaperone.

There were some more pleasant—even exciting—times. It was

Two pictures of my mother in about 1924, when she was eighteen. *Franklin D. Roosevelt Library photos*

in the summer of 1924, having just finished Miss Chapin's, that my mother spent several wonderful weeks in Arizona with her friend Martha Ferguson and Martha's family—riding, camping on the desert, and generally enjoying herself more freely than she felt able to at home. Anna wrote her mother of her adventures, her excitement, and her decidedly negative views on returning to the social scene in Newport:

Dearest Ma—

Here's a letter at last—better late than never!

Since my letter to Granny we've done loads of nice things. A week ago today we went underground in the mine here at Bisbee. They dropped us in a cage 2200 ft. in less than a minute and a half. It was a little scary, but good fun! Then we walked for miles underground, with our little miners lamps. In that dim light you could see the copper gleaming in the rocks. It was so hot that the perspiration just ran down us in rivers, and when we reached the top we nearly froze to death. . . .

. . . One night we lay out on the prairie, which is something I'd always wanted to do, and it was lovely. The rocks all around us were the most gorgeous colors. We had one or two good rides but it was so hot we didn't do much during the day.

. . .

I love it out here, the people are so friendly and hospitable, and everything is so "big". The thought of Newport is even more unattractive than ever. I'll look sweet in an evening dress. Two patches on my shoulders are burnt brown, my neck and a large V on my neck are brown, my face is brown and my arms as far as the elbows. Gee! I wish Newport would blow up and bust.

. . .

Loads of love to everyone, and piles for yourself.

Anna

Martha Ferguson's perceptive mother, Isabella Greenway, wrote her friend Eleanor near the end of the visit of Anna's "direct, refreshing ways. . . . I find her so balanced—and rational along with her gayer lighthearted ways and would value her opinion on anything." And yet, Isabella saw the two girls as still children in their ways. "Do you suppose," she asked Eleanor, "you and I were as immature as M and A in some ways twenty years ago when we were on the brink of matrimony—and they talk now of the sophisticated age!" Isabella wrote again to Eleanor ten days later: "We miss her awfully. . . . My love of her is simply firmly established for life now and I thank you *heartily* for giving me the chance to bring it to life! She was *a brick*—and the best of it I ever knew thru some real desert discomforts. . . . I was so struck by her tolerance (beyond her maturity)."

Anna and Jimmy had traveled to Europe with Granny in the summer of 1922. When my mother again accompanied Granny to Europe in the winter and spring of 1925, she was almost nineteen and her interests—including as varied activities as receiving the romantic attentions of an English lord and visiting the slums of Rome—conflicted with Sara's strong sense of propriety. Although Anna did not talk easily with anyone in her family about boyfriends, there is no doubt that several were in evidence, and indeed that she had come to find real pleasure in the social activities her later memory covered with a blanket of distaste. She kept a diary during part of the year 1925, recounting mainly her experiences on the European trip with Granny. In reading it, I was reminded of Isabella Greenway's words about Anna's balance of gaiety and rationality, and Isabella's overall sense of surprise at the adolescent youthfulness of Anna and her daughter Martha. And while Isabella could hardly have known it (indeed it is hard to believe reading the diary) there was truth in her phrase "on the brink of matrimony," for Anna was to marry just a year after returning from her European trip.

---

Anna Eleanor Roosevelt
49 East 65th Street
New York City

*The Year 1925*

*Thursday, Jan. 1*

Hyde Park. We're in the middle of our New Year's house-party. I'm having a peachy time and I have an idea the others are too! . . . Last night we went to the Rogers' party and had a great time. Today we played hockey with Dicky Aldrich's house party and were beaten badly (17/00). . . .

*Friday, Jan. 2*

Hyde Park till 3:30. We had snow enough to coast this morning and had a gay old time.

How I hate to leave H.P.! I won't see it again for almost 4 months and I don't like saying good-bye to my pups and ponies. Having the whole crowd up there helped lots all the same as there wasn't time to be anything but jolly! The second Junior Assembly dance tonight was marvelous. I had such a good time I can hardly believe it.

*Saturday, Jan. 3*

New York. Dentist this morning for 2 hours! Phew! Camilla Edwards dance at the Colony. Curt went and was a dear as usual. I had a great time and closed my "deb" season with rather a feeling of regret. Went calling all P.M.!

*Tuesday, Jan. 6*

Off to Italy! Rushed around madly all morning, of course. Sidney, Curt, Kay and Eddie Douglas, Nicky and Dot came to the boat to see me off. They were peachy to come and I certainly appreciated it. I hated saying good-bye to Ma and Pa. . . . I've got so many presents and flowers and steamer letters! It *is* a nice feeling to feel that one has *real* friends. . . . Rough voyage—reading, bridge playing, made friends with a dog in cage on top deck. I loved the "American Idyll" [a book given to her by Sidney]. If only everybody could feel that way—I mean husbands and wives.

*Saturday, Jan. 10*

Granny and I have been bickering all day. And it's been my fault all the time—I've started arguments and disputed everything she said. There's no excuse for it and it's entirely selfish. I can't even be self-righteous and say I felt strongly on the points we argued. Oh! Damn!

*Sunday, Jan. 11*

Only 2 of my "thank you" letters have been written. How I hate letter writing and yet how I love to get letters. Laziness again!

*Thursday, Jan. 15*

Fabienne and I for the second night went up on the top deck and talked with 2 officers. It's piles of fun but gee! You have to be careful, because they're so free with their arms and hands and some of the things they say about women etc. would shock most American young men to death. It wouldn't be exactly safe for a girl to go up alone with these officers, that's all I can say!! Wouldn't Granny be het up if she knew!!

*Thursday, Jan. 22*

[After arriving in Italy, a horse-drawn-carriage drive up to the convent of San Martino.] I sat up on the driver's seat and drove the horse half way up to San Martino. I don't believe I ever attracted as much attention before!!

*Friday, Jan. 23*

[In Rome] I wrote or rather finished a long and painful letter to Robert this morning. I do hope he won't misunderstand me and get mad, and I hope he won't be much hurt. . . . A letter from Sidney was waiting for me and Oh! it was nice to get it.

[A thirty-page letter from Robert arrived on Saturday, January 24; no mention of its content.]

*Tuesday, Jan. 27*

The curse—so stayed in and wrote all morning.

*Wednesday, Jan. 28*

[Granny had gone out with a woman guide in the morning.] They wouldn't take me for the same reason as yesterday!

[On February 2 she noted that letters from Doug, Sidney, and Robert arrived; and the following day two letters from Curt and two more from Robert.]

*Friday, Feb. 6*

We "did" the Coliseum with Miss Cook this morning. I loved it but I'd far rather wander around the old passages and sit in the sun at the very top by myself than stand and listen to that long-winded old hen for 2 hours!

[Anna wrote her mother from Rome on February 11, and the letter is revealing both of her then current attitudes toward the young men in her life and of the kind of confidence and affection that had grown between her and her mother:]

---

Hotel Windsor
Via Veneto
Rome

Dearest Mums— Feb. 11th 1925

Your letter of January 30th and the two kids screaming letters have just arrived. I'm so happy at getting a letter from you that I have to sit down and scribble you at least a few words.

Tonight Granny is having quite a dinner party here. Granny is having an old Baron something or other and Mr. and Mrs. Randal MacIver, and

I'm having nearly every person I know in Rome! Namely: Mr. Holman (2nd Sec. of Brit. Em.) and his sister and cousin Miss Andrews and Copley and Lord Castlereagh. We *were* all going to see the Coliseum by moonlight but the moon will not oblige tonight so I guess we will either go to one of the big hotels and dance or stay here and talk. . . .

Ma, you can't imagine how many letters I've been getting from Robert, it is something fierce! As soon as I landed in Naples I wrote him the letter I told you I was going to write him, telling him a few things which I'm afraid he won't appreciate much. Of course, I haven't had a letter in answer to it yet and I haven't written since, but I'm very curious to see what his answering letter will be! I've also had loads of letters from Sidney and several from Curt, and they all seem to take for granted that they are the one and only in my thoughts! I don't suppose I can help that but honestly Ma, I'm perfectly certain that when I get home I won't be any more anxious to be engaged than I was when I left. That doesn't mean I don't like any of these people as much as ever but it just means that I have so much fun with other people that I'm not in the least ready to say I'm sure I like one person more than any others on earth. I know you know all this all ready, but I just felt like saying it so I did.

Miss Bates* and I are doing a great deal of sight-seeing and I'm getting to love certain things. I do so wish you were here—I miss you like everything too and I think when I see you I'll have so much to say I'll talk for a full week straight. Tell the kids I loved their letters and please write again.

As always loads and loads of love,

Anna

---

[The diary continues:]

*Thursday, Feb. 12*

Granny saw the Pope this a.m. and Mussolini this p.m. so she had a gala day!

[In her entry of Sunday, February 5, Anna had written of her fascination in watching people in church: "They seemed to be worshipping so blindly and without a question as to what it all meant." Later, in Milan, she wrote of her religious feelings and satisfaction in the "pure Gothic style" of the cathedral there. But her view of Italian religious life remained mostly skeptical:]

* Miss Bates was an English governess who had been sent for hastily after Anna's adventures had persuaded Granny that closer supervision was needed.

*Wednesday, Feb. 18*

The more I see of Catholicism the more it seems like Paganism. The poor people are always being made to give money and say a certain number of prayers which will absolve them from a sin or give them 10 years less in Hell. There is always a reward. How can the Priests give God's forgiveness?

---

NINE

# *A Marriage of Convention*

ANNA and Sara arrived home in the late spring of 1925, and talk between them and with Eleanor centered on what Anna should do now that she had finished school. "In my home environment," she recalled much later, "it was taken for granted that the boys in the family went to college (emphatically, if at all possible, where their fathers had matriculated). My mother mentioned several times that she and father thought it would be wise for me to learn 'to do something' by which I could earn my living if necessary. College for me was never even discussed that I remember. My grandmother . . . on the contrary, was most outspoken: girls who went to college were very apt to be 'old maids' and become 'bookworms'—the latter a dire threat to any girl's chance of attracting a husband!"

It is not clear that Anna wanted to go to college at that time, or indeed to undertake serious study of any sort. The decision arrived at, accepted only with great resistance by Anna, was evidently influenced by her father. She later wrote: "When I was eighteen or nineteen, Father and I had serious talks about my studying agriculture, the idea being that I would be able to help him with his many agricultural projects on the acres around our house at Hyde Park. These included a farm where there were chickens, cows and pigs, acres of woods, some fruit orchards and some grain fields."

In any event my mother's parents persuaded her to enroll in what she called "a short-horn agricultural course" at Cornell University in the fall and winter of 1925–1926. The summer before, again at parental initiative rather than her own, she did a six week course—

presumably in practical agriculture—at the Geneva (New York) State Experimental Station. As already noted, she had long had a special affection for animals, especially dogs and horses, and there was a family tradition of gentlemanly farming at Hyde Park; but she had no desire to go to Geneva, and she and her mother did not speak to each other on the trip there. She had written to her mother earlier, in a hardly mistakable tone, that she was "perfectly sure I *don't* want to take the full year at Cornell. . . . I also think that 6 weeks this summer, 4 months next winter and then back to Geneva if I like it will be certainly giving agriculture a fair trial."

There is no indication—and not much likelihood—that she took her studies in Geneva or the four-month course at Cornell very seriously. Eleanor wrote Franklin, raising an issue that was to loom larger with all the children in the years to come: "Just now I am more worried about Anna than anyone. I do hope at Cornell at least her name will mean little and she'll get some of the foolishness out of her." Elliott, some weeks later, wrote from Groton (where he was having his own academic difficulties): "I don't know what the Alpha Phi [a Cornell sorority] is yet, but I understand Anna got into [it] just so she could go to a certain dance. Pretty soft I think!! Several Yale boys have been up here and have mentioned her. They think she will probably get flunked out or something like that because she never seems to be at the college at all."

Elliott's estimate may not have been far wrong, at least as an indication of where his sister's heart lay. Toward the end of her 1925 diary (whose last two thirds is blank pages) a flower is pinned to an empty page, and there is an accompanying note: "A souvenir of my six weeks at State Agri. Exp. Station at Geneva, this summer! Part of a bunch given me by George the day I left." A few pages later, two flower petals, and the note, "Souvenirs of a proposal!" And at the diary's very end, "The remains of a gardenia given me in a bunch of violets by Curt the day we sailed. It lived 5 days, then I pulled out the dead petals and pinned it here. Just a little souvenir of New York and 'Coming Out.' "

The course at Cornell was apparently concluded in the university's infirmary, from which Anna wrote her mother, "I am rather ashamed, Ma, of my inglorious way of terminating my college career, but I don't exactly see how I could have helped it!" The date was February 8, 1926, and she had been in the infirmary for six days suffering from abdominal pains, fever, and chills.

Despite occasional affectionate references to "Curt" in her diary and letters of 1925, my mother's engagement in March of 1926 to Curtis B. Dall has a perplexing feeling of suddenness about it. She had written her mother the previous spring that she was not ready to choose one special person from among her suitors, and there is no evidence that she had changed her mind or fallen singularly in love during the following year. Her dislike of schooling, the absence of other socially acceptable alternatives, and the general assumption that young women of her age and social class married when they had completed school, may have played a part; and in particular, Granny would very likely have been urging Anna in that direction.

My mother's feelings for Curtis Dall at the time of their engagement are not recorded. She was to say, many years later and after she had divorced him, that she married to get away from the constraints of her family, and particularly the tension and feeling of oppressiveness she still associated with her mother and grandmother. An underlying motive, coexisting uneasily with her desire for freedom, may have been a wish to be properly cared for by an older man (Curtis was ten years her senior): as the young Sara was cared for by the older James; as Eleanor dreamed of an idyllic life with her father; and perhaps as Anna may have wished, inside herself, to be her father's helpmate.

My half-sister Eleanor (Sisty), Curtis's and Anna's first child, recalls asking her mother, after her parents' separation, why she had married Curtis. Anna, who was sitting at her dressing table at Hyde Park doing her hair before dinner, could not answer and began to cry. Sisty was greatly embarrassed; it was the first time she had seen a grown-up cry. Curtis's and Anna's two children now explain their mother's decision to marry in similar terms: he was of respectable family, had some charm, and was the first older man who came along and, as my sister put it, "gave her the biz."

Curtis Dall was a tall, lean man with a long, good-looking face and a receding hairline. At the time of the engagement he was working for the investment banking firm of Lehman Brothers in New York, selling stocks and bonds. By profession and evidently in personal manner, he was both conventional and conservative, and in that lay, perhaps, another reason for Anna's decision to marry him: it is rather doubtful that he appealed to her spirit of adventure, but the image of security that he must have offered very likely attracted the still anxious child within her, unsure of the wholeheartedness and availability of those who cared for her.

Nearly forty years later Curtis recalled that he and Anna met in December, 1925, but it was almost certainly—as her diary attests—a year earlier. He had served in the navy in World War I, and proudly devoted his Thursday evenings to membership in a National Guard unit, as he put it, "loaded with tradition, reflected in erstwhile spit-and-polish discipline and good horsemanship." He was at home in this "congenial man's world" and on Wall Street, and took pleasure in a variety of social events: "rides in an open carriage in Central Park . . . , numerous dinners and dances, and weekends in the country visiting cousins. There were many activities such as tennis and riding during the summer. On Saturdays in the fall, there were football games which meant enjoyable trips back to Princeton for class gatherings, to witness exciting events on the gridiron and to mingle and hob-nob with old friends."

Curtis and Anna were married in early June of 1926. She had just turned twenty, and was nearly as untutored as her mother had been in the ways of sexuality, marriage, and family; and her mother was not one to whom she felt she could turn for counsel. The night before the wedding, she recalled, "my mother asked me if there was anything about 'the intimacies of marriage' I would like to ask her. My answer was a firm 'NO': I had learned a little, so very little as I later discovered, but I had definitely learned at that particular time what one did and did not talk about with one's parents."

Her father arranged for Dr. Endicott Peabody, Groton's longtime headmaster, to conduct the ceremony at St. James Church in Hyde Park (the same church in which she was baptised as an infant, and where her ashes are now buried). It was a traditionally large and

*Underwood & Underwood*

Anna becomes Mrs. Curtis B. Dall, June, 1926.

*Franklin D. Roosevelt Library*

formal affair. The bride wore a white gown with lace veil and long train. Among the boxes of papers my mother stored away there is a leather-bound book in which Eleanor recorded each wedding gift: 480 in all! After the ceremony, my grandmother recalled, "a big luncheon-reception was held at home in a tent spread over the lawn. To this event came all the dozens of Roosevelts on both sides, and friends from everywhere."

Anna and Curtis sailed on the S.S. *Empress of France* for a European honeymoon. She wrote her parents from the ship:

Dearest Mums and Dad,

We got your wire as soon as we got on board—We loved it!

Both of you can well imagine what kind of a time we are having. Absolutely perfect, are the only possible words that describe it.

Gosh! We owe a lot to you two. And don't forget that we think a great deal of you.—

Our cabin is peachy and we've chosen nice space on the starboard deck, about amid-ships, for our deck-chairs. Now we are going to reserve a "table for two" in the dining room (excuse me—I meant "mess-hall"!)

With a great deal of love to all the family and loads and loads to both of you,

Anna and Curt

It seems clear from her letters of the first months, and even the first three or four years of their marriage, that Anna entered upon the venture with some real hopefulness and some genuine affection for Curtis Dall; though she was to tell her five- or six-year-old daughter just after her separation from Curtis in 1932 that she knew a month after she was married that she had made a mistake. If, as she later said, her principal desire in marrying was to escape the fetters of family, it must have worked only in a very partial way; and it seems likely that my mother was possessed of some ambivalence in the matter. She was given a small allowance by both her father and her grandmother. Sara also, despite Anna's disinclination and Eleanor's frank anger (Sara did not tell Eleanor or Franklin of the gift, and asked Anna to keep the secret), offered the newlyweds an expensive apartment in New York, to which they moved in the autumn of 1926. Just before Anna's first child was born in 1927, Sara secretly arranged with Franklin to have it appear that her one-thousand-dollar gift for medical expenses came from him. "Eleanor," Sara wrote, "has already given [Anna] a cheque for her nurse."

Like her mother and her grandmother Anna before her, Anna was pregnant very soon after her marriage. None of them—Anna and Elliott, Eleanor and Franklin, Anna and Curtis—had significant time to explore the newness and challenge of marriage by themselves before children began to appear. My mother was pregnant within a few weeks of the wedding, and my half-sister was born at her grandparents' East Sixty-fifth Street house on March 25, 1927. Anna's labor, as is common with first children, was prolonged. Eleanor wrote to Franklin: "Such a 36 hours as we have had! . . . everything was prepared but we waited all day. It wasn't hard and the new way is marvelous but it was long and tedious for the child. However, after an active second night the young lady appeared at 5 a.m. . . . She weighs 7½ pounds, her eyes are blue, so far her hair is black, her mouth large, her ears very flat. Anna is tired but sleeping a lot. . . . Mama is thrilled."

My sister, given her mother's and grandmother's name, Anna Eleanor, was raised as a baby in the traditional manner. She does not remember her first nurse, a Swiss woman named Freida, but vividly recalls Nan-Nan—"dear old Nan-Nan"—a vivid, warm, delicate black woman from the Virgin Islands, who stayed about two years and with whom my sister remained in touch for the rest of Nan-Nan's life. Sisty loved her deeply, and she must have secured great warmth and nurture from her. Anna was anxiously following the then current behaviorist school of infant care, which prescribed rigid schedules for feeding, bathing, exercise, and rest, and she evidently spent quite a lot of time with her child; my sister's early memories are of real closeness with her mother. But her relationship with Nan-Nan must have provided more security and continuity in the face of at least one prolonged period of her mother's absence when Sisty was just two. "I was very fond of my nurses," my sister says, "and I always knew Mummy would come back sometime."

Anna and Curt undertook a second extended European trip, of

Anna and baby "Sister" (Anna Eleanor Dall), 1927. *Franklin D. Roosevelt Library*

Curtis, Anna, and their daughter, with Chief in the background, about 1929. *Franklin D. Roosevelt Library*

about three months, in the winter and spring of 1929. Sisty—"Sister," as her mother referred to her then—stayed, in Nan-Nan's care, with Anna's mother. Anna wrote her mother several times from Europe, and her letters reflect an evident concern for her baby. "We are having a glorious time," she wrote in mid-March, "but sometimes I'd like just a glimpse of her."

Sometime in the late 1920s Curtis and Anna bought about thirty-six acres of wooded and open land on Sleepy Hollow Road in North Tarrytown, New York, and arranged to build a large white house there. Curtis recalled, long after his and Anna's divorce, and in notably first-person language: "I acquired some land on the northwestern bank of Lake Pocantico, and built a house overlooking the lake. . . . From my lawn, I could . . . catch a glimpse of the Hudson River, as it flowed by Tarrytown. . . . I had no immediate neighbors. . . . On the lake's upper reaches, there was considerable wildlife. Many pheasants lived in the area and wild ducks, in season, came and went. In the summertime there were herons of varied size. . . . In the early fall, eagles occasionally glided down from the north and would often soar above the upper lake, in high circles, seemingly motionless. It was a lovely countryside!"

The setting must have vividly reminded Anna of her Hyde Park home; and if there was loneliness to be endured again, she likely found some familiar companionship in the surrounding woods and water. There is little evidence of how my mother spent her time during the some six years she lived with Curtis Dall. There was a cook and housekeeper, Katy, a plump, warm woman; Mingo (my sister called him Go-Go), a butler who also drove the car and shopped; and of course Nan-Nan. All three lived in. My mother still had her aging and favorite dog, Chief, and later acquired two handsome Irish setters, Jack and Jill. She was, my sister says, bored around the house. She supervised the household, entertained a good deal, did some work with the Girl Scouts, and briefly organized, with some friends, a party-arranging business. There was little to distinguish her life from the conventional social pattern of neighboring young upper-class matrons, and she found it uninspiring.

In 1928 Anna's father was elected governor of New York, and the campaign and subsequent political events offered her a welcome opportunity to be at his side once more. She told a story of the period during which he was considering his response to those asking him to run: "By this time I had a year-old baby girl and, having dropped agriculture as an avocation, apparently I felt competent to offer political advice. I telegraphed Father, 'Go ahead and take it. Much love, Anna.' His answer, by wire, was: 'You ought to be spanked. Much love, Pa.' " She was an excited companion throughout the campaign and, she wrote, "never before had I had such an intense interest in an election night."

On April 19, 1930, Anna's second child, Curtis, was born. (Throughout his childhood he was known as Buzzy.) She wrote her father the following month: "The baby is flourishing. I am looking after him, as Nan-Nan has bronchitis, and find that my back is still pretty weak. I'm so thankful we are not going to rent our house this summer, and expect to 'stay put' here."

Anna's husband had been raised in a tradition of assumed male prerogative and superiority. He was impressed with the prominent economic royalists whose estates bordered their home in Tarrytown. Duck hunting and the world of money were evidently his principal interests, and Anna shared in neither. He was charming and could joke, my sister remembers, and was sometimes genuinely affectionate; but "you didn't want to cross his path," for there was a rigidity and "an uncontrollable bit of temper" in him. She recalls two incidents in particular from the years in Tarrytown. She used to sing as a very little girl, but became shy in the presence of company. When she once refused to sing at his request, he became very angry and sent her out of the room. Anna followed her upstairs and comforted her. Another time she had been picking flowers—bachelor buttons—for her mother, and he asked her, "Aren't you going to pick flowers for your father?" Sisty said "No, just for Mummy," and he slapped her.

In the spring of 1929 Curtis left his job with Lehman Brothers and joined the Buffalo investment firm of O'Brian, Potter and Stafford as a partner in charge of their New York office. When the stock market crashed the following October his economic fortunes turned downward with it. The early 1930s, he later recalled with pardonable understatement, "were full of gruelling, hard, uphill work with many headaches." My mother adds: "1931 saw me and my small family broke and without a home of our own. We moved into Father's and Mother's home in New York City."

The manifold stresses in the family during that period must have made for some added insecurity in my brother's first years and my sister's preschool period. "Sisty," my mother wrote Eleanor before the family had left the Tarrytown house, "seems to be going through a sort of a 'fear' stage. This morning for the second time she yelled and cried and held her hands to her ears, after hearing a cock crow lustily about an ⅛ of a mile away. She was playing *alone* outside, which she hates! Let's hope these complexes are easily overcome, and don't take too long to run themselves out!"

Although Curtis and Anna were still living together in the East Sixty-fifth Street house in the early summer of 1932, and they appeared together on family and political occasions, they were sleeping in separate bedrooms and were effectively estranged. My brother does not remember living with his father.

It is striking, in retrospect, to see the dissolution of my mother's first marriage in such close juxtaposition to the renewal of her absorption in her father's world. The image of the hero-father was now growing to extraordinary, near-archetypal proportions as he became president of the United States in the midst of a profound national crisis. She went to the Democratic convention in 1932, and was enormously excited by her father's achievement. Years later she recalled her feeling at that time: "Starting with the Democratic convention in Chicago . . . I have to confess to feeling more exhilarated than at any time before or since—or at least that's the impression I have almost 34 years later. And this feeling was to continue throughout the campaign, and afterwards as we moved into that historical old mansion, the White House."

It was in that spirit of exhilaration, so centrally focused on her excitement and pride in her father, that she and John Boettiger met. Their love was conceived in the midst of an extraordinary adventure, and perhaps each saw, behind the other's face, the magical visage of

FDR arrives in Chicago on July 2, 1932, to accept the Democratic party's nomination for president. With him are James Farley, who managed his campaign, and his children Anna, Franklin, Jr., James, and Elliott.
*UPI-Acme*

Anna and Eleanor with Franklin en route from the railroad station to his cottage in Warm Springs, Georgia, during the presidential campaign, October 24, 1932. *Wide World*

FDR. Anna recalled later the air of adventure that surrounded her and John's coming together. She saw it as a real romance, a striking out on her own, into a different and perhaps rougher, more masculine world than she had known. Literally it was to become a move away from life with Father to life with a man of her own; but perhaps it was also an extension or adaptation of that primal family romance, and thus in some respects an extension or kin to her marriage to Curtis Dall. For if Curtis was a more conventional, less exciting and venturesome man than John Boettiger, so—in just those terms—was there a marked difference between the Franklin Roosevelt of 1926 and the FDR of 1932.

PART TWO

# *John and the Boettigers*

TEN

# *No Path Ahead*

ON SUNDAY afternoon, October 29, 1950, Theodor Swanson, a New York public-relations executive, had just returned to his apartment from a walk with his wife and children in Gracie Park. The telephone rang. It was the manager of the Weylin Hotel on Fifty-fourth Street; he was calling, in agitation, to tell Swanson that the latter's partner, John Boettiger, had attempted suicide by swallowing a large number of sleeping pills. He had been treated by Dr. Aristides S. Marcovici, the hotel physician, and was now unconscious in his room. Swanson ran for a taxi and went immediately to the hotel. He found my father still unconscious but with strong pulse and respiration. Assured by Dr. Marcovici that there would be a twenty-four-hour guard and that there was nothing more he could do until John was conscious, he returned home. Swanson was back at the hotel the following afternoon. "I found John in bed, with a male nurse in attendance. He was obviously still partially under the influence of the drug he had taken. . . . We discussed the reasons for his attempted suicide, with . . . seeming lucidity on his part most of the time. . . . For my part, I tried every approach I could think of—ranging from the kind of rugged talk good friends can use with another, to sympathetic understanding to joking. . . . He assured me that what he had done was carefully considered, that he hadn't been drinking when he took the pills. 'Ted, I have thought this all out. I have explored every detail and this is the thing to do.' "

That evening Swanson spoke to his own personal physician, Dr. Byard Williams, whom he had asked to visit my father. Dr. Williams reported that he required immediate hospitalization and psychiatric treatment, and that John, after initial adamant opposition, had "practically agreed" to enter the psychiatric wing of New York Hospital the following morning. (In a letter a few days later to my father's wife Virginia, Dr. Williams said, "When I saw him his mind was functioning quite well and the only evidence of lack of balance was his inflexible determination to die.")

Under the circumstances Dr. Williams, in conjunction with Swanson, arranged to have a young male nurse, Joseph Payne, stay in my father's seventh-floor room that night. Payne later reported that his patient had spoken to him intermittently during the night. He talked of his wife Virginia, expressing love for her and sorrow that he had made life hard for her; he spoke to a picture of her, and kissed it. He talked of his former wife, my mother Anna, with affection, and expressed the thought that she still might love him. He spoke with fondness of his former mother-in-law, Eleanor Roosevelt—"a wonderful person"; and with respect of her husband, a brilliant man, he said, of great magnitude. At one point he asked, "Why didn't it work? Next time I'll take a whole drugstore full."

Toward morning, my father asked the nurse to open the window; he wanted fresh air, and was warm. Payne opened the window about ten inches. My father rose. Payne tensed as he approached the window. But after opening it all the way, he returned to bed. To be safe—Payne said later he felt my father was "playing possum"—the nurse placed a heavy arm chair in front of the window, its back facing into the room, and seated himself in another chair, about five feet from the bed. At 6:15—the early morning of October 31, 1950—my father threw back the bed covers and moved toward the window. Payne grabbed him by the arms. He said to Payne, "Joe, let go of me. Good-bye and be a good kid." Payne later recalled, "He pulled me right along to the window. He thrust aside the chair. I was still grabbing his arms and I was half out of the window with him. I had to let go or go along too. I watched him go down. He landed on the curb on the Fifty-fourth Street side. It was horrible."

My father had written several letters before his suicide attempt two days earlier. One was to his wife Virginia, whom he had married only a year previously. With her daughter Victoria she had been visiting family in California, and it was there that Ted Swanson reached her by telephone on the evening of October 29. Virginia left for New York as quickly as she could, but was met at the airport with the news that her husband had succeeded in his second attempt at suicide a few hours before. His letter to Virginia was carefully written, not only for her but because he anticipated that parts of it would be published. He wanted to make a final statement about his life and his decision to end it, and to assure that no blame for that decision would fall upon Virginia or his friends and associates. "It was a most difficult letter to write," he told Ted Swanson in another farewell note, "and I am not happy with it, but it is the best I could do." Both a private and a public act, my father's last letter to Virginia eloquently conveys what he wished would be remembered of his life and the circumstances of his death.

Virginia, my Darling, I have reached the end of the road. I can see no path ahead that offers any promise of a useful life.

I am filled with sadness that the manner of my leavetaking is such as to bring an unwonted grief to you and others who love me. How comforting it would be if one could slip away quietly and unnoticed!

I would hope to leave with you and my other loved ones the sense that here departs an uncomplaining man who has tasted far greater joys of life than are given to most men.

In thinking about others who have taken their own lives, I have always felt that when a man in good reasoning arrives at the supreme decision that his usefulness in life falls short, his self imposed death should not invoke condemnation or dismay.

I do not challenge the thought that the man who dies to escape his responsibilities is less than admirable. But if he weighs the assets and the liabilities of his life, and the scales fall on the debt side, then his decision might be accepted, at least by those who care for him, as right.

It has seemed to me that the fates have held my life to have been lived. My Darling, I have struggled against such a decision, even up to yesterday when I talked with more people in my efforts to find a right way to carry on. But today I have a full sense of finality. I have searched myself most earnestly, and I have concluded that my course has been run.

The crushing irony in this scheme of fate is that in my personal life I am supremely happy. You have given me deep, inward happiness born of your boundless capacity for devotion and loyalty, companionship and love. Your beauty is of the mind as well as of the body. From you and Victoria I have received great gifts of human relationships. Bless you both, and my equally staunch and devoted Johnny, and may the fates deal more gently with you all, the rest of your days.

The insurance which I leave will help you three in your material needs. This, and the memory of our happy days together, are all that I can bequeath.

I am anxious that you and some others know the thoughts which are in my mind and contributed to my decision.

Some men achieve high purposes and accomplishments in life, and later slip gracefully into an acceptance of lesser aims. I could do this, and would do it gladly, so long as I could feel that I could provide a reasonably good life for my family, and so long as I had a feeling that my tasks were useful ones.

I could never take refuge in a life of intellectual asceticism, nor could I submit to a life of mediocrity. It would be frustrating beyond my power to bear to submit my family to a meager life, even though I know that your love and faith would endure. My Darling, you are made for much better things.

I am a newspaper man. Twice in 29 years I left my profession and entered other work. Both times I was privileged to work with able, successful and sympathetic colleagues. But in my present association, as in the other, I have felt ill adjusted and unable to exert what abilities I possess to real advantage. Quite frankly I feel I am more of a hindrance than a help to my present working companions.

You know how earnestly I have tried to find a place in my own profession. I have sought out publishers and editors of newspapers, and newspaper brokers, all over the country, and in every honorable way I have endeavored to discover a suitable newspaper pursuit. I have uncovered situations in which I knew in my heart I could render highly useful services, to those with whom I proposed connections as well as in society itself. But the proposals failed for one reason or another, and in some instances because people, while conceding my fitness, found it difficult to overlook my past associations.

They could not reconcile the strangely conflicting relationships I had with Franklin Roosevelt, Colonel McCormick and William Randolph Hearst. I must confess that were I on the other side of the table, I myself might hesitate to join efforts with an amorphous character such as I might seem to be!

But the people where my writings were observed, in Chicago and Seattle and Phoenix particularly, know that I searched for the truth and was not afraid to print it.

Life for me has never been dull, and for all the interesting and exciting and worthwhile things I have been permitted to do I have high gratitude toward all those who helped me in the doing. It's been a wonderful world filled with wonderful people!

My spirit rises now in happy memory of all the years I have lived, from the days of my earliest recollections, when my mother gave me her full devotion, through the years gay and full with joys and loves and good jobs to be done, down to the present in which I have cherished your glowing devotion.

Good night, Darling.

I love you.

John

P.S. Please, Darling, don't come to New York now. I want you and Victoria to think of me in our happy times. I am leaving a note that there's to be no funereal folderol.

To my mother, from whom he was then separated three years, but with whom he had shared an extraordinary love, he wrote:

Dear Anna

This is to say goodbye and to say thanks for all our wonderful years together.

I'm sorry to have failed in so many ways, but my memories are so filled with happiness and a sense of having accomplished a great deal. You know I always believed in fate. I still do and today, after years of having fought against the decision with all I could produce, I have added it all up and it seems to me that the fairest thing is for me to take off while I can still leave something for Johnny and Virginia.

. . .

I know you will make Johnny into a wonderful man. May he give you the happiness I couldn't.

Please send my love to LL and Tommy, and to Sis and Buzz.

And my love and a world of good luck to you and our Johnny.

John

LL, as earlier noted, was his longstanding private name for Eleanor Roosevelt, and Tommy was my grandmother's secretary.

My father was careful to spell out, in his last letters, the nature and whereabouts of his insurance policies. In fact, those policies were his only significant material asset at the time of his death. The firm with which he was then associated had lost its major clients and was nearly out of business. Virginia had some independent income, and had sent him a check from California a short time before his death. He mailed it back to her with the words "I love you" written across the front.

To me, his eleven-year-old son, who had last seen him a year before when he and I spent a day together in Los Angeles, he wrote this letter:

My dear Johnny,

Goodbye my son. I love you dearly. I have faith and pride in you. You will make a great and useful man.

I wish I could watch you grow.

I love you.

Pops

My mother did not show me this letter for many years (though I secretly searched her files for reference to my father, and found the letter, sometime in 1952). "For the present," she wrote Virginia on May 4, 1951, "I have decided not to show Johnny the farewell letter his father wrote him or any of the other letters, because Johnny still hasn't reached the stage where he talks naturally and normally about his father. As you say, we can never be quite sure of what goes on deep inside a child, and Johnny has been almost completely 'bottled up' about his father since he died. . . . So, all I can do at present, it seems to me, is to bring John into our conversations whenever it seems natural and easy, hoping that before long, whatever bothers him about his father's death will come out in the open and can be talked out."

Until very recently I lived with the experience of my father's death so powerfully marked in my consciousness that, in effect, there was no room for his life. I knew my Uncle Bill, his brother, and Bill's wife Grace, for I had spent several weekends with them at their North Hollywood home during the year before my father's death. I remembered them as warm and loving to me at a time of great loneliness. In the years following I exchanged cards and letters with them, and saw them on one other occasion, but I did not write frequently. Until recently, when I at last felt free to turn my attention to that part of my history beyond the years of my own life,

I knew virtually nothing of my father's family or his life before the years he was with us.

In the early winter of 1976—my thirty-eighth year—while preparing for this writing, I made a two-week visit to my Boettiger relatives. All of them, in my father's generation and my own, now live in California. It was a remarkable occasion for us all, and I came away with a new and potent feeling of identification with the hitherto neglected half of my own history. The Boettiger family has lived through its share of vicissitudes and has known its tragedies. It is a family shadowed by suicide: in addition to my father, his half-brother Louis killed himself, and one of my cousins as well. Depression plagued all three. But it is also a family that has manifest great resilience in the face of adversity—illness, economic woes, and marital strife—and a family, most notably, of a great, sentimental fellow feeling. I am very much one of them, and it is largely from their willingness to share of themselves and their stories that the following pages are derived.

ELEVEN

# *Two Families*

MY FATHER was born on March 25, 1900, in his parents' modest but comfortable apartment on Robey Street in Chicago. His mother Dora was twenty-five: expressively affectionate, excitable, a strongly built woman with dark hair pulled back from her wide forehead and gathered at the back of her neck. My father inherited her physical features: the overall solidity, the wide, high cheekbones and vivid eyes, and the prominent and slightly rounded nose. Her husband Adam had a similarly distinguished nose but was otherwise quite different: slim and straight of body, rather angular, even stiff, in his dress and manner, more reserved in his affection. He was thirty-four at the time of my father's birth, and worked as a clerk or accountant for the Union Trust Company on Dearborn Street.

Dora and Adam were both children of German immigrant parents, and both Chicagoans since their birth. Dora was born Dorothea Ott, the fourth of five children—three girls and two boys—of John and Frederika Ott.

A formal photographic portrait of my great-grandfather John Frederick Ott, taken when he was perhaps in his early or mid-sixties, shows a wonderfully lively face, a largely bald head with a warm smile showing through a white beard and full mustache. He looks, in his small wire spectacles, quite a lot like Saint Nick. And, indeed, his grandchildren remember him that way, jovial, with candy in his pocket and an inviting lap. His own children, particularly his three daughters, were deeply devoted to him.

John Ott was born into the German peasant family of Peter and

Dorothea Ott in the northern European duchy of Holstein on August 30, 1840. His granddaughter told me that he herded cattle as a youth. He may well have had some Lutheran parochial schooling, and learned, through apprenticeship, carpentry. In April, 1863, he left his homeland, as did so many other young men in those years, to avoid the onerous conditions of conscription into the Prussian army. (Prussia was about to wage war on Denmark, with the status of Holstein very much at issue.) His passage from Hamburg to the United States aboard the clipper ship *John Bertram* took fifty-three days, many of them stormy. But the most notable event of the voyage was his meeting aboard ship a young and sturdy countrywoman, Frederika Hock. Although drawn to each other, they were separated in New York, the ship's port of entry, and John Ott traveled on to Chicago alone to find a home for himself and look for work.

An enterprising young man, he quickly found a job as a carpenter, and one day, working above the street on a building being constructed, he was surprised and delighted to see Frederika walking on the sidewalk below. " 'Rika! 'Rika!" he called excitedly. She waited as he climbed down, they shared their stories with one another (she had found work in Chicago as a maid for a German minister), and their romance was renewed. He is said to have asked her when proposing, "Why not have two hearts beat as one?" They were married on June 5, 1864.

Five years after his arrival in Chicago, having saved enough money to go into business for himself, my great-grandfather became a contractor and builder. "He was successful from the first and the fidelity with which he executed all his trusts laid the foundation for a valuable and enviable reputation."* The building trades of the city were taxed to the full in the wake of the renowned Chicago fire of 1871, and a story is told, in particular, of the spirited response of one John Ott: "Histories of the great Chicago fire tell of many cases where the work of reconstruction was begun before the blackened

**Album of Genealogy and Biography, Cook County, Illinois*, 11th ed. rev. (Chicago: LaSalle Book Company, 1899). Unless otherwise identified, quotations in the following accounts of the lives of John Ott and Adam Boettiger are taken from their brief biographies in this source.

Frederika and John Ott.

bricks and stones were cold, but there is authentic record of only one instance in which the rebuilding of a burned structure was commenced so quickly that the still-smouldering ruins set fire to the first scaffold erected. John Ott of 626 North Robey Street was the hero of that instance, which was due to the great energy that is a marked characteristic of his life. He erected the first building on North Clark Street (at No. 625) after the fire, and the scaffold was built amid ruins which were so hot that it was set on fire and quickly consumed. Another scaffold was promptly raised, and the building that followed still stands as a monument to the pluck of a typical Chicagoan."

In 1874—the year before his fourth child, my grandmother Dora, was born—John Ott founded a lumber yard on the north branch of the Chicago River at the foot of Lessing Street. His grandson Wilfred, my father's brother Bill, remembers loving the drives out to the yard with Grandpa in his horse and buggy, and the marvelous smell of fresh sawdust. John built a beautiful big home for his growing family, at the corner of Evergreen and Robey: a parlor, living room, dining room, and big kitchen on the first floor; a playroom for the children downstairs; four bedrooms, two with attached sitting rooms, on the second floor; and an entire third floor given over to a ballroom for festive occasions.

One such occasion was the visit of John's brother Frederick, who was mayor of a town in Germany, and appeared suitably beribboned for the occasion. The German burgomeister may well have envied the American burgher. John Ott was thirty-five in the year of his daughter Dora's birth, and he must have looked upon his progress in life with secure satisfaction. Son of a peasant father, he had himself worked on the land and then successively mastered a trade; navigated a hazardous and dislocating change of country, language, and culture; established himself—and then his new family—quickly and firmly in a strange and vigorous urban world; and now become, with his thriving lumber yard, a successful businessman.

John Ott's wife Frederika is remembered by her grandson Wilfred—my Uncle Bill—as looking like a typical German hausfrau. Her portrait as a mature woman reveals a remarkably strong visage, a broad face with the high cheekbones and prominent nose she bequeathed to her daughter Dora and thence to my father. In contrast to the conviviality of her husband, she was a rather quiet person, but affectionate. If one may judge from her portrait, she could also be stern. She was born in the same area of Germany as her husband, and worked on a farm before emigrating. Unlike her husband, and despite some effort, she never learned to speak English, and German was regularly spoken in her home. She ran the big house on Evergreen Street with the help of Mrs. Abraham, a housekeeper who came in regularly for twenty-five years.

Frederika's parents followed her to the United States and developed a chicken farm in Blue Island, a community outside Chicago. Her mother (also Frederika) lived until just past her one hundred first birthday, and is well remembered by my father's generation. My great-great-grandmother Frederika was "smart as a whip," never wore glasses, lived many years with no teeth, and in her one hundredth year—1917—was knitting washcloths for the boys overseas. She read the Bible every day in German, and until her last months walked a mile to church on Sundays. She was evidently never sick, and drank coffee all day long. (She and her daughter, who lived together after both their husbands had died, used to retire with a little pitcher of coffee by their bedsides for nighttime use.) My Uncle Bill recalls, as a young man, taking the two "girls," his grandmother and great-grandmother Frederika, for rides in his family's convertible sedan. His grandmother would regularly say, "You're driving too fast. It's too bumpy," and his great-grandmother, then surely in her late nineties, would as reliably counter with, "Don't pay any attention to her, Wilfred, keep on going. I like it." He remembers them both with great fondness as "nice old ladies."

John and Frederika Ott's household, in which my grandmother Dora grew up with her two sisters and two brothers, was often a lively center for family gatherings. It was not unusual for thirty or forty people to get together, Uncle Bill told me, for music and German songs and a variety of toasts. The most memorable of the latter was one in which everyone raised glasses and drank in turn to all those present having their birthdays in a given month. They began

My great-great-grandmother, Frederika Damboldt Hock, on her one hundredth birthday.

with January, and, Bill said, "By the time we got through December most of them were feeling pretty good." He remembers the Otts, in general, as a big, warm, affectionate family, full of sentiment and celebration; and it is that spirit that he and others recall most vividly in his mother Dora.

When my son was named Adam in June, 1966, the name seemed a strong and fitting choice for a first child. I had no idea at the time that my grandfather and great-grandfather were named Adam too. It was, perhaps, a lesson in the inescapability of family history. The eldest Adam Boettiger, like John Ott, was a German immigrant, and left his homeland as a young man for the same reason: to avoid conscription. He was born in the grand duchy of Hesse-Darmstadt on November 12, 1829. Despite some searching of municipal records by one of his sons, nothing is known of the family in which he was raised. He was, it is said, "educated in the parish school until fourteen years old, and was then confirmed in the Lutheran Church." He served a three-year apprenticeship as a brick and stone mason before leaving Darmstadt in June, 1854, at the age of twenty-five. There are two extant stories of his dramatic voyage to the United States.

In the Cook County *Album of Genealogy and Biography,* it is written that "he went down the River Rhine to Rotterdam, and then to Havre, when he took passage on a sailing ship that carried over five hundred passengers. The ocean voyage of forty-six days was a very unpleasant one and fraught with many trying and sad incidents. The cholera broke out on board ship, and one hundred and sixty-eight people died and were buried in the sea. After this the black small-pox broke out just before coming in sight of New York." Dorothy Partington, Adam's granddaughter, says of the voyage that the captain was drunk most of the time, the ship traveled far off course to the north, among icebergs, at which point the passengers mutinied, locked the captain up, and themselves took charge of the vessel for the remainder of the voyage to New York.

Like John Ott, Adam Boettiger came directly to Chicago from New York; and three days later was employed as a mason by the Illinois Central Railroad Company, which was building a freight depot.

He soon became a foreman of masons, and stayed at his trade with the Illinois Central for eighteen or nineteen years. Then in 1873, at the age of forty-four, he was appointed a city building inspector by the Chicago commissioner of public works. "As this was shortly after the fire of 1871, he had very much work to do. He superintended the erection of the Halsted Street viaduct, the Lake Street bridge and the Harrison Street police station." Seven years later he was appointed chief building inspector for the city of Chicago, and held that post until his retirement in 1894.

Adam Boettiger's and John Ott's working lives were in many respects similar: both emerged from modest beginnings, mastered a building trade, and rose to a solid bourgeois respectability in the New World. But Adam evidently had not John Ott's strong inclination to be his own master. Both became effective supervisors of other men's work, and both stayed close to the world of their original trade. Adam, however, spent most of his working life as a manager within large bureaucratized organizations: first the railroad and then the city. Their grandson—my father—had a life-long fantasy wish to be his own boss like John Ott. But he was more at ease and more successful working for others, and in that respect more a Boettiger.

Three years after his arrival in Chicago, great-grandfather Adam married Louise Voss, who had come to Chicago from Braunschweig, Germany, just a year after Adam's immigration. They too—like the Otts—had five children, but only three lived into adulthood: William, my grandfather Adam, and Louise. The red-brick house in which the family lived until great-grandmother Louise's death in 1895 was on Lincoln Street in Chicago. Dorothy Partington, William's daughter, remembers her paternal grandmother Louise as "a little lady, a very nice-looking little lady," to whose house she used to go as a child and be given a piece of bread and jelly. But nothing is remembered of her personality, and there are no surviving photographs. The *Album of Genealogy and Biography*, whose strong points do not include fine portraiture of women, says that she proved to be "all that a man could desire, to lighten his burden of hardships and responsibility."

Great-grandfather Adam, however, lived on until 1914, and is

Adam Boettiger.

vividly remembered by his surviving grandchildren. He was a big man, fairly heavy-set, with a full white beard. He may have been more relaxed with some grandchildren than with others: Dorothy Partington remembers him (perhaps earlier) as a very friendly old man upon whose lap she could sit combing his beard and hair. But others—my father's brother Bill and half sister Louise—recall a sterner man of whom they were a little afraid. He was rather retiring and gruff, says Bill, not very warm, with a decidedly uninviting lap; "a stubborn old Dutchman." He liked to work with his hands—in the one unsatisfactory photo I have of him, his workmanlike hands and arms are notable—and Uncle Bill remembers him as an old man, long after his wife's death, coming to the house often to do carpentry and repair work. He visited around a good deal with his children's families, and liked a drink or two now and then. There was a saloon on the corner of Robey and Division, Dorothy Partington recalls, with which "he was quite familiar." One night he failed to come home to his son William's house for dinner on time, and had to be fetched, a little high. (Dorothy remembers that because at the dinner table, where everyone spoke German in her house, her grandfather suddenly broke into English.) After Dorothy and her family moved farther away—to Hinsdale, Illinois—her grandfather Adam would visit by train. He always carried a Gladstone bag, she recalls, with his clothes on one side and often bananas on the other, for the children. Toward the end he contracted a painful eczema, and died at age eighty-five. Having no use for automobiles, he wanted and was given a horse-and-buggy funeral.

The image of Adam and Louise Boettiger's household is vaguer than that of their friends, John and Frederika Ott, partly because Louise died so early that among my informants only Dorothy Partington had any memory of her at all—and that a fleeting one. But I have the impression that the Boettigers were more contained, less outgoing and convivial than the Otts. One shadow that must have darkened their lives was the death of two of their children. Dorothy Partington remembers the name of one—Julius—who, she thinks, died just after his adolescent years; but the family did not talk of them.

The Boettigers and the Otts lived near one another. Both families were members of St. Peter's Evangelical Lutheran Church. Both men were active in civic affairs and in Chicago's German community, and were members of Goethe Lodge No. 329 and Humboldt Encampment No. 101 of the Independent Order of Odd Fellows. But the clearest testimony to the two families' closeness was that two of the Ott daughters married sons of Louise and Adam Boettiger.

The families initially thought it would be a fine thing to introduce their two children whose names—William and Mary—seemed to say they belonged together. The occasion was arranged, and in fact bore the anticipated fruit: William Boettiger and Mary Ott—the eldest children of both their families—were married in the third-floor ballroom of the Ott family's house in 1886. Dorothy Partington was one of the four girls that were children of that marriage.

The second Ott-Boettiger marriage was that of my grandparents, Dora and Adam, but that union took some time in coming and was to some extent a product of the two families already being close. At the time of his and Dora's marriage my grandfather was a widower with two young children. His first wife died in childbirth, and I gather the child as well. Evidently my grandfather—like his parents in living with the death of two of their five children—did not speak of the loss. One can only assume that, added to the death of two siblings earlier in his life, that loss significantly lengthened the shadow of death with which he lived so privately. And the shadow was soon to darken again. In 1895, only two years after his wife's and newborn child's death, my grandfather's mother died. He was twenty-nine.

Since his older brother William had married Mary Ott nearly a decade before, Adam had come to know well Mary's sisters and brothers, and it was perhaps natural in the wake of such compound losses in his life that he found as a second wife a young woman who possessed the Otts' characteristic vividness and nurturant warmth. When they married—the year was 1896 or 1897—Dora Ott was in her early twenties, Adam in his early thirties.

My grandparents' first child, Wilfred—my Uncle Bill—was born in the couple's apartment on Crystal Street, near Humboldt Park.

My father's parents, Adam C. and Dora Boettiger, on their wedding day.

Not long after, they moved to Robey Street, where my father was born. The two-story building to which they moved was constructed and owned by Dora's father, John Ott, and was next door to the big Ott family house. So Adam's and Dora's first two children started their lives with a special feeling of connection to their Ott grandparents and aunts. And their lean and somewhat sober father Adam found a loving and convivial second family.

Soon afterward, probably shortly after the birth of Adam's and Dora's twin girls in 1903, the family moved again to a large, comfortable four-bedroom Victorian house with a big back yard and vegetable garden, on Smalley Court, a quiet two-block-long street near Logan Square. They lived in that house for a decade, and it is there that my father spent his most formative years.

TWELVE

# "My Own Baby Boy"

LITTLE is known of the circumstances of my father's birth in the Robey Street apartment except that, like his then two year old brother Bill, he was delivered by a midwife. His earliest picture shows a husky, healthy looking infant with the wide Ott forehead, in a beautiful lace dress somewhat reminiscent of his mother's wedding gown. My father was named Clarence John Boettiger, and he was called Clarence by his family and friends, evidently until after his high-school years, when he dropped the name because it sounded too effeminate.

One of my favorite pictures of my father, taken when he was two or three, shows him still attired in a dress, holding hands with his brother Bill. Neither looks particularly happy, and it is that picture that most reminds me of the nickname my grandfather gave his son Clarence as a little child: Bowser. The name was taken from a newspaper comics character, and reflected a quality of his early personality that his brother and sisters all remember: a seriousness, even a grumpiness, and a clear tendency to quiet introversion. Dorothy Partington remembers him as "not a noisy kid at all, always kind of off by himself. He had a big arm chair in their dining room where he'd crawl up just like a dog, all hunched up in the big chair." He was very quiet, she repeated; he never said very much. At the same time, he was "a cute little kid, with big eyes." That latter quality is best captured in another picture—one of his own favorites—taken when he was five or six. He is dressed in a new outfit—coat, suit, and cap—bought for him by his favorite aunt, Mary, and he was enormously proud. (The sleeves of the coat, it will be noted, left some room to grow.)

John's first picture.

*On the facing page:*
The two brothers, Clarence (John) and Wilfred (Bill), about 1902.

John at age five or six, dressed in a new coat and ca gifts from his Aunt Mary.

It is tempting to identify the dour and isolative quality of my father's personality as a little child as the precursor of his later tendencies to moodiness and depression. Uncle Bill, who has a kindly tendency to look to the brighter side of lives, says his brother outgrew his grumpy isolation. My own hunch is that it went underground to emerge again during periods of anxiety and stress. In any event, the sources of that quality in his life within the family are lost. One relevant event, at least, is notable. The birth of twin sisters when Clarence was three was very likely important in his life, demanding, as it must have—for all of the fact of their having a nurse—so much of his mother's energy. And the story of his father's reaction to the birth of the twins is perhaps similarly indicative. The midwife knocked on the door of the bathroom, where he was shaving, to tell him of the arrival. He opened the door, mug in one hand, brush in the other, his face full of lather, and upon hearing the news exclaimed, "Whoopee! A pair of queens!"

As an adult my father spoke strikingly little of his childhood years. At the end of his farewell letter to Virginia, though, he recalled "the days of my earliest recollections, when my mother gave me her full devotion." His bond with his mother throughout his life was clearly extraordinarily close. Aunt Louise remembers that when his mother was bedridden after her first stroke in the mid-1920s, he would write her every week, and she kept the letters in a packet, tied in a ribbon, under her pillow. "I've never seen such beautiful letters," Louise said. "He'd always say, 'my sweetheart.' "

My grandmother Dora was ample, warm, and physically affectionate. Her son Bill says she was a lively and "a very busy lady" who loved being with family and friends and getting "dolled up" for parties. (He remembers his parents dressing with particular excitement to attend a reception in honor of President William Howard Taft.) She seriously studied piano as a girl, attending a musical college in Chicago—her daughter Marie still has a small gold medal attesting to her accomplishment—and she wanted to go on to be a concert pianist. Her father John Ott said no, Dora's younger sister needed her turn and wanted to study voice. But she continued to play for the family, and inspired two of her children, Bill and Marie, to love the piano. And she brought to her husband and children the lively Ott family tradition of music and song, parties and recitals.

My grandmother was an immaculate housekeeper and had some help from a servant girl who lived on the third floor. Bill remembers his mother's lace curtains, which had to be washed frequently because of the dust from coal-burning furnaces; she had wooden frames with hooks all around to dry them on, so they wouldn't shrink. She was an excellent cook, particularly of good German dishes, bread, and pastries. Until late in their childhood, he said, she used a wood or coal stove.

My grandmother taught a women's Bible class each week at the local Methodist church. Her daughter Dottie showed me her mother's Bible, inscribed "From the Dorcas Bible Class to Mrs. Dorothy Boettiger, with love and appreciation of your devoted service as President of the class."

By all accounts then, my grandmother Dora was a warm, loving mother who devotedly and competently raised six children: the two eldest, Louis and Louise, and her own four—Bill, Clarence (John), and the twins, Marie and Dottie. Uncle Bill described my father as "the baby boy of the family," of whom his mother was particularly proud. Bill felt, in fact, that she preferred Clarence to him. The two boys also had their favorite Ott aunts; Bill's was Bertha, the youngest, and Clarence's was Mary, the eldest. Bill remembers that my father loved to be with his Aunt Mary—"he was a kind of pet of hers"—and that sometimes when he was punished he would go to her house (also on Smalley Court) and stay for dinner. (Bill's comparable devotion to his Aunt Bertha was such that he once, when staying at her house, wrote a letter home to his mother and signed it "Your loving nephew, Wilfred." His mother, he added, may sometimes have resented her sons' closeness to their aunts.)

The only surviving letter from my grandmother to my father was written shortly before her death of a second stroke in 1931. Soon after their retirement to San Diego ten years before, Adam returned home one afternoon from his part-time accounting job to find his wife on the floor paralyzed. He got her to a hospital, and with much nursing and care she recovered substantially, but never regained

Dora and Adam in about 1918.

her earlier robustness. She died at age fifty-six—"too early," her son Bill said to me simply and with a catch in his voice. In hearing him I was reminded of a story my mother told me.

Anna and John were sitting alone in a speakeasy one evening in late 1932. Suddenly—"out of the blue," my mother said—my father broke into tears. It was, he told her, the first anniversary of his mother's death. When she died he had tried to travel quickly to California to be at her funeral, but the plane or train was delayed and he did not arrive until she had been buried. The significance he attached to that event—the self-blame and anguish for his failure to reach his mother in time—was very striking to Anna, though she recalled that he seldom spoke of her again. Of one occasion Anna may not have known, for it was in a letter to his thirteen-year-old stepson, written in early September, 1943. "You know Buzz," he wrote, "Pops had a very precious Mummy, too, one who always did the sweet things for me that Mummy does for you. I'm afraid I didn't always behave toward her as I should, and about the time I really began to realize how wonderful she was, my Mum got very sick and died. It was a terrible blow to all of us, but most hard for me, I think, because she was far away from me at the time."

So the single surviving letter from Dora to her son John may well have been his last communication from her. It was written after John had sent his parents a copy of his book, *Jake Lingle.* My Aunt Dottie has their copy of the book now, and showed me the inscription:

> To my beloved Mother and Dad whom I could never repay for the love and the will to live and to learn and to write which they gave me.
>
> From their ever loving devoted and grateful son,
>
> John

It seems remarkable that a thirty-one-year-old son, in the flush of professional success, would speak of his parents' gift of the *will to live.* Such a remark may suggest that even then the very fact of life was less a given than an achievement requiring conscious determination to sustain.

Here is my grandmother's letter:

San Diego, California
My own baby boy: October 9, 1931

Great excitement reigned in the house of Boettiger, when the long-looked-for, handsome volume arrived, and there was at least one happy, proud Mother and Daddy in this dreamy city of San Diego. I just can't tell you in mere words of my feelings, of all the pride and joy which is mine. I can only say: "Thank God for this gift, this dear son."

How many times I have read those simple sweet words of yours written on the fly-leaf, just for "Mother and Dad". Oh, son of mine, we feel that we have been a million times repaid! When I think of some of the sons portrayed in your story, alas, those poor Mothers and Daddies, what agony and suffering they have endured through having sons!

I thoroughly enjoyed the arrival of it. I went deliberately at it, wishing to prolong the pleasure. So first I looked the package over, my name on it, then I untied the knots instead of cutting them; then off came the wrapper. My son's book was in my very own hands, but the treat was not yet over, I knew. I looked at the paper cover, every single bit of it, lingering over it, enjoying every second. Then, I opened it. I read Dutton's commendation, slowly, appreciatively, gratefully. Then—my son's message—could anything bring more happiness to a mother? Then, I took off the paper cover—mother's eyes saw her son's book—her hands held it, turned it over and over—what a glorious moment for a mother! Oh, dear boy, now comes a lump in my throat. If you could have looked into mother's eyes at that moment, I am sure you would have seen a little bit of Heaven there!—Eager fingers turned the pages, the debonair face of "Jake" was carefully scanned, and how appropriate the title-page, very well done! If I had had anything to say about the binding, I would have chosen just what you did, couldn't have suited me better. The black and gold is exquisite, perfect. Your name stands out beautifully, you are all gold to me, always. Then came the Foreword, read with great interest. I am sure it will serve its purpose well. The index and the pictures, what a thrilling time I had, and what a happy one!

. . .

Now I think you know really and truly what a joy you are to me, and how happy we are with the treasured gift. We send you congratulations and every good wish that your book will go over *big* and bring you fame and riches. Hope you are all well. . . .

Write *soon* to your proud and happy

Mother

What an extraordinary letter! If I did not, independently, have some confirming sense of my grandmother, if I did not know her children, I would be tempted to call it unbelievable. But, on the contrary, I believe it may convey with singular truth her character and her relationship with my father. Her devotion to her son is palpably, almost tangibly conveyed. And toward the letter's end there may be a hint of wishing to convey that which had been tinged with some doubt: "Now I think you know really and truly what a joy you are to me." Her letter embodies an effusiveness to which I can imagine a son reacting with some ambivalence: pleasure at being loved so wholeheartedly, but also embarrassment, even a wish to keep his distance. His mother's response to the book was sensuous, caressing: the book was, for her, less to be read than to be looked upon, touched, lingered over. That, too, he may have found both attractive and frustrating. For the first time, in reading this letter, I found myself wondering whether my father's wariness of women (to be noted further below) as well as his romanticism had its origins in his experience of his mother. And guilt was the natural companion to such ambivalence: "I'm afraid I didn't always behave toward her as I should."

If Dora ran the household on Smalley Court and did the disciplining of the two girls, it was clear that Adam was the traditional head of the house, and it was he who kept the boys in line. He had an eighteen-inch black wood ruler whose presence on the shelf was invoked by both parents from time to time, but which was only used on the boys. And that, said Uncle Bill, was not too hard nor often. Unlike Adam's stern brother William, who clearly and strictly controlled the lives of his four daughters* and insisted that only German be spoken in his home, my grandfather's presence was firm but quiet. He was an unusually contained, well-ordered, conscientious man, who was never without his stiff white collar—even fishing, or gardening, or dumping the garbage. He was an avid Chicago Cubs fan, and took his boys frequently to the team's home games. An active member of his local lodge, he also read a good deal, and was fond of playing cards with his wife and sometimes with his children.

Adam Boettiger spent virtually his whole working life—thirty-

*William's daughter Dorothy was to tell him later in life, when he had mellowed a good deal, that he was fortunate to have had no sons, for they would have run away.

My grandfather Adam on a visit to his son's family in Seattle, Washington, in about 1938.

three years—with the Union Trust Company in downtown Chicago. He rode the elevated train to and from his work each day; Logan Square, five blocks from the family's house, was the end of the line. When he retired and moved to San Diego with his wife and twin daughters in 1921, he was assistant secretary in charge of the bank's collateral holdings.

Scrupulous in habit and manner, modest in ambition, competent and respected in his work within the small, stable world of the bank with which he had grown so familiar, caring of his family, Adam was known mostly as an honest and sober person. "I always remember with pride," my father once wrote me, "having heard so many people say of my father: 'He is completely honest; he's never done a crooked thing.' He never cheated anyone. He didn't get money rich but he had great inner satisfaction and as you see, he gave his children cause for a fine pride in his integrity." There is a beautiful picture of my grandfather as an old man, taken on a visit to his son John two years before Adam's death: a lean, handsome, composed face, with full white hair and mustache, vivid eyes, and the omnipresent stiff collar. He visited our family's home in Seattle a few times in his last years, before I was born, and my sister and brother remember him as careful, friendly, and dignified.

But for all of his reserve and quiet, well-ordered existence, there was evidently in my grandfather Adam a romantic streak that must have been nurtured by his vivid wife. They liked to listen to records together. His son Bill recalls that one of his father's favorites was called "Gypsy Song." Bill still loves to recite with gusto a romantic ballad—"Lasca"—to which he and his brother Clarence often listened with their parents and then memorized and recited on family occasions. That poem is worth recalling in this chronicle, for there is something in its theme of wildness and adventure, passionate love and tragic death, that is at one and the same time so unlike this solid middle-class Chicago family and so reflective of an underlying spirit that even its straightest, most upstanding member, my grandfather Adam, possessed in some measure.

The ballad is the story of a free-ranging cowboy and his bold and beautiful Mexican love, Lasca: the sudden coming of a storm, stampeding the herd; a "mad chase down the wind" trying to escape the trampling hoofs; and then, clinging together on the ground:

> A body that spread itself over my breast,
> Two arms that shielded my dizzy head,
> Two lips that close to my lips were pressed,
> As over us surged the sea of steers.
> Blows that beat blood to my eyes and ears.
> When I could rise—Lasca was dead.
>
> I gouged out a grave a few feet deep
> And there in earth's arms I laid her to sleep,
> Where she is lying, no one knows.
> The summer shines and the winter snows.
> For many a year the flowers have spread
> A pall of petals above her head.
> The little grey hawk hangs aloft in the air,
> The sly coyote trots here and there,
> The rattlesnake glides, and glitters, and slides
> Into a rift in the cottonwood tree.
>
> The buzzard sails on, and comes and is gone,
> Stately and still like a ship at sea.
> And I wonder why I do not care
> For the things that are and the things that were.
> Ah, half my heart lies buried there
> In Texas, down by the Rio Grande.

Allied to his romanticism there was a capacity in my grandfather for genuine affection. And if he was not openly emotional, he was certainly capable of some fun. His nieces and nephews sometimes called him "Uncle Daddy," and while he could pick out only a few tunes, he organized a zither club and played at family occasions. A letter to my father received from one of Adam's former Union Trust Company colleagues remarked on his keen sense of humor. A few of the photographs I've seen manage to catch a slight smile and something of a twinkle in his eyes, a suggestion of muted playfulness. Once when my parents invited him to some gathering at Will Hays's ranch in California, Adam told the guests the following story with a perfectly straight face—straight, that is, until the inevitable bombardment of questions elicited a smile at the end.

As a younger man he was once walking, he said, near a park in Chicago. He happened to come upon a young woman in tears. Being the gentleman he was, he stopped and asked if he could be of assistance. The young lady replied, between sobs, that terrible things had been occurring in the park recently and she was afraid to walk across it to her home. So, said Grandpa Adam, he gallantly offered to accompany her. Upon arriving at her building without incident, she thanked him profusely and invited him to come in for tea. He demurred. She insisted. And he agreed. While she was setting up the cups and saucers there was a loud knocking at the door. "Oh!" she cried, "It's my husband!" Telling him quickly that her husband was a violent man and would be greatly disturbed to find another man in the apartment, she pressed him to hide in a closet. Through the door, said Adam (who by now had gained the wholehearted attention of his listeners), he heard the husband enter the room and immediately ask suspiciously about the cups and saucers laid out for two. A woman neighbor was coming by, his wife replied, and then called to say she could not. His suspicions momentarily allayed, the husband then spotted Adam's hat and coat, and, in a rage, demanded to know where the man was hiding. Through the keyhole of the closet my grandfather was horrified to see his adversary pull a pistol out of his jacket. In fear, Adam backed farther into the closet, only to upset some china on a shelf, which crashed to the floor. In a second the enraged husband threw open the closet door, pointed the gun directly at Adam's chest, and fired.

That ended the story, and the hush that followed was quickly superceded by anxious questions—"What happened then? Were you hurt?"—and the questions in turn by a dawning awareness that this quiet, dignified old gentleman had made the whole thing up.

That my father was devoted and respectful of his father, and that his father loved and was proud of his son in return, there is little doubt. If the two were rather reserved with one another, it reflected an inclination to reticence that they shared; neither, by nature, was as extroverted or gregarious as my grandmother Dora. Of the handful of surviving letters from Adam to his son John, there is one that conveys most clearly his rather formal manner, his humor, and the love and pride of father for son. My grandfather's uniform and exquisite handwriting reflected both his well-ordered temperament and his night schooling in penmanship as a young man. The letter is the companion to my grandmother's reproduced earlier in this chapter, written on the occasion of the publication of my father's book, *Jake Lingle*. Together, these two letters wonderfully reveal Adam's and Dora's differences in style and temperament.

San Diego, California
October 9, 1931

Dear John:

The long looked for achievement of my baby boy has finally arrived and I join with your dear Mother in voicing my pride and pleasure in possessing such a wonderful son. You have now started on a career that will produce manifold rewards and you certainly deserve the emoluments that will accrue to you for your untiring efforts and zeal in your journalistic work. I am sure Col. McCormick and the whole staff of the Tribune are proud of you but not nearly as much as are your Mother and Dad and we sincerely hope that the Publishers will dispose of a million or two copies. That ought to put you on easy street.

. . .

Our daily routine in this dreamy old town doesn't vary much. We work in the garden and use a lot of precious water in sprinkling the grass and plants. Sweet peas are just beginning to come up which will bloom at Christmas time. Soon we will have lots of rain and then I won't need to sprinkle. That saves labor and water tax for which we are thankful in these hard times.

With much love . . . I am as ever

Your dear old
Dad

Eight years later, a few months after my birth and only a few months before my grandfather Adam's death, John used his father's closing phrase in signing and sending him a picture of the grandson he had not seen and would never see—held aloft in his father's arms.

To my dear old Dad with a hope I'll do as well for my Johnny as you always did for yours.

John

## THIRTEEN

# *Clarence*

THE picture of life in the house on Smalley Court, where my father spent most of his childhood years known as Clarence, is one of a large, lively family, not uncommon then in its close ties with other kin—cousins, aunts and uncles, and grandparents. The image of my father's childhood now in the minds of his surviving siblings is, on the whole, well nurtured, benign, filled with the manifold ordinary activities of growing up and with the regular excitement of holiday celebrations. There is only a little in that image to connect with his own adult memory of anguishing feelings of inferiority.

My father wrote me an extraordinary letter from North Africa when I was just four. (He was anticipating the possibility of his death in the war, and that my mother would translate to me what was translatable and safely keep for later what was not.) In it there is the following paragraph: "Think well of yourself. I labor under a definite inferiority complex, which tortured me as a child. I struggled against it, and maybe some will say I 'over-won' the battle, but *I* know I'm not an egotist, and never could be. But I try to give others the thought that they can have confidence in me, whether I have it in myself or not. This may seem like deception, but one never knows how well one can do a thing until he ventures it and he may never venture it unless he sells his ability to handle it to the people in control." Of course, the first "people in control" are one's parents, and it may not be straining credulity to find in this poignant passage implicit reference to feelings of doubtfulness and inferiority—needs to "sell his abilities"—in relation to those primal people in his life.

Later in the same letter there emerges another related theme that is rooted as centrally in the experiences of his growing up. As an adult he was much taken by the romanticism that I have described elsewhere in his family. He believed deeply in, and perhaps depended greatly upon, the existence of absorbing romantic love, the kind of love that is ultimately derived from, and leans again toward, the symbiotic union of mother and infant. He wrote in his special letter of 1943: "I hope you will always remember how completely Mummy and I love each other. Neither of us has ever known or heard of a love as perfect as ours. . . . You are the personification of that love, and since history records that children born of great love (in or out of wedlock!) are specially gifted, you might be said to eclipse all other human beings in that regard!"

Beside that powerful belief in romantic love and its nurturant potency, there coexisted a darker shadow: an enduring, anxious, and often depressing doubt of his own adequacy as a man. And that, surely, has its roots in the patterns of love and identification which one experiences as a child, particularly with one's parents. "In your relations with the other sex," he wrote his four-year-old son, "be *careful.*. Get to know them well, study them, but try very hard to keep your emotions, especially your biological urges, rational and introspective. Get experience with women before you marry one, or even before you think of marrying! . . . [Mummy] and I made grave errors in our first marital ventures. I think it has made us dearer to each other to have suffered, and seen the hell that bad marriages can bring, but I believe we would have loved each other with utter perfection anyway. In other words, don't get eager for any woman enough to marry her, until you (and she) have tasted enough of life, *and of each other,* to be *certain.* . . . Learn to dance early and well; it will help to buck any unnatural shyness with girls. I was horribly shy in this respect, and it plumped me into a marriage which was a flop from the very beginning. *Don't do that!*"

The experience of "unnatural" shyness, for which he must have felt some shame; the defensive need for careful control of those inner enemies, one's emotions and sexual urges; the guardedness in relation to women; the compensatory attachment to a grandiose image of love's "utter perfection"—all that, together, suggests that he lived with an endemic insecurity and stressfulness in relation to others.

These reflections on the shadow side of my father's personality are not intended to discredit the truth or significance of the accounts that follow, but simply to suggest a companion presence that would not otherwise be evident.

The Boettiger household on Smalley Court was a large one—two parents, six children ranging from the adolescent Louis to the infant twins, the live-in girl who helped Dora with housekeeping, and frequently other family as well. So it is not surprising that it was often noisy, full of the sounds and movement of children and their friends. The only time in the course of an ordinary day that the whole family gathered together was for dinner at the big round dining-room table. That was the one occasion, too, when the greatest limits were placed on the children's inevitable quarreling. In a soft, firm voice, Dora would say, "Children, *not* at the table."

Each of the children had jobs to do. Bill remembers mowing the lawn, and having regularly to remove the ashes from the coal-burning furnace in the winter. On Thursdays, when the housekeeping girl had her day off, the children together washed the dishes. On one such occasion, young Clarence demonstrated an as yet unsteady ability to stand on his head, and succeeded in crashing into a stack of dinner plates, sending them to the floor in pieces. In terror and shame he bolted out the kitchen door. Hours later, when he had not come home, his sister Louise set out to find him. And she did: sitting on a curb on Fullerton Avenue, his chin in his hands. "Come on home," she said. "No", he replied. "Dad will spank me." She finally gave him a guarantee that there would be no spanking, and he came reluctantly home, scooting up the stairs before anyone could see him.

Smalley Court was then in a largely German neighborhood, with some admixture of Scandinavian families. Their immediate neighbors were named Bauman and Hinsdorf. It was a time, Bill says, when Chicago was rather clearly divided into ethnic neighborhoods,

The house on Smalley Court in Chicago, where my father grew up. His twin sisters are in the foreground.

Bill, Clarence (John), cousin Silvio Massari, Jr., and the twins, Dottie and Marie, about 1908.

and he remembers fights occurring now and then over border issues and violations of one another's territory. At one point the city changed school-district boundaries and Bill was going to have to go to school in a Polish (the family said Polack) community. His mother wouldn't have it, and made a special trip to the superintendent of schools' office to secure permission for him to return to his old school. She evidently was successful: both he and Clarence attended the Charles R. Darwin School.

Bill and Clarence shared a room, spent lots of their time playing and working together throughout their childhood years, and remained particularly close in their feelings for one another throughout their lives. For Clarence, Louis and Louise were probably too old to be companions (Louise remembers that she and John actively disliked each other as children) and the twins were both too young and too threatening of his valued place as the baby of the family. So the partners were Clarence and Bill; and they were often joined by their cousin Silvio Massari,* who appears between Adam's and Dora's four children in a photograph taken when my father was eight or nine. Bill and Clarence had a "vegetable route" in their early adolescent years—delivering vegetables to neighboring families. And under the guidance of a slightly older boy, Ben Stevens, they started a neighborhood newspaper, the *Logan Square Herald,* in 1910.

The *Herald* continued publishing, and I have a copy of the issue of December 18, 1936, with note taken in the lead article of my father's appointment as publisher of another newspaper, the *Seattle Post-Intelligencer.* "Those fellows were very ambitious," the article said of the *Herald*'s origins. "We say that because it took a lot of grit to move a press into [the upstairs of an old horse barn]. The boys used to go around during the week picking up news, after which they helped the publisher, Ben Stevens, make up and print the Logan Square Herald. They folded the paper by hand, and while the ink at times was still wet, the boys left their printing plant to deliver the papers." Other activities, Bill recalls, that he and my father per-

* Silvio was the son of their Aunt Louise, their father's sister who lived on Logan Square near Smalley Court. Silvio's father, Silvio Massari, Sr., was in the business of making flavor extracts—vanilla, lemon, etc.—in his home, and the house smelled wonderfully of them.

formed for the *Logan Square Herald* included soliciting subscriptions and advertising. It was my father's first undertaking, at age ten, in the profession that he always considered his only true calling. "We were always anxious to earn some money, pocket money or movie money," said Bill. "Our parents had a pretty big job taking care of six kids."

My father was fond of sports, especially baseball and football. He loved the Cubs games, and one of his lingering and severe disappointments was making the Englewood High School football team—the Chicago city champions in the year 1920 when he was a senior—and never getting off the bench to play in a real game. The experience must have fed his feelings of incompetence, and football for him was the quintessential masculine sport. Similar feelings may have contributed to the failure of his parents to persuade him to take up violin playing, and certainly made him dislike the name Clarence. As he approached adolescence he was a sensitive and rather private child, I suspect, easy to hurt, quick to anger and quick to withdraw. His sister Dottie recalls that once, when he was about twelve, she took his diary from him. He chased her in fury and distress, and when she locked herself (with the diary) into the bathroom, he put his fist through the glass of the door window to get it back.

Vacation trips in the summer were evidently a high point of the family's year. Both Bill and Marie wonder in retrospect how their father could have treated his family to as much as he did on his relatively small bank salary. Dora would take the children shopping for vacation clothes ahead of time at Marshall Field's department store: new shirts and swimsuits and fishing gear. And on the way to the store they would stop at the bank to get money from their father. Marie said, "To me it looked like all we had to do to get money was to go to the bank and Dad would hand it to us." Adam had an annual two-week vacation, and would sometimes send the rest of the family off a week or more ahead of him. They would go to a resort in Michigan or Wisconsin, on Mackinac Island or Silver Lake. Rush Lake in Michigan was another favorite spot.

But more special still in the childhood memories of my father's brother and sisters were the family's holiday celebrations: birthdays, Thanksgiving, the Fourth of July, and especially Christmas. In their parties in general they observed an Ott family tradition of music, songs, toasts, and little recitals by each member of the family—a poem, a skit, or a musical performance. Bill remembers birthday parties organized and decorated by his mother in the basement of the house on Smalley Court, and big celebrations on Independence Day: "Father would come home with a big sack full of fireworks—the whole works, firecrackers, Roman candles, sky rockets—go out to the back yard and shoot 'em off. I think everybody did their own fireworks display in those days in the back yards—displays going on all around." Sometimes the family would go out on the Fourth of July to Aunt Mary's house in Hinsdale. There was a parade, they made ice cream, saw a wonderful town fireworks display in the evening, and then all the kids of both families slept together in the attic.

Christmases, of course, were the best of all. These are Bill's words:

"We always celebrated Christmas on Christmas Eve, an old German custom. For some reason Father always had to go to the Lodge on Christmas Eve. We thought it was terrible because here we were, Santa Claus was coming, and why wasn't our father there? But he would sneak off somewhere, maybe down in the basement or the next door neighbor's or someplace, and put on his Santa Claus costume, and all the trimmings, you know, and probably a pillow under his suit, and his whiskers and a mask, and all. He'd put all that on, and a stocking cap of some kind. And then pretty soon we'd hear the doorbell ring, and say, 'Gee, that must be Santa now!'

"In the meantime, why, the Christmas tree was all closed off; it was in the sitting room behind the parlor. They would keep the door closed to that sitting room so we couldn't enter that for maybe two weeks before Christmas.

"And then all of a sudden the doorbell would ring, and we'd say, 'Ho, Ho, Ho! Here's Santa now!' So sure enough, here comes Santa Claus, my father all dressed up, of course, with a sack full of toys, and maybe two sacks. For years we didn't know who it was. He'd distribute all the presents. Also, I remember, why, we used to have to speak a little piece before Santa would deliver our presents. In German. [He recites in German.] It starts out, 'Dear, dear Santa Claus.' I've forgotten what the next two lines mean, but the last one says 'I will always be a good boy. I will always be obedient.' And then he'd deliver the gift, pat you on the back, and say 'Good boy.'

"Pretty soon, after Santa left, my father came home from the Lodge. He'd be surprised and disappointed to have missed Santa. Then he'd go all the way around, you know, to see what we all got for Christmas, what Santa left.

"But one thing he missed doing one Christmas, and I guess it gave him away. I don't know whether John noticed it, or I did, or who, but we noticed that he had his usual slippers on—house slippers. So we recognized the house slippers and we thought, 'Gee, I wonder how Santa Claus got those house slippers.' [He laughs.] I think that ended the masquerade.

"The Christmas tree would be all lit up just before Santa got there. Candles. They had to stand up straight, you know, so they wouldn't drip or leak. It was dangerous, as I think back. Pretty, though, lit candles, all the flames flickering, you know. Those were good times."

One of my aunts recalled that on the occasion of those recitals for Santa Claus my father would get so nervous he would stammer and forget his words, and the other children would help him get through them.

The family left Smalley Court in my father's early adolescence, and moved to a more suburban setting in Morgan Park. It must have been about 1914, as Clarence was starting his years at Englewood High School. The house was lower and more dispersed than their home on Smalley Court, with a big yard in front and an empty lot next door where the twins tethered a pony. The family was beginning a period of dispersal. Louis left home to go to the University of Illinois. Bill brought his fiancée Beatrice to the Morgan Park house for his parents' approval; they married in 1916 and moved to Gary, Indiana, to start a new family.

When the United States joined the war in 1917, Bill joined the army and served at Fort Sheridan. My father enlisted in the navy on April 8, 1918, hoping to get overseas. But it was to be another disappointment. He was first stationed at the Great Lakes naval base outside of Chicago. My father's mother, the twins, and their cousin Dorothy Partington all went there to see him on some special field-day occasion in which John Phillip Sousa reportedly directed thirty-four combined bands. Out comes Clarence, recalls Dorothy, as a stretcher bearer, which he evidently found humiliating. Dorothy said his mother cried when she saw him. Later he became a pharmacist's mate, third class, and served for a short time at the Naval Training Station in Hampton Roads, Virginia. But he evidently took no pride in his first military service, and was given a medical discharge on March 31, 1919.

Back in Chicago, my father returned to school and graduated from Englewood High in January, 1921. On the graduation program there is an item indicating that Clarence J. Boettiger read an essay at the ceremony entitled "Restorative Surgery." The notes for it in his handwriting are among the very few records of his youth which he kept. He spoke of his own plans (perhaps influenced by his naval service) to become a physician, a specialist in ear, eye, nose, and throat surgery. He spoke about the practical issues of a doctor's life—the range of doctors' incomes then prevailing, the advantages of specialization. Most striking to me—probably most revealing of his own motivation—was his strong emphasis on the physician's "standing among his fellow men, loved by his patients, esteemed by all." And he added: "Being a highly educated man, the doctor is sometimes chosen to act in public affairs. At all times his rank in the community is recognized and respected."

His brother Bill believes that he began a course of study at Rush Medical College in Chicago. If so, it could not have lasted more than a few months. He very likely was in need of more funds. His father retired from the bank that year, sold the house in Morgan Park, and took his wife and twin daughters to San Diego. In any event, whatever plans my father had for higher education and a career in medicine were abandoned. Afterward, throughout his adult years, he felt his lack of college education and degree as a significant disability,

John in his navy uniform.
He was eighteen.

The Englewood High School football team, Chicago city champions in 1920. John is in the middle row, second from the right.

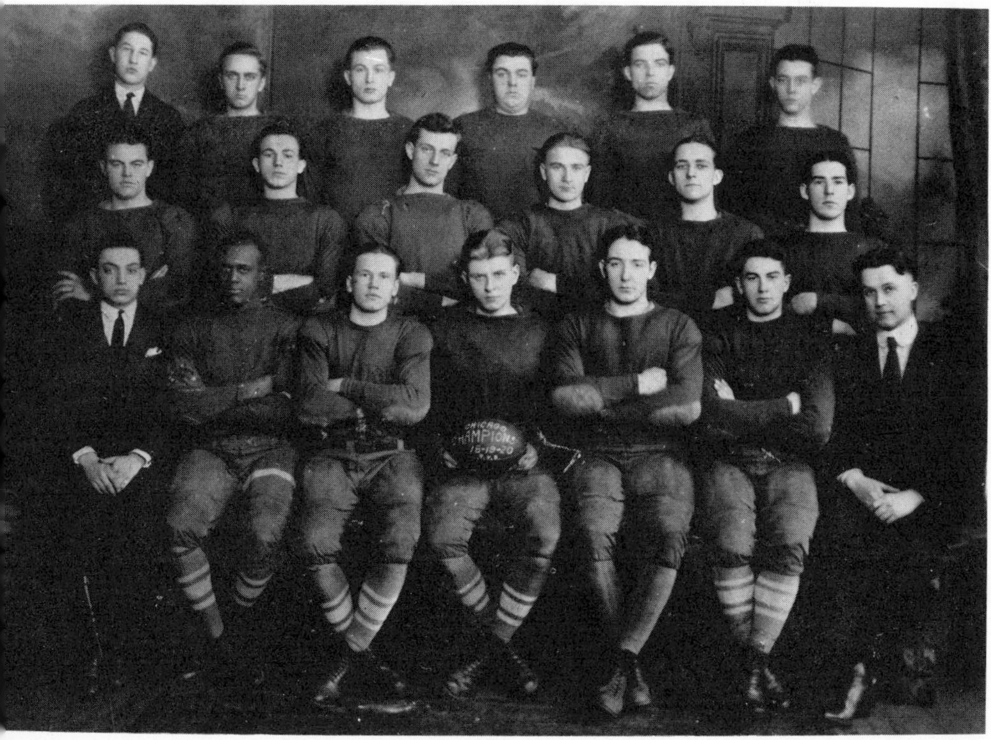

and he came to urge college and a life of reading and intellectual pursuit upon his son.

Bill recalls that John (it was then that he gave up the name Clarence) took his first job as a newspaper reporter to make money to renew his medical studies. There is no doubt that he intended it as temporary work. But he found himself excited and decided to stay on. That first job, starting in the late summer of 1921, was with the City News Bureau, a metropolitan news service jointly sponsored by the several daily papers in Chicago and a regular source of apprenticeship for aspiring reporters. In August, 1922, he moved to the *Chicago Evening American*, and in the following May he began a nearly twelve-year period as a reporter for the *Chicago Tribune*.

At almost the same time, three consequential events occurred in my father's life, which surely had a complex interdependency. First, his family—the parents for whom he was still and would remain their "baby boy," and his sisters—left Chicago for California. Second, he found work—the kernel of a professional identity—that challenged and excited him and at which he began immediately to demonstrate some competence. And third, he decided to marry, in effect to adopt another family, and one in evident need: the woman he chose was almost certainly in financial straits and had a daughter about four years old and an infant son.

Very little is known of Alice's history before marrying my father in Chicago on April 29, 1922—not even her last name. None of John's surviving siblings attended or remember the occasion of his wedding. His decision to marry was evidently a precipitous one. Many years later, advising a young nephew contemplating marriage, he wrote: "If it is some girl you have just met, for God's sake don't rush off on that kind of a tangent. I speak from experience, and I ought to know!" It was, of course, the marriage to which he referred in his 1943 letter to me as a grave error and "a flop from the very beginning." In that same letter he links his decision to marry with his "horrible" shyness, and there is indication that he had, at the time, very little experience of women outside of his own childhood home.

FOURTEEN

# *The* Tribune *Years*

MY FATHER'S years with the *Chicago Tribune* were years of very considerable professional success, and the life must have been a stimulating one as well as a welcome relief from the stresses of his marriage. One of his earliest friends and colleagues was Willard Edwards, who wrote to me recently of the atmosphere of newspaper life in those years, and of my father's place in it:

"To understand a newspaperman, such as your father, who worked in the Chicago of the 20's, one must try to understand the city of those years and the role that journalists played in it. The Hecht-McArthur play, 'The Front Page,' is usually considered a hilarious burlesque. The fact is that the players were not only real in name but in character. I attended the opening night in Chicago when half the audience came from gangland and remember, at intermission, a loud comment: 'That's just the way those bastards are!' None dissented.

"We all drank a lot and drinking was regarded as part of the business. If you could handle it, get your story and write it, nobody thought to criticize. When Prohibition ended, hard drinking went out of fashion in the newspaper world.

"There was a fierce competition, largely unknown today, between rival newspapers which excused a breaking of all rules in the interest of securing an exclusive story. There was also, in Chicago, a circulation war which sometimes brought sluggers from the Tribune and Hearst's morning Herald-Examiner into bloody encounters. There was also, I am sorry to say, a toleration for venality in government and, to a minor degree, in the newspaper business. Reporters became friends with gangsters in the course of covering crime stories and a few did not scruple to augment their income illegally.

"The Federal building was notorious as a haven for fixers. The Daily News man covering that beat enjoyed the comforts of a Lake Shore Drive apartment and a butler! In the county building, lawyers paid reporters in cash or whiskey to have their names advertised in divorce stories. At Christmas, City Hall reporters collected loot that could exceed $1,000, a magnificent sum in those days. The more serious graft . . . was better hidden. . . .

"I recall this sordid picture only to emphasize how difficult it was for a newspaperman to remain untainted in those days and to note, with emphasis, that John Boettiger to my certain knowledge, always maintained a high standard of honor. There was about him, and I say this with affection, a kind of innocence. It would never have occurred to him to be influenced in any way in the performance of his duties. He was, in later parlance, a square of squares, a man of simple honesty and integrity. All his friends recognized this and sometimes ribbed him for a lack of 'sophistication'. He took this with good humor. There was never any malice in it.

"You ask, 'What were the real issues in his life?' He was, as the record shows, an outstanding reporter, a strong writer, who moved steadily upward in his field from the very beginning. He was recognized for administrative potential as an editor and executive. He was undoubtedly moved by a strong ambition to climb to the top of his profession. He was conscious of the lack of a college degree and embarked on a vast reading program. But his own ambition never blinded him to the aims of associates and he was generous to a fault in helping them get ahead. My own career, such as it has been, owed much to him. It was a privilege to have known him."

My father and Willard Edwards met in 1921 at the City News Bureau; he helped Edwards gain a job on the *Tribune* in 1925, and later his assignment to the paper's Washington bureau. "He worried about my serious failings which included a drinking problem (at age 18!). When he arranged an interview for me with the night city editor of the Tribune as a job applicant, I can see his anxious face and hear his pleading tones as he urged me: 'Now, for God's sake, show up sober!' I did and was accepted largely because John, then a highly regarded 'beat' man (county building), had described my potentialities in glowing terms."

Another *Tribune* colleague and friend, Manley Mumford, came to the paper within weeks of my father's arrival in 1923, and vividly remembers those early years:

"John, when he first came, was quite shy and reserved and did not make friends easily. As a matter of fact, during the days when he was on the local staff, he was never one of the boys, but was strictly business. Never popular, he was always respected, because he was a conscientious, hard-working, careful reporter, with no flair for cowboy antics. One of his earlier assignments was to cover the county building: sheriff, coroner, divorce courts, and the like.

"In his early days John was a little stiff. Tall, ramrod straight, unsmiling, he appeared a little Prussian. At one time, some of us made up a name for him, 'Johann Wolfgang von Boettiger'. He didn't seem to mind and gradually lost his stiffness and became much more mellow.

"John had not graduated from college, as I remember, but he was always improving himself. He had in his home Dr. Eliot's five-foot shelf of the Harvard Classics and was constantly reading. I remember him asking me for a copy of *The Iliad* once. He was not a good writer, at first, but improved rapidly.

. . .

"None of us had any money in those days as salaries on the *Tribune* were low. I started at $40.00 a week and I suppose John had about the same. The reporters in those days worked from 1:30 P.M. to 9:30 P.M., but often were stuck on a story, and didn't get off until much later, perhaps midnight. There was no overtime, of course."

His skills were recognized early by the *Tribune*'s editorial leadership. Articles under his byline were appearing on the front page by 1925. He wrote on a great variety of topics in the late 1920s, largely political and police matters: alleged corruption in the governor's office in Oklahoma City, a dramatic murder in Wisconsin, an exposé series on various cities' pollution of the Great Lakes. For a time he served as assistant to the day city editor, J. Loy Maloney, and took over that responsibility when Maloney was on vacation or otherwise away. Maloney wrote to me from Florida just before his death in 1976 to say that in that capacity John Boettiger was "the best." By 1930 he was clearly one of the paper's top reporters, known and trusted by the *Tribune*'s lord and master himself, Col. Robert R. McCormick.

Levering Cartwright described the period of my father's last years in the city of his birth:

"Your father was the ace general assignment reporter and commanded the top wage of $100 per week. Mine was $20. He was bronzed, handsome, with a commanding mien. He was firm in his questioning and had a natural writing style that conformed to the standards but possessed distinguished clarity. He had an underlying sense of humor and was sentimental at heart. He made extremely fast friendships with politicians and conversely developed strong antipathies. I remember one Saturday when he was doing an obituary of an office holder who was one of those that he all but idolized. Bob Lee, then assistant managing editor, brought the copy to me. It was uncommonly flowery and lengthy. 'Just give this brother an ordinary funeral,' Lee told me."

Walter Trohan, another *Tribune* reporter, who spent a good deal of time working with my father on various assignments in Chicago and later in Washington, also remarked on his austerity, adding that there was another nickname given him by some—"the Hun"—and that he didn't like it. Trohan attributed that reserve—seen by some as arrogance—to an underlying shyness. He even used my father's own phrase: John seemed "stricken by an inferiority complex." Trohan told me—and others confirmed—that my father was increasingly recognized by the *Tribune*'s executive staff as having great promise, and was regarded by his colleagues as having excellent prospects of becoming city editor and managing editor in the long run. "He had a good, sharp mind, knew news and how to assign reporters."

In June, 1930, when a fellow *Tribune* reporter, Jake Lingle, was shot to death and one of Chicago's gangs implicated in the slaying,

John Boettiger was assigned exclusively to the case. That assignment, said Walter Trohan, was a measure of the extent to which my father had become "trusted as a man of unquestioned loyalty and great ability" by Colonel McCormick. The search for Lingle's murderer—including an untangling of Lingle's complex relationships with leading figures in Chicago's criminal and police organizations—took several months. My father not only covered the story but virtually co-directed the investigation, and was on hand when Lingle's killer was apprehended in a Chicago apartment building on December 21, 1930.

John won high praise from *Tribune* readers and staff for his series of vivid stories about the events of the Lingle case, and he decided he had the material for an absorbing book. *Jake Lingle, or Chicago on the Spot* was published by E. P. Dutton in 1931 and received favorable reviews. Its sale, however, was brief and limited in quantity; given his—and his father's and mother's—hopes and expectations, that must have been a significant disappointment. *Jake Lingle* is manifestly a reporter's book: a story painstakingly and ingeniously followed, told clearly, simply, and straightforwardly, if frequently with a melodramatic flair more common in the journalism of that day than now.

There is a striking photograph of John Boettiger in his reporting years, probably taken in the late 1920s. It is a dramatic formal portrait: a leaner face than in his thirties and forties, a handsome face with strong, prominent features. His hat is pulled down over his forehead in rakish, romantic elegance. There is a theatrical quality about the picture, almost as if it were a Hollywood studio's vision of the reporter-hero exposing crime and corruption in the city that had become its symbol. A receding hairline does little for that image; hatless and in double-breasted suit in another picture of that era, he looks rather middle-aged and respectable. I suspect he coveted both roles: the polar qualities of dignity and adventure, responsibility and romance that were so present in his years of childhood. It is remarkable, for all of John's greater ambition and the considerable difference in professional milieus, how reminiscent of his father Adam are those *Tribune* colleagues' accounts of John: his honesty and in-

John as a *Chicago Tribune* reporter in the late 1920s.

tegrity, his conscientiousness, his stiffness and reserve, his "underlying sense of humor," and his sentimentality.

His successful pursuit and coverage of the Lingle case brought from Colonel McCormick an offer that was to affect deeply the course of my father's life: to cover for the *Tribune* the 1932 presidential campaign of the governor of New York, Franklin D. Roosevelt. The *Tribune*, whose editorial and news policies reflected so palpably the conservative views of its authoritarian owner and publisher, was no friend of Roosevelt, and there is no reason to suspect that John Boettiger's own political views were markedly different. Although little is known of his politics during his Chicago years, it appears that his sympathies had leaned to the Republicans in the 1920s. And at the time of the Chicago Democratic convention in 1932—a place where he and my mother might first have seen one another but did not meet—he was an avid supporter of the candidacy of Maryland's conservative governor Albert Ritchie.

So it was sometime in the summer of 1932 that the *Tribune*'s correspondent met the daughter of the Democratic candidate. John arrived in Albany in midsummer, but soon became ill with an infected throat and was hospitalized briefly. Governor Roosevelt, no doubt out of some mixture of kindness and political sagacity, learned when he was to be released, and had him driven in an official automobile to recuperate at the Roosevelt family home in Hyde Park. It seems likely that Anna and John met during that stay.

Both were still married, and both were emotionally estranged and separated from their spouses. Indeed, both had strong romantic inclinations to adventure and had failed to find embodiment of that common spirit in their initial choices of a partner. Both had married young—my mother at twenty, my father at twenty-two—one out of a wish to escape the tensions and constraints of family, the other perhaps out of a wish to reconstitute a family that had dispersed. The two wishes were not dissimilar, and neither had satisfyingly materialized.

By the late summer of 1932 it was clear to others that Anna and John were in love. Reporters came upon them kissing on the platform between two cars of the campaign train. A new friend and

FDR's campaign train. Anna is standing at her father's right, her face obscured by a microphone. John is directly below her.

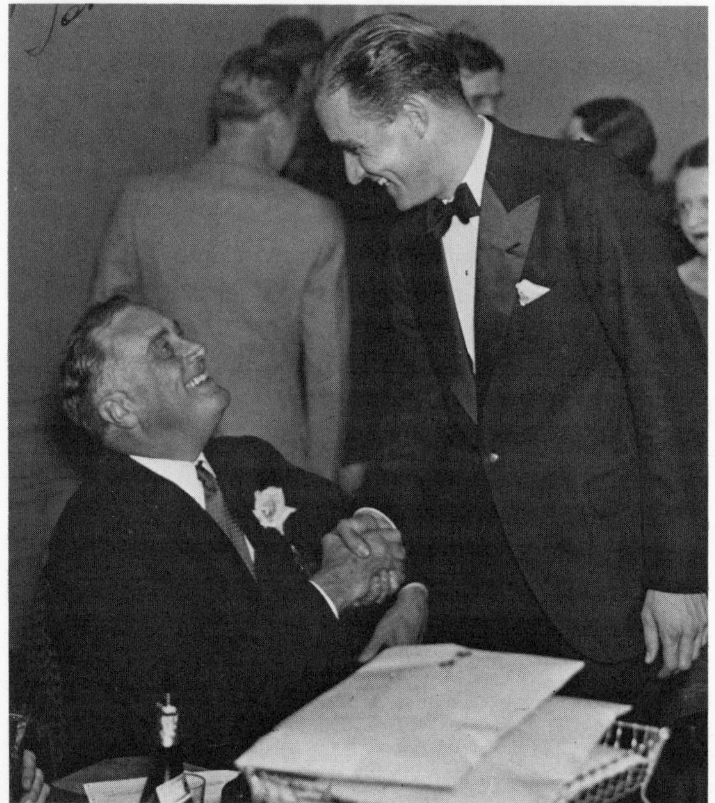

The *Tribune*'s reporter congratulating the president-elect, November, 1932. John sent this picture to his father. *UPI-Acme*

reportorial colleague, Ernest Lindley, shared a compartment with my father on the first long whistle-stop tour through seventeen western states in September. He told me that Anna and John were already a couple, deeply attached. They would gather for drinks in Ernest's and John's compartment in the evenings, with Anna's brother Jimmy and his wife Betsey. Talk would center on the growing excitement of the campaign and its chief protagonist, the impact of whose charm and persuasiveness John had already begun to feel.

PART THREE

# *Anna and John*

FIFTEEN

# *Beginnings and Ends*

THE NEXT two years were a period of considerable transition for Anna and John: a sometimes painful, often exciting time. Centered in their growing love, the life of each nonetheless moved in its own distinctive orbit. They saw each other as often as possible, and knew that the tasks and changes each was undertaking were rooted above all in their common desire and expectation of a life together.

With FDR's victory in the election that November, John stayed with the president-elect, following his activities for the *Tribune.* When the new president was inaugurated in March, 1933, my father was made assistant chief of the paper's Washington bureau (a promotion, said a later article in the *Tribune,* earned because of "his striking and able performance of his tasks," but embraced by John for personal reasons of which the *Tribune*'s managers were only partially aware). The following month he told his wife Alice that he would no longer live with her.

The divorce decree, dated November 7, 1933, reads like a brief for the complainant (Alice): she consistently good, true, chaste, and affectionate; he guilty of "extreme and repeated cruelty." He was directed to pay Alice thirty-five dollars per week as alimony and support "until her remarriage or until the further order of the court," and she got the Ford and the furniture. No mention is made of Alice's children, so it is unlikely that he had legally adopted them. (My father was significantly attached to the children. He corresponded with both for several years after the divorce, paid for one's studies at the University of Wisconsin and for a year of college for the other.)

John shared a room at the Wardman Park Hotel with Edward Roddan, a fellow newsman and close friend who was later to be one of my two godfathers. Roddan remembers his roommate as "personally well disciplined. . . . He was orderly in his habits; he never drank too much or smoked too much, common failings in our trade. He kept regular hours." Roddan also recalls, "I was perhaps more liberal than John in my political views. He was probably infected to some extent by the far right views of his publisher." He was quick to learn the ways of official Washington, and adept at finding the sources and gathering and writing the news of FDR's dramatic first months in office. Another salary raise came in September, 1933, with a letter from the *Tribune*'s managing editor praising his work. Rumor within the *Tribune* organization was that he would be the next bureau chief in Washington.

Despite the continuing development of his relationship with the president's daughter, John often wrote critically of the New Deal. I am reminded particularly of a decidedly uncomplimentary feature story detailing the absent "war records" of the "generals" of the New Deal; and I try to imagine, without much success, John and Anna discussing his observation, "Critics have found it interesting to note how closely America is being shoved into the same paths which resulted in the establishment of the German, Russian and Italian dictatorships." On September 28, 1934—his marriage to my mother less than four months in the future—he wrote his boss:

Dear Colonel:

We have been assembling material for some time for use in a series of stories on the propagandists of the New Deal.

Without question, there are more newspapermen working for the Government in Washington by several times than there are newspapermen working for newspapers. It has seemed to me that a survey of the whole Government showing how many press agents are at work, what their titles and various duties are, would be interesting to show the vast character of the New Deal's propaganda mills.

Before going to the large amount of work which such a survey would entail, I thought it best to ask you if you agreed with me that such a series would be of interest.

Manly is working on a series exposing the personal grafts of the New Dealers which I hope to start Sunday morning.

Very truly yours,
John Boettiger

The colonel's response was scrawled on the letter, which was returned: "Yes. Do enough to protect yourself against contradiction and to be interesting. Don't get every last case."

But it is also clear that my father's political views were changing, and that as he found himself moving closer to the president—and the president's family—he found his position at the *Tribune* less and less tenable. In September, 1933, McCormick pulled one of his stories out of the paper's city edition because it was "unbalanced"; and the colonel wrote a sympathetic acquaintance three months earlier, "I am constantly after our correspondents in Washington, but find it very difficult to keep them from putting in their own language the point of view of the officials." The following June there was a telegram from the Chicago editorial office to the Washington bureau chief, referring to the length of a current story: "Have cut Boettiger to 500 because last night Colonel said giving too much space to 'Roosevelt handouts.' . . ."

I asked John's good friend on the *Tribune*, Willard Edwards, about my father's changes of views in the early thirties and their impact on his position with the paper. "I believe," he replied, "I can point to the moment when he realized that he could no longer work as a *Tribune* man and maintain friendly relations with the Roosevelt administration."

"The time must have been early 1934 when I first served with the Washington bureau of the Tribune on a temporary basis. . . . John obtained an exclusive interview with President Roosevelt in which the President outlined his hopes and ambitions for the future. An exclusive Presidential interview is always a coup for a Washington newspaperman and he was elated. The story, of course, was favorable to FDR and the Tribune editors gave it a good play on its merits as news, presumably without consulting Col. McCormick. I will never forget McCormick's message to Henning [the bureau chief in Washington] after he read it—'After reading Boettiger's story today, I recommend sulpher and molasses' [a home remedy for spring fever]. John was stunned and heartsick. It was definite notice to him that he could never report any administration development which seemed to hint, in the slightest degree, that FDR was not a monster. Altho I was not in Washington when he made his crucial decision to quit the Tribune, I am sure that this incident precipitated the serious thinking which must have gone into that decision."

When his letter of resignation came, a month before his already rumored marriage, it was still with reluctance, for he was concluding a remarkably successful eleven-year association, and must have known that had he stayed with the *Tribune* he might one day have been its managing editor. His decision came in part for reasons to which Willard Edwards refers and in part out of a wish—strongly reinforced by Louis Howe and others at the White House—not to embarrass the president and the Roosevelt family. A few weeks later, after the wedding, he was asked by a reporter if he resigned from the *Tribune* because he was becoming the president's son-in-law. "I think I'll duck that one," he replied.

Dear Colonel McCormick: December 11, 1934

The subject of this letter is one which I would infinitely rather discuss with you face to face, because I could talk to you quite frankly, and explain matters in detail to my better satisfaction.

Since this appears to be not feasible, I will have to content myself with this confidential letter. But if you wish, I shall be very glad to come to Chicago, or to meet you in New York to tell you the whole story.

For personal reasons—reasons which probably have been made known to you from various sources—I find it best for me to resign from THE TRIBUNE.

I have come to this decision after months of inner debate, and, as you must be certain, with great reluctance. I did not come to you with the problem because I felt it was one I had to decide for myself, and when I concluded that I must leave the paper, I knew in my mind that you would agree unhesitatingly that my reasons for leaving were such that you could see no other course open to me.

At a time like this my recollections go flooding back over the great adventures I have had on THE TRIBUNE, and to the inspiring contacts I have had with you. To say that I am grateful for the opportunities given me is to put it mildly. I have endeavored to measure up to them with energy and loyalty through all the years.

I am very eager to have your best wishes for me in my future years.

Faithfully yours,
John Boettiger

The colonel first replied by telegram—"OKAY OKAY OKAY BUT WAIT FOR MY LETTER"—and the letter that followed was warm and bespoke a considerable relationship of trust and respect:

Dear John: December 13, 1934

I have your letter and understand perfectly.

While I cherish an avoidance of the personal affairs of other people, I have not been able to ignore the repeated questionings of friends. If you had found it compatible to remain with us, I would have been glad to have you. Your personal affairs are none of mine or The Tribune's, nor do I find anything other than delightful in your plans. If in view of this letter you care to reconsider your decision, do so. I will not take any steps towards putting a man in your place until I hear from you once more.

I can clearly see that your position in Washington would become intolerable, and also I see that for a while any occupation that requires you to come in contact with strangers would prove embarrassing. On the other hand, I can arrange a transfer to give you executive work in Chicago.

When all this is said, and I am saying it in great sincerity, I will add that I suppose that a continued connection with the Tribune will at best be difficult. If you finally decide to go choose your own moment. God be with you, and may every happiness and success attend you.

Yours sincerely,
Robert R. McCormick

In early 1933, as her father was preparing to assume the presidency, Anna was living with her two children in the Roosevelt family's town house on East Sixty-fifth Street. She and Curtis Dall were separated; a legal agreement was drawn up by Harry Hooker, the family's attorney, and signed that spring. Some time before, Anna had asked her father to tell Curtis that she was going to seek a divorce. According to Curtis, Anna never discussed the matter with him directly. If that is so, it is consistent with a pattern of avoidance she had learned early in relation to her father; it was always exceedingly painful for her to face directly the disappointment or anger of the significant men in her life.*

* In Freidel's first volume on FDR, he describes Sara as "a strong and vital personality; nevertheless her world rested upon an unquestioning acceptance of the dominant role of the

Anna's brother Elliott was about to divorce his first wife in mid-1933, and it appears that my mother delayed her own plans so that her father would not suffer the political embarrassment of two of his children divorcing at the same time. Whatever the reason, it was not until the following summer that she traveled to Nevada with Sisty and Buzzy to obtain a divorce. They stayed for the required six weeks' residency in a secluded log house overlooking Lake Tahoe, and the decree was granted on July 30, 1934. Sara, who remained fond of Curtis Dall and was of an earlier age, wrote her granddaughter from a vacation in Scotland: "I like to think of you and the children at beautiful Lake Tahoe, but the thought of Reno gives me a sinking feeling in my heart! I know there is much that I do not know and that I could not understand." The decree provided for support payments of $100 a month from Curtis for the children, and for rights of visitation with them. That same summer he took them, as he did in several subsequent summers, to the vacation home of friends in Plum Lake, Wisconsin.

By 1934, Sisty and Buzzy had become, as one newspaper account put it, "the famous White House grandchildren," a fact of some concern to their mother, who wanted them out of the limelight. Buzzy, now three, was a quieter, more introverted and reticent child than his sister, and frequently found himself her subordinate in play. They had both lived in families and households in conditions of stress and transition—from Tarrytown to New York to the White House; from life with their father to life without; from the relative isolation of New York to the populous household in Washington. But Sisty was born into a more stable home, two and a half years before the Wall Street crash; and Buzzy hadn't the advantage of his sister's relatively secure and continuing identification with her mother.

On visits to the White House as well as in New York, Anna conscientiously supervised a familiar regime of nurses and governesses: a supervision with some of her mother's austerity and stiffness but

stronger males around her." Anna wrote in the margin: "Some of this in me with regard to J.B." It was, of course, a pattern well rooted before she met John Boettiger.

more relieved by humor and a capacity to identify with her children's rambunctiousness. The latter qualities, of course, were her father's gifts to her; and now, for a few minutes each morning when Sisty, Buzzy, and their mother were visiting the White House, his playfulness extended to a new generation. Sis and Buzz still remember the game of Whiffenpoof, in which a grandfatherly hand was transformed into an excited and unpredictable bug that moved here and there, then suddenly pounced on a happily squealing child.

Anna possessed her mother's ambivalence toward the position of special privilege in which they now doubly lived: by virtue of the family's long-established social position and now by added virtue of being the nation's First Family. Her wish to protect her children from elaborate attention in the media, her care in teaching them that the applause and parades were not on their behalf, her own self-consciousness and insistence on appropriate behavior on public occasions—all of that reflected the extraordinary degree to which she now found herself living, inescapably and indefinitely, in her parents' shadow. It was as if the world had now confirmed and established beyond recall an identity already well fashioned: she was, first and always, Franklin and Eleanor Roosevelt's daughter. It was an identity whose primacy she was henceforth to cherish and resist but never escape.

In the early autumn of 1933 my mother and her two children moved into the White House. In late 1933 and 1934, she continued a series of part-time writing and editorial jobs begun while still in New York. She acted as her mother's assistant in fulfilling a rather unlikely responsibility, editing a magazine called *Babies—Just Babies*. She responded to correspondence generated by her mother's monthly columns in *Women's Home Companion*. And she hosted a radio program, wrote a series of short articles for *Liberty*, a national magazine, and co-authored *Scamper* and *Scamper's Christmas*, children's books about a rabbit and a young girl and boy who lived in the White House.

Clearly modeled as they were on Sisty's and Buzzy's White

House adventures, publication of the Scamper books suggests some ambivalence in Anna's attitude toward public attention. The degree to which she then found herself living in her parents' public shadows may be reflected in her choice to portray Babs and Dave, the children in her books, without their own parents. They live in the White House with their grandfather the president, their grandmother, Scamper the rabbit, two dogs, numbers of servants, many visitors, but no mother or father.

Eleanor Roosevelt knew of her daughter's romance with John Boettiger and was pleased. She had met my father at the start of the 1932 campaign and had soon become very fond of him. In the second volume of her autobiography, *This I Remember*, she wrote: "There was one young reporter I had come to know fairly well since he had been assigned to Albany by the Chicago Tribune after my husband's nomination. He had travelled up and down from Hyde Park for week ends and had been on the campaign trips. His name was John Boettiger, and he was later to marry our daughter and to become one of the people for whom I have a very special and personal feeling. I used to tease my daughter by saying that I knew John before she knew him."

My father's first letter from his future mother-in-law was written during the campaign: a thank-you note to four reporter friends who had given her a traveling bag. It is touching testimony to her warm responsiveness to offers of friendship, and to her growing access to her resources of humor.

My dear "boys",

If you are "uncles" then I must at least be your grandmother! As you know the old are always particularly appreciative of attention from the young and so your entirely unexpected birthday greetings and present gave me much pleasure.

I shall use the bag constantly and it will be particularly enjoyable because it came from you. You were dears to think of it and this note takes you my thanks.

You four have a real place in my affections, and even though I know I sometimes disturb you, I hope you will always count me as a real friend and when these hectic days are over, I hope when you are free, that you will

Anna with Sisty and Buzzy at a horse show, in about 1934. *Franklin D. Roosevelt Library*

Anna in attendance, while Eleanor speaks to a women's group, in 1933 or 1934.

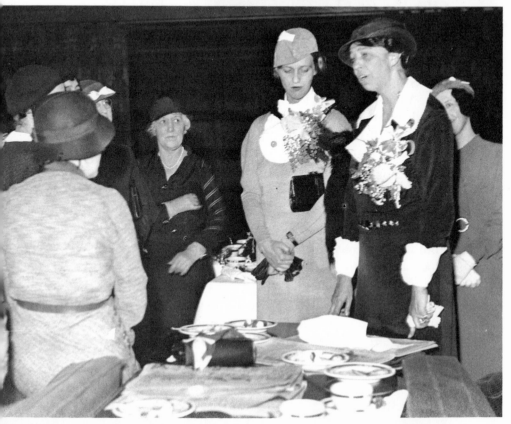

always remember that for you and yours at any time the door of my home is wide open.

With thanks again to you all,

Believe me,

Your affectionate friend,
Eleanor Roosevelt

Eleanor responded with genuine empathy to my father's unsureness in moving into a new and imposing social world, and to his difficulties in resolving his relationship with Alice. She wrote reassuringly and hopefully to him at Christmas, 1932:

My dear John,

This little line goes to you instead of a Xmas card and please forgive the writing as I'm on the train and it is very wobbly! I think of you often my dear boy and I want you to know that I am very fond of you, just for yourself and not for anyone else's sake. A Merry Xmas to you and may the New Year bring you much more happiness than you have had in years gone by.

We'll be sending you our thoughts on Xmas Day.

Affly yours,
Eleanor Roosevelt

Her love for John Boettiger grew as his relationship with Anna flourished. She wrote him in July, 1934: "I loved seeing you in Chicago, John dear. I've grown to love you like one of my very dear ones and I'm grateful beyond words for the happiness you've already given Anna and I trust you for the future."

Anna's and John's love may have offered Eleanor an image of the kind of intimacy she had fantasized and deeply wished but never realized. "I hope," she wrote John around the time of their marriage, "that every year . . . you will be able to write that the happiness is continually deepening—Somehow I feel it will, that together you will go thro' life's sunshine and shadow finding that joy and sorrow but draw you closer together. I am glad you both love me and that I have been able to help in small ways during the trying times, but it is your own fineness that brought you both to a happy day. I love and admire you both."

It is an extraordinary experience to read the love letters of one's parents. Those that follow, drawn from many written in the year and a half before their marriage in January, 1935, evoke a mixture of feelings: a sense of irony and some old bitterness and sadness, knowing what is to follow; some embarrassment in the presence of such ardent and repetitive declarations of love, and some wonder about the underlying anxieties, offered no room in these exchanges; a stab of anger and shame at the emergence, in one of my father's letters, of the sort of thoughtless, impersonal anti-Semitism which still lingered, mostly unattended or consciously outgrown, in the unenlightened shadows of both of their families; and pride and pleasure that my parents had known such a deep, absorbing love, and that, as my father later wrote me, I was a child of their love.

The tenth of October, 1933, was a special anniversary—perhaps of the first time they made love—and they exchanged the following letters.

My Darling—

A thousand thoughts, all precious beyond expression, come to me now as I look backward over the year.

In a sense this is not an anniversary, Darling, for it seems that I have ever loved you, even as I always shall.

So full of the most glorious adventures with you, however, I suppose that this past year shall always live indelibly in my memory, Darling, and if I could live it over and over again, as I surely shall in that lovely vale of dreams, I would ask naught else.

I LOVE YOU, my Sweet, always and always and always.

Every day, every second with you has made you the more dear to me, and as we look ahead to the years before us, I pray that they may be laden with the greatest happiness for you.

What joys you have brought to me, and what I may have given to you, shall always, my lovely Darling, be the boon of my life.

And so, Beloved, this day's message to you, one that shall always be ever new and alive, and coursing through all of me, is—

I LOVE YOU!

Yours
John

Anna's letter begins with a characteristic down-to-earth observation (she was the more practical soul of the two); but she is as ardent as John.

My Very Precious One

The day's work is just finished at 11 p.m., and this is the first chance I've had to sit down alone. But, Darling, you've been so constantly in my thoughts all day. Our Oneness and our Love seem, and are, so very close to me. This is an anniversary for us, Honey, because it seems to bring to life—at the magical thought that we've actually been each other's for a whole year—the myriad memories we have of our ever growing living LOVE, our many glorious adventures and experiences, and the almost breathtaking realization that during this year we have found through each other that dreams sometimes do come true—and for me have proved more wonderful than my wildest imaginings.

Darling, you have, and are, giving me *so* much happiness; and you have opened up a great many more, very lovely, avenues to life, which I had thought about, and guessed at—and a year ago, didn't really think I wanted to go any further!

And Honey, your happiness means more to me than I can possibly tell you. Oh, my Sweet, unless we had that Oneness and instantaneous response to each other's touch, moods and thoughts, we would never have known that marvelous feeling of soaring in the clouds, just the two of us, replete with happiness.

Honey Darling, you'll have to forgive me—this morning with YOU, and your oh, so precious letter which I read right after lunch today, have made me a bit scoofy! Right now I want to take your head between both of my hands and cover your face, your ears, your neck and your hair with kisses—then lie down with your arms around me with my head in its favorite spot on your shoulder, snuggled into your neck—and slowly let that feeling of you steal over me, till I'm full to the brim of YOU, and US, and our LOVE.

I'm really so full of you just now that I'd probably burst if I were really with you!

Sweetheart, you *are* everything in life to me, and I LOVE YOU, with all my heart and soul, now and for *always*.

Your,
B.*

Only one earlier letter survives, written by my father shortly before that first anniversary. It reminds me vividly of the strong current of romanticism in his childhood family—of the poem "Lasca," and the warm sentiment passed so generously from the Otts to the Boettigers.

My Darling—

I am wistful tonight, my Dear, and a picture I crave is of you and me, sitting on a soft couch somewhere in the complete quiet, where we might

* Short for one of my mother's nicknames, "Beetle," shared, to my knowledge, only between the two of them.

watch a smouldering fire and just be together. Or perhaps out in the pine woods somewhere, lit by the stars and the moon, stretched out on a blanket of needles, just feeling the touch of you and staring up at the limitless sweep above, where no one cares who you are, what you may do, who you may love with all of your heart.

The moon is full tonight and I wonder if you saw. It is full of lunacy, my Darling, and of inconsistency, for it doesn't stir a passion in me, but it does reach me with an urge, so very strong, to be where I can see it lighting your face, crowning your hair, filling us to the brim with its peace and companionship and understanding.

. . .

In my spell of lunacy, Darling, I am wondering if I could woo you to the same soft mood, were you here tonight. I don't really wonder. I know I could, without the need of wooing you to it, for you would love it, even as I do.

. . .

Come and dream with me, Darling, and soon.

The lines "where no one cares who you are, what you may do, who you may love with all of your heart" no doubt reflect a preoccupation and impatience with the secrecy of their relationship. It is a theme that runs strongly through these letters. Part of the concern, as I have earlier noted, was that at the time neither was divorced; and both were anxious not to provoke outcries of scandal in the president's family. To a degree the secrecy was part of the adventure, with cover stories, clandestine rendezvous, and notes mailed to a post-office box rented in a friend's name.

But there was an oppressive cast to the secrecy, too, reflecting a hardly admitted awareness of the costs of living—even when avoiding it—in the public eye. In one of her last letters before their wedding, my mother reports a striking dream, expressive of this theme and indicative of a shadow that their marriage would not dispel. She dreamed "that you and I . . . were sitting in some apartment together discussing plans for us. It was such a glorious dream until suddenly we heard some whispering. You jumped up and opened the door into the hall. There—were dozens and dozens of reporters and sob sisters, who burst into gales of laughter and began quoting things they had just heard us say. Sweet little nightmare, n'est-ce pas?"

And it seems likely that there were a few more personal dark moments in those bright, passionate, and impatient months. John Boettiger was moving into a new orbit of unprecedented prominence and power, and while he no doubt found it intriguing and exhilarating with Anna beside him, he must also have encountered again some of his old shadow presences: the feelings of self-doubt and inferiority that so painfully dogged his youth. But if there is reference to such in the letters, it is coded in generality. "I love your understanding," he wrote his wife-to-be shortly before their marriage, "without which we should have lost this most precious thing we both now covet above everything, and I shudder to dwell long upon those very severe tests of your understanding. Yet I marvel on them. Bless you for that understanding, Beloved, and for your infinite tact."

In October, 1934, the second anniversary of their love, and the last such anniversary before their marriage, my father looked backward and forward in a letter that seems to capture most vividly the wonderfully extravagant spirit of my parents' love in those earliest years.

My Beloved—

Today I am dwelling on days gone by, and glorying over them, and dwelling, too, on days to come, and losing myself in a future world so beautiful that I tremble with the joy of it.

You, my Darling, are the treasure of my past and the all of my future, and in writing to you my thoughts for *OUR* day, I find them crowding each other so that they challenge the putting them down on paper.

O, life is so utterly precious with you in it, my One! I thought I was living before that first day when I held you in my arms, and learned how blessed is love, that day whose anniversary quickens my heart so today. But I never lived till you came into my being.

. . .

Will you stop now, as I have done a dozen times since starting this letter, and let your thoughts drift back? O, my Sweet, doesn't it leave you breathless and very happy?

Then came other days, my Love, full of the loveliness which has enriched my memories—OUR memories—beyond compare.

Days under the pines, when the miracle of your great understanding heart was shown to me.

Days in the snow, with a biting wind whipping color to your cheeks.

Long days in the sun, gorgeous loafing lazy days.

Days on horseback, holding hands as we rushed on, laughing with joy.

Days of quiet, of long talks in which we explored each other, and found so to the very brim what we've always sought in companionship.

And days when we explored people, and things, and happenings, long perfect evenings alone—when perfection meant only that we might be alone.

Days and nights, when the urge to binge was strong in us and we went "on the loose", and loved it so!

Days of peace and solitude on a rock beside a stream that rushed noisily enough to banish all else but US. We shall never forget *OUR* rock, my Darling.

Impatient days when things conspired to separate US, but even those days rich because nothing *could really* separate *US!*

Darling they seem like a million days, so many are their joys. I love them all.

. . .

I want so to hold you fast in my arms, today of all days, to hear you say it has been so sweet to you, too, and to plan with you for the days to come.

But comforted am I with the thought that this shall be our last anniversary apart.

I LOVE YOU, my Precious One, with all of me. I am yours, yours alone, for always.

I LOVE YOU! LOVE YOU! LOVE YOU!

Your
John

(I have loved writing this. It has seemed almost as though you could hear me. O, I'm *happy,* Darling!)

I LOVE MY BEAUTIFUL *ANNA*.

J.

When John left the *Chicago Tribune* in December, 1934, he had another job waiting (thanks to the assistance of his friend Joseph P. Kennedy, then head of the Securities and Exchange Commission). He became executive assistant to Will Hays, president of the Motion Picture Producers and Distributors of America. The Hays Office, as it was universally called, had been established in 1922 as a public relations and self-censorship arm of the movie industry, and was best known for its administration of a twelve-point Production

Code assuring that films did not transgress current American standards of decency. Hays himself had been postmaster general in the Harding administration, and a former chairman of the Republican National Committee. He was a staunch, teetotaling, nonsmoking midwestern Presbyterian, and an extraordinarily effective public-relations man. John liked and admired him.

As Hays's assistant, John later wrote in a summary sketch of his working career, "I reorganized [his] press relations staffs in both New York and Hollywood, made many contacts by personal visit and otherwise with newspapermen and publishers over all the country, and explained to them the accomplishments and purposes of the Hays organization. I also worked with Mr. Hays on many of the problems of the industry relating to its trade practices, its relationship with civic organizations—women's clubs, religious organizations, PTA groups and the like—and in general, participated as Mr. Hays' assistant in the manifold problems relating to the running of the motion picture industry."

The new job was politically acceptable to the White House, and carried a salary more in keeping with the imminent change in John's social status. Judging from his letters to my mother, he evidently enjoyed the glamor of his association with Hollywood and the movie industry. "The day at M-G-M was damned interesting. I can now tell you all about sound, synchronization, mixing, lights and—Jeanette MacDonald. . . . I lunched with Louis Mayer, president of the company. . . . He is really a very entertaining dodo, and we got into some swell discussions." My father even wondered in one letter about the possibility of their moving out to Hollywood. But I wonder if there may have been an underlying disquiet as well, a sense of having forsaken his real work for a field—public relations—that journalists characteristically view with contempt. I remember that paragraph in his farewell letter to his wife Virginia: "I am a newspaperman. Twice in 29 years I left my profession and entered other work. Both times I was privileged to work with able, successful and sympathetic colleagues. But in my present association, as in the other, I have felt ill-adjusted and unable to exert what abilities I possess to real advantage."

SIXTEEN

# *Honeymoon*

WHILE I have no account of my parents' honeymoon trip, my mother many years later recalled that it was not without stress and anxiety for my father. Small wonder, for in marrying Anna Roosevelt he married as well the most prominent, scrupulously watched, and variously judged family in the land. And in so doing he entered a social world far from his roots on Robey Street and even from the reporter's craft and identity that had so sustained his early adulthood. For now he was on the other side, more the observed than the observer; and he had long been unusually sensitive to his standing in others' eyes. For all of his confident and competent public manner, his large-framed masculine charm, he was still a shy and anxious man, still deeply unsure of his capacity to stand securely on his own, still intensely vulnerable to criticism and susceptible to humiliation. He married Anna Roosevelt with a great and marveling joy, a resurgence of adventure and romance he had probably not known since early childhood. But he became President Franklin D. Roosevelt's son-in-law with profound if muted ambivalence and not a little fright; and the latter identity was inextricably bound up in the former. Small wonder, indeed, if he knew some anxiety on that honeymoon trip. However secluded their brief retreat, it could not have shielded him from the extraordinary sea change his life was undergoing.

Anna, too, could hardly have been free from anxiety, for she brought with her into that marriage some burdens of her own: a troubling insecurity and mistrust lingering from her early childhood; some identification with her mother's fears of desertion and betrayal by those—particularly those men—closest to her; a companion sense of lurking inferiority (as if betrayal or desertion might somehow be provoked by her own inadequacy); and a profound, demanding, and often constraining sense of responsibility as her father's daughter.

But too much can be made of this shadow theme. Honeymoons are often emotionally strenuous affairs. If Anna and John were dogged from the start by a shared experience of self-consciousness and anxiety, they were also deeply in love and shared a great and venturesome excitement at beginning a new life together. Those same constraining apprehensions also fueled their love, their feelings of devotion and dependency on one another. Their private letters conveyed a conviction that the two of them together were halves of a single whole, a whole more tangible, more real, than either of them individually as man or woman. However problematic the undertone and eventuality of that conviction, it was then, and often in succeeding years, wonderfully confirming. I imagine (it is, I hope, apart from its plausibility, a son's pardonable fantasy) that in those first married days alone Anna and John occasionally enjoyed a freedom simply to be, beyond the memory of either. A newspaper photograph of the two of them, on their return from their honeymoon, reveals a spontaneous, open pleasure, a lack of guardedness or pose, that is truly beautiful—and never quite recaptured in the pictures and films of their married life together.

A month or so before, John had found them a small apartment at 112 Central Park West, and there they settled for the rest of the winter and spring of 1935. For the remainder of the school year Sisty and Buzzy stayed at the White House with a small and reliable community of caretakers and under the watchful eyes of their grandmother and greatgrandmother. They were completing their second year as the resident and much attended White House grandchildren. For all of Anna's admonitions that they avoid unnecessary public attention, and Sisty's echoing chastisements to her little brother when on some occasions he made his presence known more boldly than she felt appropriate, they both found their role as the nation's most famous children an exciting one. (Some months earlier

On their return from a short honeymoon, John and Anna face reporters in the Roosevelt family's New York home, January 21, 1935. *Wide World*

*The New Yorker* printed a cartoon of a mountaineer struggling triumphantly atop a hitherto unconquered peak, and naming it "Mt. Buzzy Dall.") Their notoriety, the continuing appearance of interesting visitors and events, the numbers of people throughout the White House staff who took pleasure in the occasional companionship of two engaging presidential grandchildren, the sheer variety of absorbing places to explore in the house, through the grounds, and on forays into city and park, and even their detailed and supervised daily schedule—all of that offered some security or appeal, and compensated to a degree the disquieting awareness that their mother was too often preoccupied or away.

The children were fond of John, though Sisty with less ambivalence than her brother, who felt some natural jealousy. They called him "Uncle Jay," and had seen him often as a guest at the White House. My brother was distressed that they were not told in advance of their mother's plans to marry again, and were not brought to New York for the ceremony. My sister remembers hearing the news of the wedding as "no big surprise."

With the children's move to New York in the summer of 1935, Anna and John rented from one of the Rockefellers a large and rather elegant duplex apartment at 2 West Fifty-third Street. While far from the scale of the White House—Buzz recalls my mother telling them, "Well, it's not very grand, kids, but . . ."—it was big enough to comfortably accommodate the children, their Belgian governess, Mlle. Deschamps, and a live-in couple, Katy and her new husband, a tall West Indian man named Ivan. I wonder if John overheard Anna's remark to the children, for their new home was also a far cry from his and Eddie Roddan's bachelor digs at the Wardman Park Hotel.

In subsequent and more troubled times my parents looked back on those first two years of marriage in New York with considerable nostalgia. It was a time of more spontaneity and relaxation, of more freedom to be thoroughly with one another, than they were ever to know again. While my father was later to disparage his public relations work for the movie industry, he liked working for Will Hays. And he *did* enjoy the association with stars and moguls (the more so, perhaps, for being now something of a star himself), and seemed not to find the work unduly strenuous. Once the children were settled into their carefully detailed school and governess routines in New York, Anna began to organize women's activities for the Democratic State Committee. But Anna's and John's life together and their love for one another were clearly at the center of their world. While the press paid a good deal of attention to their social activities, they were able to enjoy relative anonymity in New York when they wished, and the burden and seduction of their roles as presidential daughter and son-in-law may have seemed less encompassing.

Nonetheless, the roles were not to be avoided, and neither John nor Anna wished wholly to do so. They visited Denver in August, 1935, and the *Denver Post* announced: "Trying hard to be plain Mr. and Mrs. John Boettiger, the son-in-law and daughter of President and Mrs. Roosevelt arrived in Denver quietly and without fanfare." The paper referred to them as "the No. 1 American newlyweds" and quoted John on his work: "I never had more fun in my life than I did as a reporter. There are times, however, when it gets you jittery. Now I am in very interesting—I might say exciting—work and it is a relief to be able to sleep nights instead of staying awake haunted by the fear that I might be scooped."

On the same trip west they spent a two week vacation in Montana's Glacier National Park, and while there made the first of a number of 16-mm. family movies. The film graphically reveals their roles as public figures, even, as in this event, on a wilderness vacation. They were assigned a park ranger who accompanied them everywhere and took most of the film. Anna and John are continuously aware of being watched and filmed, and are appropriately self-conscious. In one sequence—a playful and funny but somehow poignant performance—the camera focuses upon a cabin door, supposedly in early morning. A horse stands to one side. The door opens and John comes onto the porch, stretches, and yawns widely as if emerging from sleep, then jumps down the steps, vaults onto the conveniently waiting and saddled horse, and thunders off into the distance (no doubt to return in a few moments and join Anna in what they called their most popular walk: from the cabin to the dining room).

Often they found themselves preoccupied by their public roles even as they claimed freedom from them. They had been living together nine months when John's work took him again to Hollywood for a brief trip. He wrote from the plane after their leave-taking of the number of continuous nights they had been together: "The record I am breaking tonight (damn it!) is, I figure, 9 months and 3 days. Let's try to make the next record 9 years and 3 months! Or 90 years would suit me perfectly. I talk and write and act like a newlywed, and what's more to the point, I feel like one." Then he added, "It *is* wonderful to be able to write to you, and not to worry about the letter going astray. Not that I want this letter to go astray, but it wouldn't create any political reactions if it did!"

Something of the quality of my father's ambition, as well as his ardent devotion, is conveyed in another passage of the same letter: "What we must drive at, and believe me, Beloved, I'm driving at it every minute, is to reach that point of financial and business independence where no one can say either of us has to rush anywhere without the other." The image of their independence—of being masters of their own lives and beholden to none—was a recurrent and central fantasy of their marriage; and it always coexisted with a powerful opposing impulse and obligation to enclose themselves in the orbit of presidential power. John's ambition moved, sometimes comfortably and sometimes uneasily, as if in a shifting magnetic field, between the two poles.

My father had, like my mother, some real ambivalence about the fish-bowl aspect of their lives: the special privilege, the public attention, and the responsibility to consider the political impact of all their actions. But John was newer to that world, and had not been taught, as had Anna by her mother, an ethic of forgetting oneself. He was excited by his prominence, unsettled by the reflected quality of that glory, anxious surely of his ability to please the president and act appropriately in his unaccustomed role; but still excited, aware that there was implied a real power, a real opportunity on a scale otherwise inaccessible, to become a man of public consequence, a man, as he put it in his high school graduation speech, whose "rank in the community is recognized and respected."

And around that deepest wish—to be a man of consequence—the choices and events of my father's life now began to circle with greater stake and intensity. The years I am about to chronicle were years of high achievement, much happiness, and great love. But the roots of self-destructiveness did not appear suddenly at the end, however much it appeared so to many who recognized him only in the part he was willing to share. For all of the accomplishments he knew were his, that deepest wish failed of fulfillment. For all the affection and respect he had from others, for all the power and grace of my mother's love for him and his for her, he could not find a way securely to know himself to be a man of consequence. The painfulness of that made him intensely vulnerable to public failure, and proved ultimately too much to bear.

In one respect my father's attitude toward FDR was part of an already established pattern: a tendency to subordinate himself to a powerful older man, to seek advancement, authority, and refuge under the wing of a strong, fatherly mentor. There was always that backdrop to his wish for independence. If it was paternal intimacy he sought—the intimacy he perhaps was denied by a stiff and reticent father—he did not choose well in Colonel William McCormick or Franklin D. Roosevelt, nor later as we shall see in William Randolph Hearst. And in any event, open intimacy had somehow been foreclosed, beyond the realm of the appropriate or comfortable in his relationships with other men. Still, I think that he experienced, with these three powerful and problematic men, a profound dependency and a companion need (always contained in the circle of that dependency) to chafe and rebel.

Anna and John kept in touch with her parents by telephone, occasional visits to the White House and Hyde Park, and frequent correspondence with Eleanor. The president's nature and the press of his responsibilities inclined him to write little, and when he did the notes were usually brief and often hasty. But occasionally they received a real letter from him, and must have been especially pleased with an unusually vivid and handwritten one that arrived in October of their first year together. He wrote from aboard the U.S.S. *Houston*, lying at Bahia Honda off the Panama coast.

Dearest Anna—

I have just come up to my cabin after the church service on the well deck, attended by many of the officers and men of the Houston and Portland. We are lying in this very lovely landlocked harbor 200 miles west of the canal—a very wild tropical country that can only be reached by sea—a few Indian huts on stilts, and with thatched roofs—and some dugout canoes coming out to trade cocoanuts for cigarettes.

It is hot in the sun but there is a nice breeze, and I am getting thoroughly tanned to the waist. The fishing has been marvellous and tho' Gus [the president's bodyguard] has the record with a 148 lb. sailfish I am second with a 134 pounder—9 ft. 6 inches long.

. . .

I do want to hear all about the apartment and also the children's schools. Give them a great deal of love and tell them I hope to have some good photos of the Big Fish to show them. Much much love to you and John. I heard several reports of the grand work he is doing while I was on the coast. I hope to be at Hyde Park the Sat. and Sun. before elections and count on seeing you then.

Ever your affectionate
Father

It is a wonderfully *physical* letter: off on his own, on the sea, a ship at his command, in congenial company, he was warm, relaxed, and affectionate. Never a very accessible father, he was becoming less so in the presidency, but his remarkably vivid spirit charmed and moved his daughter, and this letter may well have reminded her of the compelling and high-spirited man with whom she had ridden and sailed as a child.

Anna had lived at the White House and had worked closely with her mother during the years just before her marriage, and Eleanor had come more and more to feel a rare and treasured bond between them. As both mother and daughter had grown in years, Eleanor's feelings were less buried and found a clearer, less tempered voice. On Christmas Eve, 1935, she wrote a deeply moving letter to my mother from the White House. In juxtaposition to that of her husband above, it serves dramatically again to underline the differences in their personalities and gifts.

Darling Anna,

Perhaps I needed to have you away this Xmas to realize just how much it means to have you, and so I think I'll try to tell you in these few minutes

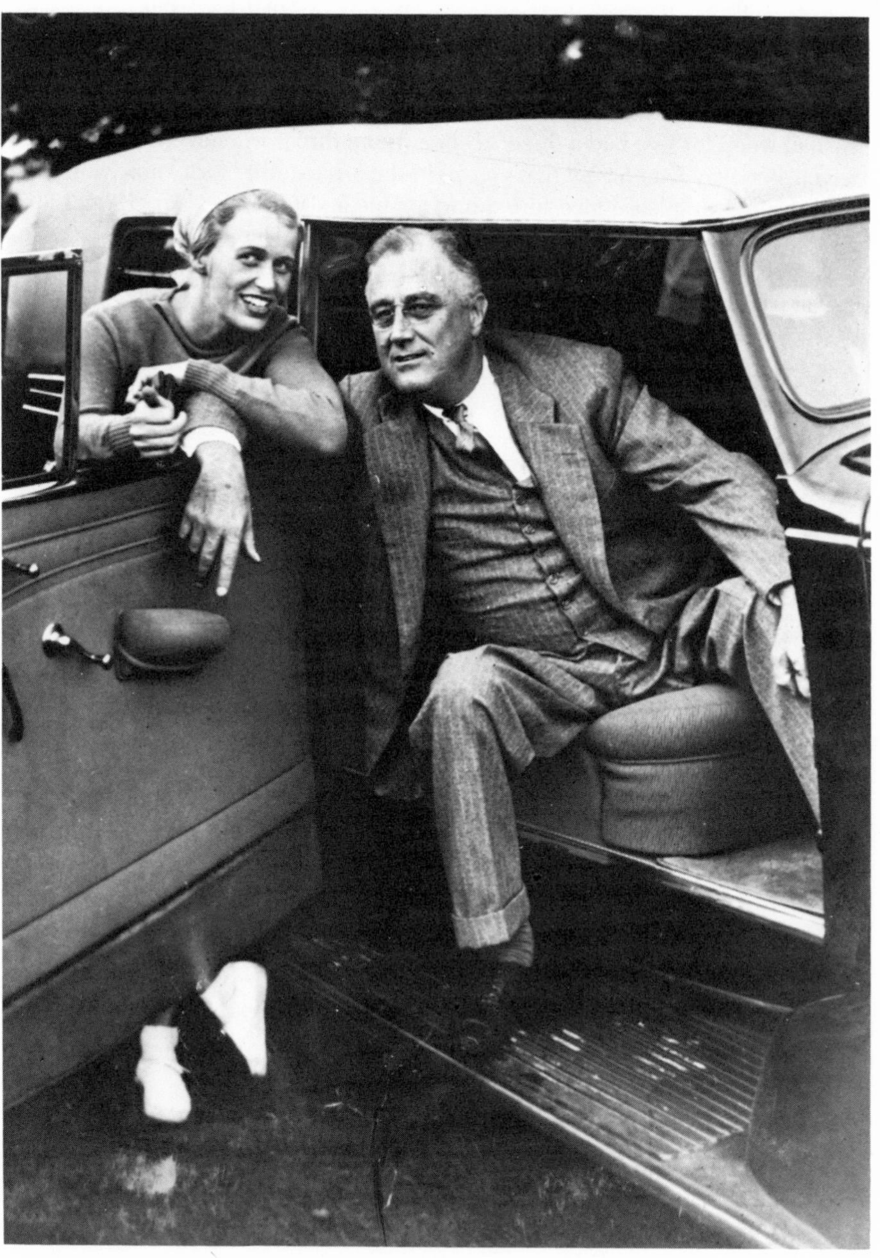

Anna and her father watch a softball game in Pawling, New York, September 21, 1935. *Franklin D. Roosevelt Library*

before dinner how much I miss you. The dogs and I have felt sad every time we passed your door. It was hard to decorate the tree or get things distributed at the afternoon party without you and I dread dinner tomorrow night for so many of your friends will miss you and if anyone says much I shall weep for I've had a queer feeling in my throat whenever I thought of you. Anyway I am happy that you and John are together for I know you will be happy. So please give him a hug for me and tell him I am grateful for him and for what he means to you every day of my life. . . . When I go to church tonight I'll pray for long life and happiness for each and every one of you who mean so much to me and may I always realize what a blessed person you are dearest one.

Mother

SEVENTEEN

# *New Venture*

DESPITE the attractiveness of their life in New York, it is clear that John wanted to return to the newspaper business and that they were actively looking for a new opportunity by mid-1936. For a time they contemplated going to Hollywood and a more direct association with the movie industry. Eleanor was distressed at the prospect of having them across the country, and wrote that she "told Pa and he said there were going to be changes in the whole industry and he felt John would be far better off to stay where he is with Will Hays."

But my father's restless ambition, his lingering newsman's discomfort with the heavy flavor of entertainment and promotion in his current work, and his and Anna's shared desire to embark on some mutual adventure in the world combined to fuel a continuing search. And in the autumn of 1936 they were offered an opportunity that involved and excited them both: directing the publication of a major West Coast daily newspaper, the *Seattle Post-Intelligencer*. At the outset, however, there were two problems that vividly illustrate their inescapable web of connection with FDR's presidency.

The *Post-Intelligencer*, or *P-I* as it was called familiarly, was one of a chain of newspapers owned by a man who had been a consistent and vocal critic of the president and most of his policies, William Randolph Hearst. And the *P-I* was in serious trouble. Its advertising revenue and circulation had slipped in recent years, and it had been losing ground to its locally owned competition, the *Seattle Times*. In the summer of 1936, embroiled in a volatile unionization dispute, the *P-I* was shut down by a strike initiated by the Seattle Newspaper

Guild. As the strike continued into the autumn, Hearst and his lieutenants fulminated to no avail about the country's impending labor dictatorship. Then, on the first Tuesday in November, an event occurred that turned matters in a new direction. In one of the great landslides of American political history Franklin D. Roosevelt was reelected for a second term. The old electoral adage "As Maine goes, so goes the nation" was rephrased "As Maine goes, so goes Vermont"; they were the only two states Roosevelt did not carry.

The impact of that victory on the nation's politics and policies has been recounted elsewhere. Its personal impact on a young family who stood close under the president's shadow was far-reaching. William Randolph Hearst, no stranger to the world of political expediency, evidently decided it was time to make some reconciliatory gestures toward the New Deal. (His newspapers had campaigned strenuously for Roosevelt's defeat in the election.) And equally no stranger to shrewd self-interest, he found a way simultaneously to serve the restoration of his immobilized newspaper property in Seattle. He quickly capitulated on most of the points of contention with the Newspaper Guild, and as the strike moved toward settlement he made a carefully arranged and attractive proposal to the president's son-in-law and daughter.

John was offered a three-year contract as publisher, beginning on the date the strike was settled and publication resumed. Unlike the publishers and editors of other Hearst papers, who were closely directed from the central offices of Hearst Publications, Inc., he was to have the authority to direct "the editorial and business policies of the paper." The salary offered was high: $30,000 a year, plus a bonus contingent upon improvement in the *P-I*'s position, if he succeeded in bringing that about. (The paper had been losing around $200,000 a year before the strike.) In addition, Anna was offered employment, for the same three-year period, "as a contributor to women's pages . . . and in connection with all matters of interest to women," at a notably more modest but still substantial salary of $10,000.

Anna and John were cautious: they didn't particularly trust Hearst, and were aware of the element of self-interest in his offer. And no doubt my father had some uncomfortable realization that the opportunity clearly hinged on his relationship to the Roosevelt family. While he was viewed as a very promising editorial talent at the *Chicago Tribune* and was of proven ability as a reporter, he had scant editorial experience and virtually no experience in business management. But the offer was enormously seductive as well: it would allow John to return to his own newspaper world, in a top position of real authority, and with prominence in a region and city both he and Anna anticipated with a kind of pioneering spirit. (She had visited Seattle with Curtis Dall nine years before, and had even then thought that it might be an exciting territory to settle.) It was an opportunity to build up their own capital resources. John had no money other than his salary; and Anna was still receiving an allowance from her father. While working for Hearst was not a wholly comfortable idea, their freedom from heavy interference seemed assured, and they had hopes that "W.R." would sell them the paper in time. Above all, the opportunity seemed theirs *together*. Their marriage was still full of buoyant confidence, and the chance to tackle this work as a team gave new form and impetus to their vision of common adventure.

Just a few days before they were to accept the Hearst offer, my father wrote FDR from New York to tell him their news and ask for his public blessing. John began the letter with the words "Dear Pa," and noted, "Thereby marking for the record the first time I have addressed you so. It is because I feel that way." The salutation bespeaks a new confidence in the relationship, as if perhaps, momentarily, the venture in the offing might confirm the President's image of John as "a real man." (He was to revert, shortly thereafter, to the more awkward "Dear 'FDR.' ")

The guild strike was settled, though the feelings it aroused and the residue of issues it left were to be a major worry to John and Anna in the next months. On Thanksgiving Day, 1936, my father formally resigned his job with Will Hays, and he and Anna took up their appointments on the *P-I*. They made hurried arrangements for packing and for supervision of the children in New York over the next transitional two months, and four days after Thanksgiving were aboard the North Coast Limited on their way West.

They were met in Seattle by a gala reception. Mayor and Mrs. John Dore and a considerable crowd greeted them at the station. Mrs. Dore presented Anna with an enormous bouquet of roses. And they were escorted from the platform to a waiting car by the city's police band and drill team. That night they were the guests of honor at a banquet sponsored by the mayor and Seattle's civic leaders. Dave Beck—the powerful Teamster's Union leader who had lent muscle to the *P-I* strikers—as well as the mayor and the state's two U.S. senators, were among the welcoming speakers. John wrote in the *P-I* the next morning, "I have spent most of my newspapering years in getting and writing the news. . . . I've been out of the business now for two years, following the lure of the motion picture business, a lure which somehow could never quite overcome the virus of newspapering in my blood. I'm glad to be back in harness." A note from Anna's father arrived a day or two after they set to work: "I am so thrilled that the plan has gone through successfully—and that you have actually started! I'm confident it will succeed and the only objection is that all four of you will be so far away."

It was an objection that Eleanor felt particularly deeply. She understood Anna's and John's choice, calling the move "a grand adventure" in a letter to her daughter shortly after their arrival, and prayed "as you do that John comes out with flying colors." But she was dismayed to have them go so far away. "I shall miss them sadly," she wrote Franklin, "but it does seem a grand opportunity and they will love it and so life is life, not always very pleasant"; and a week later, in another letter to her husband, "I can hardly bear to have Anna and John go, but they are so happy that I wouldn't let them know for worlds. But it is better than Europe for at least one can fly out if necessary." And fly she did—the following spring and then frequently over the next six years that Anna and John lived in Seattle. "I want to see your house when you get settled," she wrote that Christmas, "for I like to be able to see you in my mind's eye when I'm thinking about you." (Mother and daughter were much alike; it is a phrase I remember my mother often voicing as I pursued my own itinerant young adulthood.)

Anna and John had a quiet Christmas alone that year, in rooms they had taken at Seattle's Benjamin Franklin Hotel. They must have felt there was much to be thankful for. Anna's love notes on that occasion, tucked under the ribbons of gifts for her husband, have been lost, but there is a much folded and refolded page in my father's hand that one could imagine as a Christmas toast to his beloved: "You, my Sweet, are the most glorious gift ever given to any man, and when I dwell on the fact that I have that wonderful gift, not alone on Christmas Day, but every day through the year, I simply burst with joy. I pray that you will always be happy, Darling, and always with me."

One of Anna's principal tasks in those early weeks in Seattle was to scout the land for a large, comfortable house. Given her love for the Hyde Park estate, and her wish to preserve her family from unwanted public attention, she leaned to more secluded homes, and the place she found in suburban Lawtonwood was strikingly beautiful: a rambling and roomy cedar shingled house, with great shade trees and two acres of lawn and flowers surrounding it, and a magnificent view of Puget Sound and the Olympic range beyond. There was a beach below the house, and the sun set across the water. In short, the home and its grounds splendidly suited their sense of themselves and their place in Seattle—a tangible representation of that security and accomplishment they so eagerly sought and now felt at hand. In part it *was* at hand, but there is a no less indicative irony in the fact that the house was only available on a year's lease, and that they would move again and again—four times during their six years in Seattle.

Katy and Ivan, the housekeeping couple who had been with them in New York, arrived with Anna's Irish setters in mid-January just as they were moving in, and Sisty and Buzzy came with their governess soon after. The household was complete, the Boettigers under one roof again. It was the family's first real home, and Anna's descriptions in letters to her parents and grandmother are conveyed with a detail and pleasure both unprecedented and unequaled on the occasions of her many subsequent moves.

Sisty enjoyed the move West, and made friends easily and

The family's first Seatt
home, in Lawtonwood
Anna, John, Eleanor,
Sisty, and Buzzy are o
the lawn.

The Boettigers welco
Eleanor to Seattle.

Christmas, 1937.

Anna and John with the President in June, 1938, en route from Poughkeepsie to Hyde Park. *UPI-Acme*

quickly in Seattle. Buzzy felt more uprooted. He had come to feel a real attachment to the White House and to Hyde Park, and in fact was more comfortable with his great-grandmother and grandmother than with his mother and Uncle Jay. He both admired and resented his new stepfather. Buzzy was then, as I have noted earlier, a considerably more self-conscious and shy child than his sister, and he felt isolated and vulnerable in a new school and community. Secret Service agents, assigned to the family for their protection day and night, took the children to and from school and lingered as inconspicuously as possible until they were ready to return home. The other children, needless to say, were fascinated by the "G-men," as they called them, and that only served to increase Buzzy's discomfort. The following summer, when he and his sister were in Hyde Park on a vacation visit after their first half year in the northwest, Buzzy was asked by a cousin how he liked Seattle. His only answer was that there was a lot of slush and no snow for coasting.

Anna and John were both intensely involved in their new work, and evidently enjoyed something of a honeymoon period at the *P-I*. Anna wrote her father on January 10, 1937, "The jobs grow more interesting and absorbing, day by day, and we are loving it." She reported to him that circulation had gone up 3,500 copies since the paper was shut down the previous August, and advertising was "doing correspondingly well except in a few cases where the advertisers have frankly said that they are afraid of us as a New Deal paper!" Her own tasks kept her busy, she said: "some reorganization of our women's departments, helping with some promotion work, and attending innumerable women's clubs' shindigs." John wrote a friend and former colleague in New York that he had put into effect a program of economy, and that the Hearst organization was proving cooperative in all respects and Hearst himself had even made several good suggestions. John had arrived, he thought, at a politic editorial formula: "We will support the administration when it is not in direct conflict with the Hearst policy; we will be silent for the most part otherwise." If he was persuaded that he had been granted complete editorial freedom, he was nonetheless being careful of his boss's sensibilities.

There were two serious sources of apprehension that marred the edges of this happy picture. The first, and ultimately more important for them personally and for their marriage, was the increasingly hectic pace of their work lives, the sheer time and energy consumed by the *P-I*, their related social and promotional activities in Seattle and the surrounding area, and the stresses attendant upon a dramatic expansion of their public roles. Both had begun to have heavy schedules of speechmaking, and both brought home in the evening briefcases bulging with unattended paperwork. A note from Anna to John during one day at the office indicates something of the strain: "Would it be possible for you to get home about 6:20? Here's my selfish reason: If we can drink leisurely cocktails, eat dinner at ten minutes to seven, then I will have about a half hour before we leave for Meany Hall in which to get over that 'full' feeling. Of course, I'll understand if you can't make it—and I ought to be plenty used to 'squirming' by now!"

My sister and brother remember a characteristic scene: Anna and John returning home in the early evening to a cocktail time punctuated with "I love you" toasts and an intimacy too little open to the presence of the children, who were largely companioned and cared for by a governess or the housekeeping couple and by the ever-present Secret Service men. Buzz remembers his feelings of exclusion, his jealousy at Anna's and John's absorption in one another. Sis felt those occasions "overdramatized and phony." Whatever the feelings underlying that perception, it suggests a painful likelihood: that the stylized quality of my parents' public lives was beginning to infect their private times at home as well.

There were, of course, good family times during those Seattle years. Indeed, Sis recalls, "almost every weekend had *some* family time, usually at least Sunday dinner; and often, if there were no guests, we four played gin rummy or Parcheesi or some other simple board game for an hour or two in the evening. At such times there was never any of the 'cocktail time' ritual and I remember lots of kidding and laughter." There were also weekend rambles with the dogs and trips along Puget Sound aboard the family's cabin cruiser, *Newshawk*, of which John was particularly proud. But the stresses in their lives were hard to ignore.

"We have worries and sleepless nights," John confided to a

former colleague, "but after a bit the ominous clouds roll away and we get back into optimism again. Mostly the worry is caused by overwork, I think." He and Anna were able to get away alone for ten days in the late summer of 1937, but the swamp seemed deeper on their return. "The difficulty," he wrote to an old Chicago friend, "is that vacations are fine enough while they last, but when you get back to your desk you have to pay for all the time you have taken off in added work, and by the time you get anywhere near through the added work, the benefit of your vacation is pretty well shot."

The second cause of stress, feeding the first, was an increasingly preoccupying and conflicted labor situation at the paper and in Seattle generally. John struggled to retain his spirit of buoyant adventure, but felt increasingly burdened. He wrote a friend: "The future of the town is rosy, once we get the damn spectre of labor troubles overcome. It is a real battle, much, much more difficult than I ever imagined in New York. Maybe, if I had realized how heavy the odds were stacked against me I would never have come. But I have never regretted coming, and I relish the battle. Anna is in it up to her ears, and she feels exactly as I do about it." Up to their ears they were indeed, and such near total immersion may well have had its rewards. Both of them were raised—Anna more by her mother, John probably by his father—to find real satisfaction in hard work. But it brought considerable tension, too; and that, for all the closeness of their working lives, made for greater difficulty in being as easily and wholeheartedly with each other and with their children.

My father wrote a very long letter to FDR on May 19, 1937, summing up their first six months at work in Seattle. Most of the letter is devoted to a discussion of his sense of embattlement on the labor front. He had evidently made some real progress at first. "The unions on the paper were rather frankly suspicious of me, doubted that as a Hearst publisher I could remedy their complaints. I met them as a friend, on their own grounds, settled our differences quickly and fairly, and gradually acquired their confidence." He found himself, though, watching apprehensively "a feud of growing proportions" in the Seattle labor movement between Dave Beck, the Teamsters' leader whom he had befriended, and Harry Bridges, the Communist-leaning leader of the West Coast maritime unions who had just gone about "seizing control of the Seattle Newspaper Guild." My father feared that the *P-I* would be caught and immobilized in the midst of this Beck-Bridges feud or, worse, get swept up in Bridges' efforts to control West Coast newspapers through their union organizations.

At the letter's end, John said to the president that he didn't want anything, or wasn't suggesting FDR do anything. "I can handle our situation, I believe, although the going may get tough and not to my liking." He said he was sticking to a peaceful policy for the time being, of which FDR approved in his answering letter. In a phrase anticipating his own policy toward a vastly greater conflict about to emerge in Europe, the president remarked, "if one is to wage a war, it is best not to talk until the other fellow gets himself into an untenable position."

The labor situation gradually improved, and despite the strain of a national business recession developing at the end of 1937, the *Post-Intelligencer* was doing reasonably well under John Boettiger's leadership. Circulation continued to rise, and the paper was actually showing a profit for a brief period of months in late 1937 before the recession hit. "It all goes to prove," FDR wrote John, "that a Hearst paper, minus Hearst's management, can be made to pay if it is run by a fellow like you." At the same time, my father's liberal New Deal editorial policy—particularly as another presidential election year approached—was the object of some chafing from the Hearst executive offices in New York. While my parents' contracts with Hearst were renewed in 1939, and they were evidently on cordial terms with the man himself, John felt increasingly harassed by his relationship with the *P-I*'s parent organization. In May, 1939, he wrote a confidential letter to his old boss, Will Hays: "The business of working for Hearst (the institution, not the man) is so beset with obstacles and difficulties and worries that neither Anna nor I have the wish to stay longer. It is impossible to get the best results for your labor; gains are made at terrific effort."

"Still, with it all," he went on, "we both have loved the job here, we like Seattle and the Pacific Northwest, we love the kind of work

*Starting on the facing page, clockwise:* John and Anna at their desks in the *Post-Intelligencer* offices.

Anna interviewing cannery workers in Kirkland, Washington.

The Boettigers and their boss, William Randolph Hearst. *Pictures, Inc.*

we are doing." They had thought of buying the *P-I*, but they hadn't much capital, and the world seemed precarious in mid-1939; and anyway they were fairly sure Hearst would not sell. They had also considered the idea of buying a smaller paper, but that would provide at best "the nucleus of a satisfactory income," and they had made, as yet, no inquiries in that direction. Soon, after consultation among family and a few friends, they chose to stay with Hearst and the *P-I*.

That choice seems, in the light of the events that followed in the next few years, critical and singularly poignant. I hardly trust myself to make such an assessment: that year was the year of my birth, and I without doubt still deeply wish that 1939 had been in all ways a turning for the better in the lives of my parents. That it was not so—not wholly nor even on balance so—is still dismaying.

But that it might have been so is not only a son's imagining, for the vision was theirs: a newspaper of their own, somewhere on the northern Pacific coast between San Francisco and the Canadian border; an enterprise free of absentee ownership, divided loyalties, the cautions and fears, the tiresome compromises and endless negotiating that such division fosters; a venture that both of them might have undertaken with more confidence that it was theirs in their own right rather than through the fortunes of birth or marriage and the self-interest of others; a chance, finally, to redress the growing imbalance of the public and the private in their lives, and thus to recover that centeredness in their love of which they still spoke to one another with fervor.

And yet that the choice emerged as it did can hardly be surprising, nor can I easily fault them for it. For all of their difficulties with the Hearst organization, they were proud of their accomplishments at the *P-I*. "We have taken a paper which was in the most desperate state possible, and made very good strides with it." Their combined salaries were very high for those times. With John's annual bonuses added in, they were making about $43,000 a year. To have given up that income and purchased the *P-I* or another large paper would have required a sizable amount of external capital, and while they thought it would be forthcoming, the fiscal conservatism of a bank officer's son inclined John to avoid the risk, particularly when the nation and the world seemed again to be entering such troubled times. To have bought a smaller paper would have meant a substantial loss of income, but probably more important—at least for my father—a loss of some of the civic prominence, the public consequence, he had so long coveted and so briefly as yet enjoyed. While he was deeply discomforted by the appelation "Mr. Son-in-Law" occasionally heard and often in the minds of those resenting his policies or his position, he relished his reputation as "the liaison man of the Administration in the Pacific Northwest."

He shared my mother's self-consciousness and nervousness in the face of continuing demands for public appearances, but also took considerable pleasure and pride in the recognition he received on such occasions. Evidently stung by a critical letter from a Hearst executive in 1939, he composed a very long reply detailing the *P-I*'s successes and his determination to continue writing editorials supportive of FDR and the New Deal. He added that one prominent bank president had recently and publicly spoken of his gratitude "for the many ways in which I have produced constructive benefits for Seattle, and expressed his pleasure at 'being able to call John Boettiger a citizen of Seattle.' " Such a letter may well have reflected John's own privately recognized tendency to "sell his ability . . . to those in control," but it also summarized a striking fulfillment of his adolescent hopes for himself.

Furthermore, he played the part well. One otherwise rather critical journalist wrote: "He makes many speeches. The invitations are too numerous to fill. Audiences seek him for return engagements. Relationship to the President is not his only qualification. Tall and erect, his hair graying slightly, Boettiger has a platform presence. With his jovial manner, resonant voice and big physique, he might be a Roosevelt born instead of a member of the family by marriage."

# EIGHTEEN

# *The Turning*

THERE was another reason for not undertaking a risky new venture that year, and perhaps for expecting that their love and their family circle offered prospect of renewed devotion. I was born in March, 1939. My parents had not meant to have a child; their absorption in their work, in one another, in the manifold tasks and avoidances of being the Northwest's resident Roosevelts, and their care for Anna's eight-year-old son and eleven-year-old daughter, all combined to offer in their eyes a full—often, it seemed, overfull—life. "We didn't plan [it] . . . ," John wrote to Eleanor after they knew Anna was pregnant, "actually resisted [it] because we were not sure we wanted to divide ourselves any farther. We wanted freedom to devote ourselves pretty generously to each other." Yet somewhere, for one or both, the wish may have been there for a child of that union they so treasured. They certainly spoke and wrote as if that were so.

They had, of course, been suspecting pregnancy by early August, 1938. Appropriately enough, if perhaps sadly as well, Anna conveyed the confirming news to her husband by a typewritten note in the midst of a busy day at the office: "I have talked to the Doc and have even seen the rabbit's ovaries—and the answer is 'YES'! Vat do ya tink, Papa?!" John's immediate response was not recorded, but on August 27—probably the next day—he wrote Eleanor: "Ever since I laid eyes on Anna certain happy fates have attended my existence. . . . I was extricated from a terribly unhappy situation. My work improved and I got ahead. My point of view on many things changed and brought greater philosophic enjoyment of life. . . . Now comes this new joy which we didn't plan. . . . But now I feel it is just another stroke of that happy fate and I'm fairly explosive with joy."

Anna wrote to her father: "We are Pupping!! So, in about seven months you should be a Grandpa again! We are both very thrilled. John has never had a child of his own, and he's becoming very paternal by leaps and bounds. He's rooting for a girl because he says they are much less trouble than boys to 'bring' up. I've told him to ask you! I'm rooting for twins for he has twin sisters and I've been told that this type of prolificness (if there is such a word) is hereditary!"

The early months of her third pregnancy were not easy ones for my mother. In early October, Eleanor wrote reassuringly and a little ominously out of her considerable experience, and offered the kind of advice she had made a central tenet of her own personal philosophy: "The worst part will soon be over, and it won't be very bad til the last months. I think you will find keeping busy if you don't overtire yourself is a help right through." John was excited, but also very anxious. Anna had a history of gynecological problems, and he feared complications in the pregnancy. (My father had an extraordinary concern throughout their marriage for the general states and minor changes in his and my mother's health.) When I was five months inside my mother's womb, and developing perfectly normally, Eleanor wrote with characteristic empathy to her son-in-law, "I know so well what you mean about worrying about what might happen. I have that horrid kind of an imagination too. . . . She was quite normal last time [with Buzz's birth]. There is no reason why she should not be this time." Eleanor had planned from her first knowledge of her daughter's pregnancy to be with her at the delivery: holding Anna's hand as she had at Sis's and Buzz's births, and as Sara had held her's.

In her eighth month my mother had cut back substantially on her work schedule, and Dr. Richard O'Shea, the family physician who was to deliver me, insisted that she spend much of the last seven or eight weeks in bed; and those last weeks—contrary to my grandmother's prediction—were in fact quite peaceful ones. Anna wrote Granny on March 5, "I seem to be getting lazier and lazier every day!" Eleanor arrived in Seattle on the twenty-fifth, five days before the birth of her ninth grandchild, John Roosevelt Boettiger, at 12:43 P.M. on March 30, 1939. I weighed in at nine pounds, one ounce. The birth, my father was relieved to learn, was perfectly normal. "I feel like I can breathe again," he told his sister Marie, "I have never been through quite so much worry before."

The president wrote his daughter from his retreat in Warm Springs, Georgia: "It's just too grand! I had only been at the cottage half an hour after a long day in the car when John and Mother called. What a bouncer! And what fun we're *all* going to have with him!"

My mother's first letter from her hospital room after my birth was to her father:

Dearest Pa,

Your letter from Warm Springs meant a great deal to both John and me. I felt cheated that I hadn't been able to talk to you on the phone—and the letter made up for it, and made you seem much closer to us than the three thousand physical miles between us.

We're so happy about little Johnny! You should see big John learning how to handle him and feed him his bottle. I thought Mother would die laughing at John's concentration, facial expressions and efforts to "catch" the baby's head as it rolled from side to side!

Ma was *such* a comfort before the event, during and after. . . .

She ended the letter with the hope that he might soon visit. "Your youngest (for the moment) precocious grandson has a most excellent pair of lungs and vocal chords with which to welcome you."

My mother recovered her strength under her husband's attentive eye. I grew vigorously with my mother's care and that of a nurse (the tradition sustained) who would soon take fuller responsibility for me as my mother returned to her work at the *P-I.* Many years later, toward the end of her life, my mother told me that she did not breast feed me, as she had Buzz and Sis, because my father was anxious that she be free to return to work as soon as she was strong enough.

Judging from the pictures and home movies of the time, I was a lively and venturesome infant. I made my first cross-country trip by train at eight months, when our family returned for Christmas to the White House, and there is a picture of the assembled Roosevelt clan in which my willingness to pose was overcome by my urge to explore. I was christened at the White House on Sunday afternoon, December 31, 1939.

However genuine my father's affection for his former wife's children and his devotion to Sis and Buzz, Anna alluded to something of importance in telling her father that "John has never had a child of his own." For a man endemically possessed of doubts of his masculinity, there must have been some extra measure of pride in this birth. He wrote his Aunt Bertha, "I waited nearly forty years to taste the joys of fatherhood, which makes them all the sweeter."

Still, I think he distrusted even then his capacity adequately to father a son. His relationship with Buzz was not an easy one. He joked to his friends occasionally during my first months, "The boy . . . seems okay in every way except that people insist he resembles his old man." And I was *not* to be John Boettiger, Jr. I was recognized as a Roosevelt by my middle name; and he talked—again jokingly—of the name John relating not to him but because of my hefty size to Robin Hood's companion, Little John. (My father himself, of course, was a six-foot, two hundred pounder.)

John particularly wanted to share his new son with his own father Adam. I have earlier mentioned the picture John sent his father a few months after my birth, "with a hope I'll do as well for my Johnny as you always did for yours." Grandpa Adam had visited Seattle less than a year before my birth, but when he died in his San Diego home at age seventy-four in May of 1940 he had not yet seen his son John's only child. For whatever confirmation or redemption, whatever act of love that might have been in my father's mind, that fact clearly hurt him; and it is tempting to find in it some kinship with the failure he felt in not arriving at his mother's bedside before she died nine years before. "The thing that frets me most," he wrote Eleanor, "is that Dad was planning to be with us this month, and to have his first visit with his newest grandson, Johnny. The first thing he said when we got down there was 'Did you bring Johnny?' "

The death of one's last surviving parent is often a peculiarly devastating loss, bringing as it does the awareness to even the most determined and middle-aged grownup that finally now there is no one left to be mother or father in times of need. And, of course, to

)n *the facing page, above:* The family at home with heir new arrival, John Roosevelt Boettiger, in 1939. *elow*: Christmas, 1939, at the White House. Seated re: Eleanor Roosevelt (not shown), Sara Delano oosevelt, Ethel du Pont Roosevelt (Franklin Jr.'s ife) with her son Franklin III on her lap, the presi- ent, Anna, Mrs. James R. Roosevelt (the president's ister-in-law), and Anne Clark (Mrs. John) Roosevelt. tanding: Franklin, Jr., John, and John Boettiger. Sit- ing on the floor are Sisty, Diana Hopkins (daughter of residential friend Harry Hopkins), and Buzzy. The ewest grandchild is exploring in the foreground. *ranklin D. Roosevelt Library*

nna and John with John's father, on a visit to Boettiger relatives in California. *elow:* The photograph John sent to his father in 1939, inscribed "To my dear old Dad, with a ope I'll do as well for my Johnny as you always did for yours."

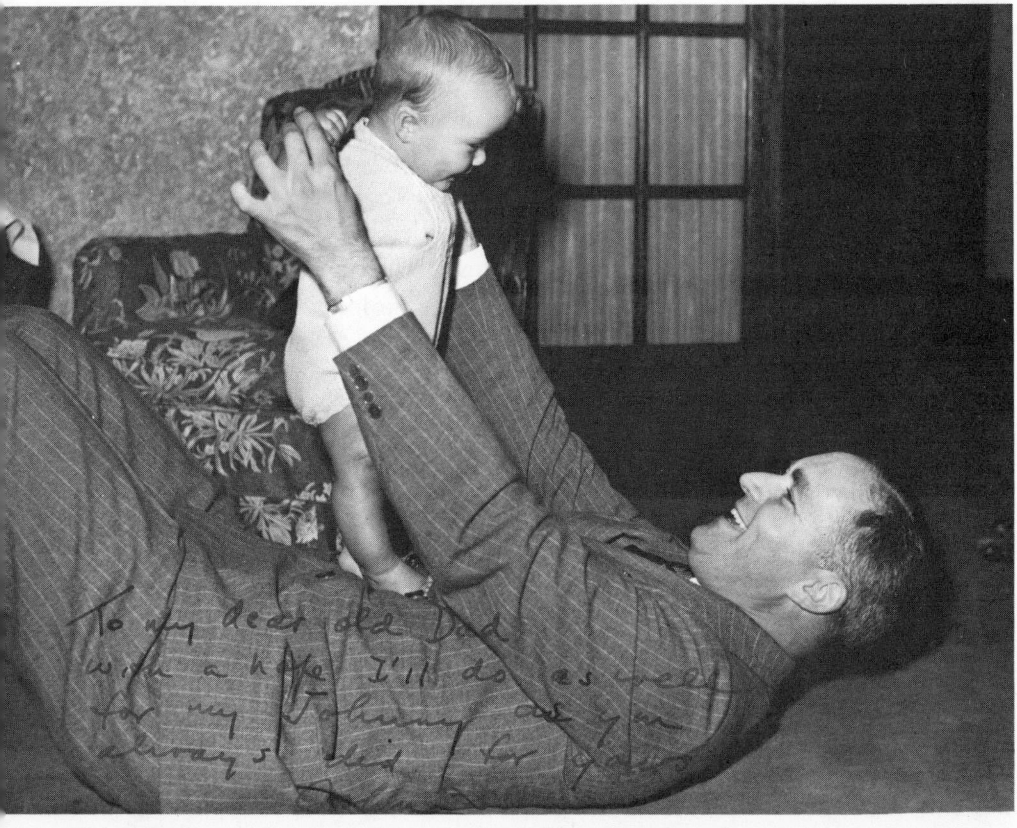

those of middle age—my father was forty, the classical point of turning—it often brings more dramatic consciousness of one's own mortality. More immediately, John endured the vigil of watching his father slowly die. "The loss," he wrote one of his few close friends, "was a very severe one and his suffering for days was a terrific strain on all of us. Some day the medical profession will have decent and humane principles in cases of that sort."

Eleanor, who as a child had drawn further into her solitary world of fantasy after the death of the father whom she took as her life and her hope, wrote touchingly.

John dearest,

I sent you a wire but I want to add this line for I know these partings are hard and from Anna I realize that the end was not easy for you to watch. I think probably your Father did not suffer as much as he seemed to and you must try to forget that and remember how much happiness you gave him these last few years. I'm glad you and Anna had each other through all this for it does make sorrow easier to bear. . . .

Much, much love John dear,
L.L.

Anna evidently took on some added responsibility at the *P-I* as her experience grew. By 1940 her title had become associate editor. While she and John were of similar mind on most issues concerning the paper, she often had a less ego-invested and more philosophical attitude. For example, in the midst of their most trying labor-relations disputes in 1937 she wrote her mother that she knew the nation as a whole—union members and leaders, employers, government officials, and many others less directly affected—was "going through an inevitable and evolutionary period which was bound to tax the patience, senses of humor and perspective and common sense balance of a great many people." She may also have been thinking of the strains in her relationship with John in adding: "Our immediate troubles to keep this paper open and make a success of it are very apt to loom large and out of all proportion if, because of continual pressure we forget to keep in mind the larger picture of what is going on not only in this country but almost all over the world."

Anna was developing in those years something very close to the distinctive mixture of political realism, strong ethical commitment, and care and understanding for the sensibilities of individual people that so richly characterized her mother. Eleanor had flown to Seattle to be with her daughter when Anna underwent some painful surgery in December, 1937, and Anna soon afterward wrote to Malvina Thompson, my grandmother's secretary: "I was certainly a grateful young pup when I saw her walk into my room Christmas morning. All the transfusions, pills, and injections that I have had have been nothing compared to the tonic of having her with us."

On Eleanor's part there was the continuing pleasure she received from Anna's and John's love—as she wrote my father at Christmas time, 1939: "The happiness you and Anna have and create around you gives me hope when other things seem dark and I'm so grateful to you both." And there was also, as Eleanor's friend Joe Lash knew at the time, a special and growing kinship with her daughter: "Anna was the one [of the five Roosevelt children] who had developed most in the way of understanding and compassion. Mrs. R.'s voice would reflect her special joy and pleasure in Anna. . . . A deep and intimate understanding had grown between them and her heart would sing when she was going to see Anna."

For all of that closeness, there remained always as well a less tangible sense of stress between them to which neither openly alluded. I remember of later years that the atmosphere in our home changed when one of my grandmother's visits was anticipated: excitement grew, but so did tension. Anna sympathized greatly with her mother's deep hurt at the absence of a close and sustaining love from Franklin; and both women knew, as well, of the relative relaxation and simplicity of his relationship with Anna. But more important was my mother's lingering sense of neglect and inferiority as a child, the painful shyness she had learned, like her mother, both to hide and put to use in the nurture of genuine compassion for like feelings in others. On one of Eleanor's visits to Seattle, the two of them joined in a radio broadcast on the theme "Education of a Daughter for the Twentieth Century." In the transcript of that program there occurs the following exchange, interesting not least for the public circumstance in which it occurred.

MRS. ROOSEVELT: There's another thing, Anna, that bothered me as a girl. I had an inferiority complex which so many children suffer from.

MRS. BOETTIGER: It took me a long time to get over mine, and I think that was your fault.

MRS. ROOSEVELT: Really? Why?

MRS. BOETTIGER: Well, I never felt I could be as capable and interesting as you and father were.

MRS. ROOSEVELT: I have heard so many young people say that about their elders, and I have come to believe that one of the essentials of education is developing a sense of self-confidence. If only our companionship could have developed as freely when you were little as it did later on, I would have probably understood a great deal more.

And perhaps Anna would have been less dogged throughout her life by the underlying conviction that she was not "as capable and interesting" as her illustrious parents.

In July, 1940, Anna listened on the radio to the Democratic national convention with mixed emotions. A month before, Hitler's armies had marched into Paris, and the remainder of free Europe, including England, seemed in grave danger of succumbing to the Nazis. The United States was embroiled in a vigorous debate over the need for U.S. assistance. President Roosevelt was absolutely convinced of that need, and had already set in motion steps to bring it about in effective quantity and with necessary speed. Hearst papers—minus the *P-I*—joined John's old employer, the *Chicago Tribune*, to warn against "being dragged into war to save England." And in the midst of this controversy Franklin D. Roosevelt accepted an unprecedented nomination for a third term as president of the United States. Anna sent her mother insightful commentaries on the convention and the campaign to come. "Somehow," she said of her father's acceptance speech, "when he first started to talk last night he sounded a bit weary to me; but as he went on his voice regained the same old ring of strength and conviction. His job is so immense that it is really frightening to think of. You have grown to be a part of that job in the eyes of most of the people—which puts such a terrific burden on both of you that all that the rest of us on the sidelines can do is to hope and pray that you stay strong and well."

A few days later my mother wrote her father in a mixed spirit of pride, love, and anxiety:

Dearest Pa,

. . .

I hate to think of the almost inevitable and constant strain which you've agreed to undertake for the coming four years, and of the private activities you were looking forward to which you will have to forego during those years. On the other hand, I never could forsee much private activity for you, even as a private citizen, once the present world crises became evident! Nevertheless, it's such a terrific sacrifice that it does make me hope and pray harder than ever before!

. . .

We all send you loads of love—and an extra lot from,

Anna

In all these six years between their arrival in Seattle and my father's decision to enter the army and seek overseas duty in 1943, the most consistent strain on their marriage, on their well-being individually, and thus indirectly on their children was the seldom avoided experience of leading public lives, of being responsible not only for themselves but for their share of the reputation of the Roosevelt family. My mother's loyalty to her father, her wish to be worthy of his love, and her desire for his recognition, were intense. And she had early gathered from her mother a self-consciousness and nervousness before the press and on public occasions, feelings upon which she imposed a strong obligation: one did one's duty, but one was always to know that the recognition received was not for oneself. In short, one accepted one's reflected prominence, privately complained at the invasiveness of press and public, and was discouraged from enjoying whatever compensatory pleasures such attention might naturally bring. I vividly remember being admonished as a child that the applause was not for me, and Sis and Buzz felt even more strongly, over a longer time, the forceful but puzzling and inhibiting impact of that family rule.

My father, sharing my mother's nervousness and feelings of constraint on public occasions, allowed himself to enjoy the "red-carpet treatment" more openly than she could, and that was one source of conflict between them. She loved him deeply, and supported him with solicitous care when his moodiness overtook him at times of discouragement. But she could also be sharply critical of his compensatory air of self-importance. My brother remembers her in a characteristically humorous but mocking gesture, looking at my father, her chest thrust out, her thumbs hooked under her arms and fingers waggling to represent the self-styled big shot.

To some degree they both could find enjoyment—even an enhancing reflection of their high romance with one another—in the celebrity status they enjoyed on public occasions. Something of that spirit is captured in this memory of my sister, who was just entering adolescence: "Popsy was immensely proud of Ma's beauty—tall, long-waisted, slim. They cut a fine figure as a couple on the dance floor. I remember several times (probably office Christmas parties) seeing them hold forth and *knowing* they were the most naturally graceful and accomplished dancers in the room. They were physically glamorous without even trying and of course it added to their general aura."

Their enjoyment of that glamor made for a vexing paradox: the very public roles that made truly relaxed privacy so rare were for both of them (if for Anna more covertly) important sources of security and gratification. As my sister put it in a recent conversation, "I think if you've played . . . Princess Anna for so many years you can't entirely get away from it." (The phrase is suggestive, for it identifies my father in the subordinate position of prince consort.) Constantly sought after, they frequently left on short business or speaking trips. My mother wrote her mother one July day in 1942, "the last few weeks were hectic enough to make Johnny look up at me most wistfully one evening and ask: 'Is Mummy going to stay in this house for just a *little* while?' I almost wept because we had to leave for Spokane that same evening!"

There were numerous business and political friends, local dignitaries and visiting firemen, many of whom they felt obliged to see, a few whom they admired or enjoyed but with whom there still existed that social crust of their public identities. "Mother's friend, Martha Gellhorn, and her husband Ernest Hemingway, are here," Anna wrote her father while they were on a short Sun Valley vacation, "as well as the Gary Coopers. The latter are really nice—the former are still somewhat of a puzzle to us. Ernest seems to have a pet fondness for a certain type of red wine which has the effect of making him most incoherently talkative—coherence showing itself only in his profuse use of unmentionable four letter words." And again, Anna complains to her mother in August, 1940, that she and John, who hadn't been away alone in months, had just planned a four-day holiday only to find that a couple of important advertisers had decided to come to town the same four days. "I'm hoping we can successfully sit on our consciences! It seems impossible for we two to keep our fingers out of too many pies—they're all interesting, and some seem so vitally important!" The difficulty, so far as the growth of their marriage and family were concerned, was that their consciences predominantly led them further into the realm of that public responsibility which Anna's parents modeled so consummately well.

There may have been others, but my sister and brother and I can remember only one couple—Stanley and Marie Donogh—with whom my parents enjoyed the kind of relaxed, fun, frank, free-flowing friendship without which the most promising marriages and families tend to founder inwardly upon themselves. Stanley was a successful Sears, Roebuck executive, a big-hearted, handsome, gregarious man who loved to work with his hands. He had a great, infectious laugh. John admired Stanley, and probably also envied his self-confidence and rugged, comfortable competence. I remember Marie as one of the gentlest and most lovely women I have ever known, and my mother's dearest friend. They were a gift to my parents, and to us all. When I recently visited the Donoghs, Marie showed me a book—Chapman's classic *Piloting, Seamanship and Small Boat Handling*—my father had presented to their yacht, *Shoreleave,* on which the four of them had enjoyed many cruises and fishing expeditions. The occasion was Father's Day, June 21, 1942, and the inscription read: "With a hope that the wisdom in these pages may see us over many shoals and that the good fellowship in our hearts may give us many smooth sailings in the tough years and rough seas ahead."

For all of the friendship and relaxation the Donoghs offered, and despite the growing closeness between Anna and her mother, there was no one to whom she felt she could freely turn to share the increasing worries she had about John beginning around 1940; and she feared to confront him directly. The language of their notes to one another—on short trips apart, Christmas cards, and letters marking anniversaries and birthdays—remained remarkably consistent during all those Seattle years, and indeed well beyond. They spoke of increasing love and happiness, of each as the object of the other's total devotion, and often signed their letters, "Your 50%er" or "Your Other Half." But scattered among these virtually ritual testimonials, Anna reveals more complex feelings. Like her mother, her characteristic way to express her worry about others was to criticize herself, as on March 25, 1939—my father's thirty-ninth birthday and five days before my birth: "My Sweet and Precious One, things may get tough for us from time to time—but, *please always* trust my complete love and loyalty for you. My 'orneriness' and my bark are tough to put up with—but as long as you know I worship you—maybe you'll continue putting up with them." And two years later, in the summer of 1941: "I'm well aware of my fault in worrying and fretting about the fear that we may lose something and not be able to find it again. And this naturally leads to making life difficult for both of us."

Anna's love for John was complemented—and complicated—by her grandmother's early and influential teaching about a woman's obligations to her husband, and by her great wish that this marriage succeed. On the whole, she saw more clearly than did John the emotional and marital costs of their public lives, but she was reluctant to oppose his judgment and feared his anger and disappointment. My sister once wrote vividly to me of those themes in Anna's life; and it is not difficult to see the shadow of Sara—and Eleanor too—in the background. "She was brought up to believe a woman must . . . be whatever the man she loved and had settled to live with wanted her to be; to not 'take advantage' of 'who she was' when dealing with that man; to cajole by being cute, supplicating or vaguely humorous; to put her best foot and best face forward in all situations [while] at the same time building the situation so that her husband would be the stand-out and the single real achiever. She wanted *above* all to make

There were some good vacation times, in the mountains and on the rich fishing waters of the Pacific Northwest.

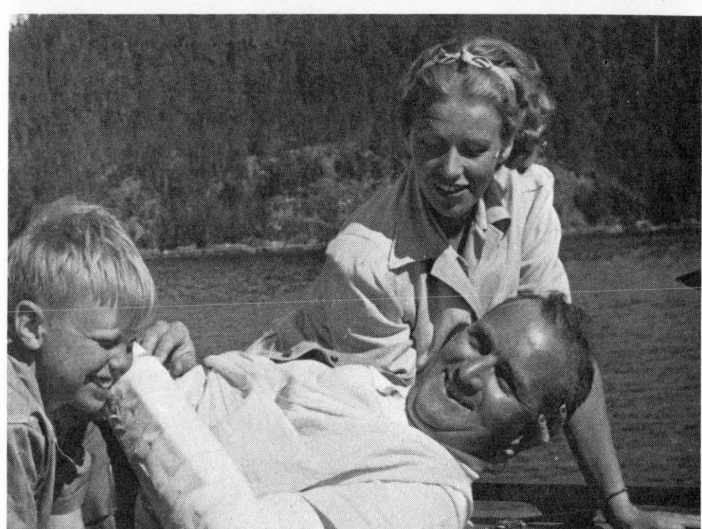

that second marriage work, to have a home for herself, her man and the kids that could survive public and family prominence." My sister reminded me, in that same letter, of a remark my mother made in her last illness, shortly before her death: "Learn to say 'No,' " she told a woman friend. "I didn't begin to learn that until it was too late."

Feeling bound by that ethic of subordination and self-restraint, Anna nonetheless found ways—including some "orneriness" and bark—to assert the very considerable power of her own personality. In this context, one can imagine some resentment growing on both Anna's and John's part. But such feelings—like the "conflicting interests, envenomed jealousies or ill-tempered words" of Sara's day—found little room for open expression or exploration. Anxiously devoted to their vision of a supreme and unqualified love, they must have found it exceedingly difficult to deal constructively with conflicts in their relationship, and may even have found some refuge in the demands of their busy schedules.

No one really knows what complex factors served subtly to turn a tide in my father's life around his fortieth year. Anna began to worry about John's increased restlessness, and the times when he would suddenly lose interest in the daily affairs of his work and withdraw into himself. In her apprehension she consulted the family physician, Dr. O'Shea, who recommended that John talk to a psychiatrist. When she told him of her conversation with O'Shea, he was indignant. In his view psychiatrists were for those who were mentally deranged, and were mostly quacks in any case.

It was in reference to the point of midlife that the psychologist Carl Jung observed a common pattern of experience, and his words seem to have relevance for my father: "We see . . . a significant change in the human psyche is in preparation. At first it is not a conscious and striking change; it is rather a matter of indirect signs. . . . Often it is something like a slow change in a person's character; in another case certain traits may come to light which had disappeared in childhood." Jung added that in his experience there is a distinct rise in the frequency of depression, particularly among men, around the age of forty. My father had reached a kind of professional peak—at least in terms of public recognition—beyond which no rise seemed likely. His father's death may have more starkly revealed his own mortality, and the years 1940 and 1941—when FDR assumed responsibilities of unparalleled stress and unprecedented power in the world—may have brought to mind both the mortality and the unapproachable achievement of that father figure. For Franklin Roosevelt to have died would abruptly alter John's own derivitive power and prominence. For Franklin Roosevelt to live as commander in chief through the greatest military challenge this nation had endured would secure unbridgeably the gulf between Anna's first love and her second.

All this is, of course, speculation. All we know for sure is that there reappeared more visibly in the early 1940s a pattern of depressive experience that my father had known periodically for most of his life; indeed, a pattern kin to the dark moods, the grumpiness, and the temper that earned him the name "Bowser" as a young child. Returning now at a critical time in his marriage and his working life, that endemic distress must have begun to evoke a natural impulse to escape the pain. And that, in turn, bode ill for his and Anna's future together.

NINETEEN

# *Wartime Separation*

SINCE World War II had begun with Hitler's lightning attack on Poland in the autumn of 1939, Anna's and John's attention was drawn to the conflict in Europe and Asia with growing apprehension. The awareness gradually came to them, as to other millions of Americans, that their lives would be deeply affected. The Japanese attack on the American Pacific Fleet at Pearl Harbor on December 7, 1941—the day, Anna's father said, "that shall live in infamy"—unified a still divided nation. "Never before," FDR declared in his war message to Congress, "has there been a greater challenge to life, liberty and civilization."

My father was then in his early forties, too old to be drafted, a man of influence and established position. His contribution to the mobilization and support of the war effort at home was in the view of most to whom he spoke more important than anything he might accomplish in the service. And for a time he was convinced of that himself. But there was a complex combination of circumstances converging on a change of view, which Anna recognized with apprehension, resistance, even bitterness—and finally resignation. Long after his departure overseas she confided: "Here's a secret: For many months I lost faith in that strong feeling I've had since I first knew you, that there was some big power watching over US and guiding US." She spoke of her "hatred of war and belief in its futility," and of "the months of brooding as to how it would affect US (ever since England declared war in September 1939)," and she came to "the point where I saw that you would *have* to go, but to where I refused to believe that any fate watching over US could possibly have anything to do with it."

It was John who had a lifelong romantic inclination to view himself as essentially powerless, subject to "fates" which determined his life for good or ill regardless of his wishes or struggles. Anna sometimes (as in this instance) accepted his rhetoric out of a wish to share his world. But she also knew that a profound source of their trouble lay closer to home. And for all her dismay, she believed it must somehow be susceptible to their will. She deeply doubted that separation would bring anything but further distraction and deterioration to their marriage.

For the practical task of resolving the strains and conflicts of their relationship, however, neither was particularly well suited. Both had some inclination to romantic hopefulness, and to a naïve faith in the autonomous power of their love: that which they awkwardly but devotedly called "US." Both were apprehensive of the other's ire or withdrawal, and thus inclined to avoid whatever might lead to serious conflict. Their years of living responsibly in the public eye and in the anticipation of public judgment compounded the reticence with which both had been trained to regard the stresses of personal relationships. Thoroughgoing friendship, in which mutual trust and care might have offered companionship and support in such matters, did not come easily to either. In the prevailing cultural climate, psychotherapy seemed terribly invasive of privacy and (particularly for John) frighteningly associated with mental illness. While both might have found some help in their own families—Anna most likely from her mother, John perhaps with his brother Bill—pride and geographical distance made that unlikely. Under the circumstances, the temptations to rely on their love to see them through, to look to their work and their public activities to confirm the value of their lives, and to suppress the seriousness of their plight, were very strong.

A decision as consequential as the one my father undertook in the early months of 1943 had to be a tangled and conflicted one, and much of that—not all, but much—was conveyed for my safekeeping in his remarkable letter to his four-year-old son on June 3, 1943. He was writing from North Africa, at a time when American forces there were frustratedly marking time while preparations continued for the invasion of Sicily the following month.

My dear Son,

I have been over here . . . only three weeks, but it has been a period marked by a growing appreciation on my part of the largeness of the task ahead of our armies, and also a clearer picture of the part any of us may be called upon to play.

In the weeks since I left you and Mummy sitting in the window at the White House—the hardest thing I have ever been called on to do!—I have had much time for thought.

Now I want to have a talk with you, my Son, to say a few things that are in my thoughts and my heart. . . .

I cannot explain to you why I am here. I had a job to do as a civilian which I conceded to be important in the war effort, *more* important, possibly, than the job in uniform. I still cannot explain why I left it, but when I try to find any logic to justify my leaving Mummy, adoring her as I do, wanting (as I have over *every second* of our lives together) to be near enough to touch her, to hear her beloved voice, I am completely at a loss.

War does funny things to people. Of course I wanted to be part of this great struggle involving the peoples of the whole world. I am sincerely hopeful that I can do a good job, and maybe even a more important task than the one I left at home. You may be sure that I will give my best to it, and when I get home to you and Mummy and to Sis and Buzz, I will know that I made my best effort, and you can put that down for your pappy!

It would be easy to say that separate lives are not important when the whole world is aflame, but Johnny, I know now that our lives *are* important, and I want as soon as possible to get them going once more, together. The same is true of all people who are fighting in this war, and if some of us, who have been close enough to the people in power to have a better picture of the *consequences* of the victories and decisions of these days, can take part, even humble part, in *working out* the victories and decisions, maybe you, for example, won't have to tear your life apart, and that of the woman *you* may come to adore as I do your Mummy, to go off on such a bitter errand.

Well, Johnny, I'll be seeing you, but in any case, carry on!

My prideful and devoted love to you always, my Son.

Pops

In its anticipation of death, its gathering of the lessons and gifts of his life, and, less clearly, its theme of fateful pain and loss endured, this letter anticipates another: that written seven years later, on the eve of his suicide, to his wife Virginia. Fortunately, both letters were preserved for years, until I was old enough to begin to read them with understanding and forgiveness.

Perhaps under the strain of an impending decision to enter the service, my father's moods of distress and discouragement increased in frequency and severity during the winter of 1942–1943. Both he and my mother, in their wartime correspondence, refer to his troubling "spells"; "there were quite a few of them," she said, "over quite a period." They agreed, in retrospect, in attributing his "spells" to his struggle over the decision to leave, but Anna, at least, was afraid of something more. "I feared," she wrote him in renewed confidence of their love the following October, "you were getting tired of something or other about me or in me. . . . When you had gone away, I still couldn't get away from the feeling that something of You had been lacking in the make-up of US during most of those last months. . . . I just felt impotent and unable to cope with whatever was wrong. So, I guess, I automatically decided that I was somehow to blame." In their accustomed modes of explanation, neither was willing to consider the likelihood that John's "spells" were expressive of a more serious, endemic melancholy.

If an old, underlying depressiveness, and a distress and doubt of his adequacy as a man were emerging again in my father's early forties, the issue of joining the service provided both relief and exacerbation. His and my mother's love, as well as his public prominence and success in Seattle, had been powerful protection against the resurgence of those old convictions of inadequacy and inferiority; yet the strength of those defenses were showing signs of dangerous weakening in the last two or three years. And there must have come to mind, as well, one old wound in particular. He had sought to fight for his country in Europe as a seventeen-year-old boy, and had found disappointment and even humiliation as a stretcher bearer in Illinois and a pharmacist's mate (third class) in Virginia.

Last, and most precipitous of his final decision to go, there loomed the figure of the president of the United States and my father's position as Roosevelt son-in-law and brother-in-law to the four Roosevelt sons: a position of notable insecurity for him. He was neither son nor not son; in the Roosevelt family but not of them. My grandmother wrote of him in *This I Remember:* "He had served in the First World War and was over-age for the draft, but he had a feeling that because all our sons were in the service he must go in, too, or my husband might feel that he was not doing his share. I was never quite sure that his reasoning was right, though I understood his feeling; nevertheless, it seemed to me that this was a war for which young men were far better suited than older men and that perhaps those who had established themselves in an occupation had a greater obligation to stay and do their job well at home. But I knew only too well how men could feel and I respected John Boettiger's decision."

The critical moment came in late January of 1943. On the evening of FDR's return from the Casablanca Conference with Prime Minister Winston Churchill and the Allied chiefs of staff, he and John and Anna were talking alone at the White House. The president's mood was ebullient, and he described the course of the war and the atmosphere of the Casablanca meetings with a vividness that kindled great excitement in his two listeners. "Do you remember," John asked Anna in a letter months later, "my saying I'd give my eyeteeth to go along on such a trip and why couldn't I? And then, my sweet, do you remember (can you ever *forget?*) his saying to me: '*Well, you are not in uniform!*' "

My father did his best to hide it, but he felt crushed by the president's comment. It came at a time when his sense of self-esteem had become more openly vulnerable and, of course, from the single man whose adverse judgment he would find most devastating. There is little doubt that he took it as a deeper and more personal criticism than FDR intended. He felt as if he had been told by his and the nation's commander in chief that he was not doing a man's work. John later wrote Anna, "I won't say that one remark of his did it, but it went farther than any or *all* influences that did make my mind up."

A day or two later he wrote to General Dwight D. Eisenhower, whom John had met and come to know during his reporting days on the *Chicago Tribune.* The two had evidently formed a mutual respect, and it is clear that my father hoped—though he did not mention it in the letter—that he might be able to serve in some capacity on General Eisenhower's own staff, then headquartered in North Africa. My parents returned to Seattle, and anxious weeks passed with no word from Eisenhower. Finally, at the end of March, John flew to Washington to see what could be done. When he arrived in the president's study in the middle of a small dinner being given for British Foreign Secretary Anthony Eden, FDR greeted him warmly, inquired after Anna and the kids, and then asked, "Have you taken your physical?" He replied in some confusion that he hadn't but hoped to. "Then," John wrote Anna, her father "told the others that Gen. Eisenhower had asked for me and I was going to the army and to N. Africa."

My father soon found out that Eisenhower had in fact received his January letter, and had cabled the War Department in Washington that he had known John Boettiger for fifteen years, had high regard for his abilities, could use him in any of several capacities, and asked that he be commissioned and sent over to be attached, not at Eisenhower's own headquarters but somewhere in that theater of the war. One reason for the last suggestion, evidently, was Eisenhower's only caution: that some political objections might arise out of the fact of John's relation to the president; but, he said, "I don't think a man offering his services should be penalized for such a reason." FDR, to my father's intense pleasure, was warmly supportive. "I can't tell you," he wrote his wife joyfully, "how perfectly wonderful your Father has been! He has just about overwhelmed me with kindness and help! . . . Never has he gone so far in *wanting* to do things for me!" It was quickly arranged that John would be commissioned as a captain, sent for several weeks of intensive training to the army's School for Military Government in Charlottesville, Virginia, and then assigned somewhere in Eisenhower's command in North Africa. He returned home to Seattle on April 1 enormously excited.

It was an excitement my mother understood but found impossible to share. The prospect of a long separation could only strengthen her already existing fears about my father and their relationship. And she was resentful, too, of being left behind, proscribed from a direct role in the world struggle, and subject to the never-questioned assumption that the woman stays to mind the house and children. She hid these feelings at the time, but later, when John had come to wonder himself whether his choice had been mistaken,

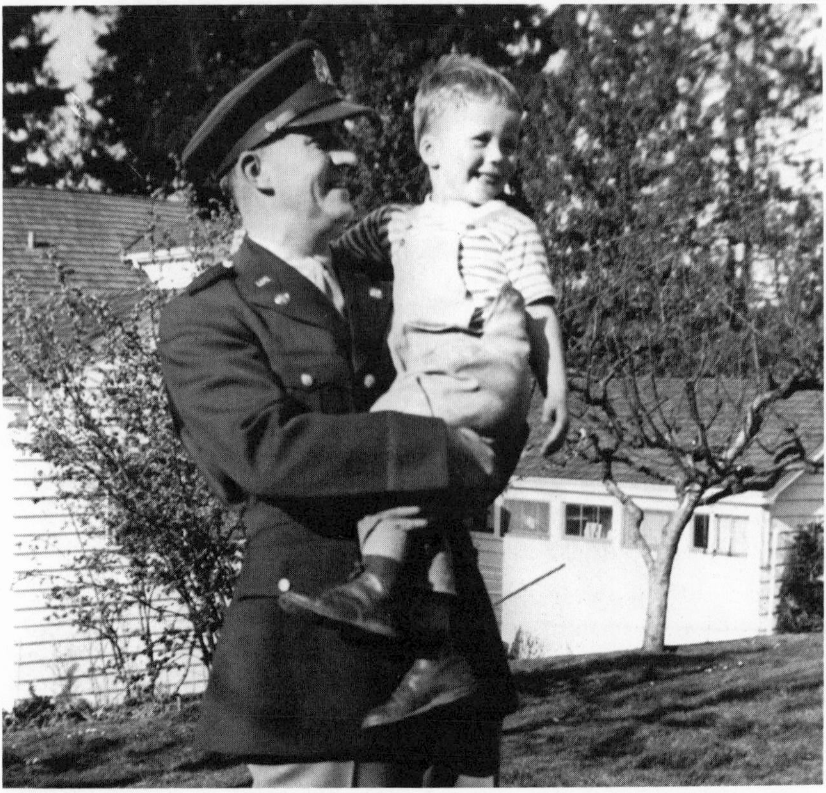

John enters the army and leaves for North Africa in the spring of 1943.

she wrote him passionately: "My main trouble was that from the moment you wrote that letter to your friend [Eisenhower] in North Africa, I began to suffer acutely. I seemed to know all too accurately what it was going to be like when you left. . . . There was nothing I could do to get 'the ants out of your pants'—without running the possibility of hurting US permanently. . . . Uppermost in my mind was a dread that if I tried to adamantly dissuade you from going into the army, you might some time regret it so much that you would feel down deep inside of you that I had been wrong. . . . Maybe I was wrong not to have told you all I was thinking and dreading—but I just couldn't."

My mother and I came east that April to be near my father while he undertook his training in Charlottesville. He left Washington for North Africa on May 12, 1943. Anna wrote her first letter to him from the White House three days later. It was full of determinedly cheerful news of family and visitors, and ended: "It's like making a completely new life for myself, with you in the background of all I do, yet so terribly intangible and indefinite. You are so constantly in my thoughts. Yet, at night, I have to resolutely force myself to think of trivialities or I can't get to sleep."

My father wrote in comparable spirit and with equal devotion from every stop along his air route: Presque Isle, Labrador, Iceland, Scotland (where he told Anna in great detail of a delightful day he spent exploring the birthplace of a favorite poet, Robert Burns), and the Moroccan capital of Marrakech. His destination—appropriately enough, given the origins of his venture—was Casablanca, the city from which FDR had just returned on that well-remembered January evening four months before.

John did not know what plans had been made for him, but he had a general set of expectations shaped by Eisenhower's message and by the training experiences in Charlottesville. General George C. Marshall, the army's chief of staff, had suggested to the president in March that John's experience particularly suited him for action as a civil affairs officer. The army school in Charlottesville had been established to train officers in the task, as Eisenhower put it, "of providing for a conquered population." They were to accompany the assault forces and "take over from combat troops the essential task of controlling the civil population."

It was the idea of accompanying the assault forces and staying close to the theater of operations that saved this role, for my father, from seeming in prospect a more responsible but equally inglorious equivalent of his service in World War I. He had good reason to believe that the Allied invasion and occupation of North Africa would be completed before his arrival, as indeed it was. The last German and Italian troops in Tunisia surrendered three days before his transport plane set down in Casablanca. So his hopes and expectations were that he would be assigned to the civil affairs division of the staff under Eisenhower's command planning "the next big push," and that he would accompany that invading force.

Those hopes and expectations were sorely disappointed. Eisenhower had evidently no specific ideas for including him in the planning of the invasion of Sicily scheduled for early July; and in the absence of such orders no one seemed ready to decide what to do with a new captain who happened also to be the president's son-in-law. As a result, he was left in a distressing limbo without meaningful work, instructed to spend "a few weeks getting the whole picture of civil affairs" in the Casablanca area, feeling, as he put it, "like a fifth wheel." And he was receiving no mail from home because of the vagaries of the wartime postal system.

Finally, on May 29, two and a half weeks after his arrival in Casablanca, Anna's first letter came, carried by a mutual army friend. It produced, he noted in his diary, "quite an emotional upheaval," and his reply is eloquent testimony to his state of mind: "Dearest One: At long last I have a letter from you and I could weep with joy to know that you are (or were on May 15) okay. . . . Two fears constantly gnaw at me. One is that you will fall ill. . . . I wish I could explain how it troubles me! The other fear is that something may happen to US. . . . I worry that you may feel *I* hurt US by going off on this business and the worst of it is that I began at the very start to berate myself for risking the one thing in all my life which counted—a blessed thing which has been the one wonderful part of my past, and is my *whole future*. . . ."

Anna's replies to this and his earlier letters might well have been a great source of comfort, but he received no more of her almost daily correspondence for another six weeks. She and I had arrived back in Seattle in late May. Her spirits wildly varied in those first days. With all three children, in their familiar home and at work on the *P-I*, there was something of an air of exhilaration at being free of the darkness of those months of worry and fear as John prepared to leave and she lived in his shadow. "Beloved one," she wrote on May 28, "your editoress has just finished her first week of working completely on her own—and I can honestly say that I have loved it!" But away from the office, and particularly at night, the anguish of loneliness was so great that for five days she could not even bring herself to write a line to John. "I was so horribly low in spirits that it actually hurt when I would start a letter to you. I started about 4, tore each one into shreds after a couple of paragraphs, because I was obsessed with the idea that I mustn't let you know just how low I was feeling and that I couldn't write without giving myself away. I was scared to death of sounding like a cry-baby!"

As she began to receive his letters from Casablanca in early June, his voice and his own loneliness helped to free hers. She hoped his period of waiting for a real assignment was at an end, knowing so well that a sense of usefulness, or even the mere fact of being really busy, made living much easier for him. And she had, of course, a wholly empathetic response to the difficulties of what they had come to call "the psob angle": a phrase by which the manifold problems of being the president's son-in-law were translated into irreverent shorthand.

At the end of May John thought his luck might be changing: he was contacted by General Eisenhower's aide, Commander Harry C. Butcher, and was transferred to Allied Military Government headquarters in Algiers. It appears, from the security-conscious and, therefore, cryptic language of his diary and letters, that he was to be attached as a civil affairs officer to a British outfit participating in the coming invasion of Sicily. (That operation was a combined Allied enterprise under the overall ground command of the British general Sir Harold Alexander.) But as the early weeks of June wore on, there was still no specific task at hand. On the eighth he wrote Anna with hopes weakened but still intact: "things may break in such a way as to make my effort and contribution really vital. . . . I do want you and the kids to have some pride in your soldier husband-father!" Finally, on June 23 he was moved to the Libyan seaport of Tripoli, where the British unit to which he had been assigned would depart for the island of Malta and thence to the invasion of Sicily. Two weeks later he and his unit followed the airborne and amphibious assault troops that began the attack on Sicily. His nearly two months of waiting for action were over.

Between his arrival and the completion of the occupation of Sicily on August 17, John and his fellow civil affairs officers were fully occupied with the manifold tasks of restoring and maintaining—as much as possible under circumstances of continuing battle—civil order, adequate food and supplies, and assistance for the wounded and displaced populations of the devastated Sicilian cities and countryside.

While sitting it out in North Africa my father had been making up and sending me, partly no doubt in compensation for his own inactivity, a series of hair-raising tales about the adventures of a young four-year-old Arab boy named Mohammed. I loved them, made my mother read them over and over to me, although at first, she reported to John, I was jealous "and wanted to know if you would bring Mohammed home with you or give him back to his parents before you came." In mid-August, from Sicily, my father sent me a true story of another little boy "just a little bit older than you."

"I was in a town . . . which was bombed in the middle of the day. Some poor people were killed and some hurt very badly, and some were buried in wreckage. After we took care of all the people we found, someone told us there was somebody left in a bombed house. We went over there, and heard a weak voice crying out for help. All we could see was a mass of tangled timbers and great heavy concrete slabs and dirt and stones and glass. . . . But we began pulling the stuff away, being careful so we didn't let things down on top of the person. He kept calling for help, and finally we uncovered enough to talk to him, and it turned out to be a very little boy about seven years old. We dug some more and he stuck out a hand to show where he was. Then we got more wreckage away and we could see his face, full of grime (and a few, but only a few, tears).

"He was very brave, wasn't he? We got a hole big enough for him to crawl out . . . but he tried and said he was unable to move his legs. So we pulled more stuff away, and then we saw that a great big concrete slab was wedged in such a way that it held him down. . . . You'd have thought he would have passed out by this time, wouldn't you, but he held out very bravely. We managed to get some water to him to drink and he felt better. At last we got him free, and lifted him out, and the crowd cheered. . . . We sent him to the hospital, and I don't even know his name, but I do know he wasn't hurt at all, really, and that today he's playing around just about as gaily as you are."

Still in Sicily on August 10, his commanding officer told John that he had been recommended for promotion to major (it was officially approved in early November). And shortly after, with great excitement, he learned that he was to participate in the planning for the coming invasion of Italy, and join the operation itself. His conduct in Italy over the next four months earned him the Legion of Merit. In the words of the citation, "he voluntarily went ashore with the first Allied troops on the initial landing on the Italian mainland, and displayed coolness and executive ability in looking after Allied Military Government personnel and supplies under enemy fire." In the months that followed "he demonstrated rare good judgement, loyalty and initiative, frequently being required to make immediate decisions of importance, when the situation did not permit his consulting his superiors."

Naples had been taken from the Germans by October 1, and in the weeks thereafter my father's military government unit had its hands especially full. In a city of a million inhabitants their problems were legion: electricity had to be restored; food and water shortages, and related problems of sanitation and threats of disease, to be remedied; and civil order and municipal authority stabilized through complex dealings with an Italian government in which many fascists still occupied positions of significance.

There were some welcome comforts and lighter moments for

John after his field experience in Sicily and Salerno. He soon moved, with other officers, into the Villa Emma, "the place having been originally built by Lord Hamilton, the British Ambassador, for his wife, later and for years the mistress of Lord Nelson and a famous beauty." He adds, in a diary entry on October 13, "The house has been rebuilt into quite a luxurious villa, right on the sea, and these last three moonlit nights have been truly gorgeous. The volcano [Vesuvius] sets up quite a show of flame at night." A few days before there had been a hotly debated public health issue in the city concerning the need to construct outdoor latrines. Although it was deemed unnecessary as a city-wide measure, John noted that in the villa to which he had been first assigned, "we did build our own latrine. . . . You could sit on the seat, in the open, and gaze upon the Bay of Naples and Vesuvius—without doubt the finest view from any craphouse in the world!"

For all the real satisfactions of his work in Sicily and Italy, my father was now increasingly troubled by word finally received from Anna at home—a packet of letters had arrived in Sicily on July 24, and others came regularly thereafter. Her initial enthusiasm at working on her own at the *P-I* had been superseded by a growing awareness that her position there was in fact untenable. Her authority as associate editor was far more limited than had been John's, and she was faced with a Hearst-appointed acting publisher jealous of her continuing prominence on the paper, far more in sympathy with Hearst's own conservative editorial policies, and almost certainly ambitious to replace John permanently in the publisher's chair. She found herself staying for what little she could do to influence editorial policy, out of loyalty to her and John's few real friends on the paper and in Seattle, and because her family was settled there. She was alternately bitter, resigned, and philosophical; but gradually more firmly convinced, as she put it in a letter to John on August 14, that "under present circumstances there is definitely no chance of my doing anything constructive on the P-I, and these are quite tremendous times to even passively stay a part of a destructive outfit." So she had begun "cautiously . . . to put out 'feelers' for something new."

She continued to miss him terribly and to fear the unknown impact of a long separation, the differences in the lives they were leading, and the changes in one or both of them that might emerge. She wrote him in mid-September of her efforts to avoid "automatically looking for you and imagining how wonderful it would be if I did see you—in the funniest darn places you can imagine! For instance, I'd stand in the shower and vividly imagine that at any moment the curtain would stealthily be drawn back, my fanny pinched, and your grinning and precious puss would show itself! You'd think such imaginings would make me laugh. But, quite to the contrary they would make me weep and ache for you! . . . Now, while I think of you in everything I do and compare my enjoyment of the moment with how wonderful it would be if you were there to share it with me, I have acquired what I call my 'alone poise.' It was something I just had to acquire. I don't enjoy it, but it was necessary."

She chafed increasingly—as she had news of her father, of her husband and four brothers in the service, of her mother traveling for weeks in Red Cross uniform, visiting servicemen and women in the South Pacific. "The blues make me lose faith in myself and bring my inferiority complex out in full force, make me so jealous and bitter about being the only member of the family who can only say when this war is over: 'I was the good little woman who stayed home and looked after her three children, and earned a good salary working for Willie Hearst.' "

So, out of all this, a determination gradually grew strong and firm in the autumn of 1943 to find a meaningful task somewhere near John—near enough to be with him at least occasionally—or, failing that, to get work of genuine significance completely on her own that would offer her a sense of accomplishment. "Otherwise," she put it in language of unusual toughness, "I'm going to always harbor a feeling of resentment; a feeling that you and I are not on an equal basis of experience; that somehow life has cheated me."

Even in the self-centered excitement of his preparation for joining the service, John had some worry that he was not leaving Anna in an easy position in Seattle. In the midst of his own disappointment and distress in North Africa, and having as yet none of her news, he pleaded with her not to "stay out there if it isn't *completely* to your liking, in comparison with what you might have [nearer her own family] in Washington or New York." And at the same time an idea occurred to him about which he felt some natural ambivalence, but whose fruitfulness he clearly perceived: "if the going gets tough or distasteful for you in Seattle, there is a job you could do for the OM.* At the same time the atmosphere is anything but restful and I fear you would be so terribly in demand that you'd never get any rest."

When he began to receive Anna's letters in Sicily—twenty-one letters and two cables arrived at once on August 11—he was deeply moved. "I wept over them," he wrote in his diary, "because they showed me so clearly what a bastard I have been to come off on this chase and what a rotten mare's nest I have left for her." Ideas that had for some time been vaguely forming in his mind began to take on new clarity and urgency, and he shared them with Anna and with Eleanor. He wanted to find, he wrote to Eleanor, without either embarrassing or involving the president, "a situation where Anna and I could work together. . . . Neither of us is giving to the war effort, separately, what we could give jointly." And he had a specific idea that he thought might be both feasible and honorable: for Anna to come to Washington—she was in any event planning to bring the children in early December for a five or six week visit—and for him to seek reassignment on the civil affairs staff of General John H. Hilldring at the Pentagon.

He made the request, and after several months of anxious waiting and continued work in Italy, the orders they both hoped for came through in January, 1944. On the seventeenth of that month John left Naples, and at 9:00 A.M. on Monday, January 24, eight and a half months after their leave-taking, my parents were reunited in New York. Sis, Buzz, and I met them late that afternoon at Union Station in Washington. I wish I could remember the occasion, for it must have been a splendid reunion.

In this account of my parents' lives during their separation in 1943, there remains one brief story, that of a dramatic eighteen-day interlude in the midst of my father's service with the Fifth Army in

*Old Man, that is, FDR.

Italy. On November 21, still in Naples and long before he knew his requests for transfer could possibly bear fruit, he was suddenly ordered to Tunis to report to his brother-in-law, Colonel Elliott Roosevelt. (At the time Elliott was commanding an air reconnaissance squadron out of North Africa.) My father soon learned what was afoot: FDR had asked that he and Elliott be temporarily assigned to accompany him to the Cairo and Teheran conferences of heads of state. As he flew from Tunis, on to Algiers, and then with Elliott and General Eisenhower to Cairo on the night of November 24, his thoughts again returned vividly to that evening at the White House the previous January: his wish to be included on the kind of adventure FDR had so colorfully depicted, the president's wounding remark, and all the events and discoveries that had followed.

He wrote Anna after his first full day in Cairo, a Thanksgiving Day concluded by a traditional American holiday dinner for the British prime minister and his staff, with enormous turkeys and "all the trimmings, up to pumpkin pie." It was a warm occasion. Churchill recalled, "For a couple of hours we cast care aside. I had never seen the President more gay." John joined with pleasure in these events, but his mind was also on Anna, and on the painful lessons, as he now viewed them, of those last few months. "Finally, my Beloved, I am on such a trip, vastly more significant and important than the Casablanca trip, and I am brutally truthful when I say to you: it is not worth the candle! . . . Do you realize that I have never spent much time around him [FDR], *since our marriage*, without you being there, too. And now I know, Honey, that you are the indispensable quantity, the perfect ingredient, to make even this sort of adventure really click! It's true, so tragically true." It was a powerful moment of unifying insight in which his enduring wishes and needs—high adventure, public recognition, movement in the orbit of a great man, and a superordinate love—gathered themselves into as true a hierarchy as he ever brought himself to know. And at the end, that arresting and profoundly appropriate phrase—"so tragically true": a recognition only half formed, for of the character and devastation of the tragedy to come he must have had only the vaguest apprehension, if any at all.

And if he was anxious and lonely, my father was also enormously excited to be where he was. For the next two weeks he was a keen observer of a series of historic wartime meetings: between FDR, Churchill, and Generalissimo Chiang Kai-shek in Cairo, then in Teheran when the British and Americans were joined by Marshal Stalin, and finally back in Cairo for further British-American meetings and a visit from President Ismet Inonu of Turkey (whom my father had been deputized by the president to fetch from his homeland in an American transport plane). John was helpful in managing press relations, and took great pride—"I practically jumped out of my skin!"—in having written the first draft of what emerged in language still largely his own as the Teheran Declaration, summarizing publicly American, British, and Soviet determination to "work together in war and in the peace that will follow." He was greatly moved as he flew on two occasions over the Holy Lands. "Naturally I thought of Christ. . . . The city of the Carpenter was plainly visible. . . . There are ancient trails through these mountains winding through the hills; possibly some of them were trod by Jesus!"

He left FDR at Sicily, where the president had stopped on his way home to confer decorations on General Mark Clark and other Fifth Army officers. "I said goodbye . . . on the plane, asking him to be sure to give ARB my love and tell her I hoped to see her *soon.*"

TWENTY

# "You Meant More to Your Father Than Anyone"

WHEN my mother arrived in Washington with her three children on December 5, 1943, she had no clear expectation that she would stay longer than the few weeks whose high point was to be a family Christmas at Hyde Park. "The way things happened, however, it was April 20, 1945 before I moved out of the White House." She was determined to find work of more relevance to the war effort, and to be rid of the painful waste she experienced increasingly at the *P-I*. She loved being near her father again; and when John's assignment to the Pentagon was confirmed in early January, 1944, it was clear that she would stay. The story of her work is best told in her own words, for they vividly convey her devotion.

"In December, 1943, Father returned to Washington from the Cairo-Teheran Conferences. With no preliminary talks or discussions, I found myself trying to take over little chores that I felt would relieve Father of some of the pressure under which he was constantly working.

"After a couple of weeks I asked Father if he'd mind if I resigned my job on the newspaper and stayed on to help him. In my work for him I never had an official job or title or salary. Father and I never had any discussions as to what my job or jobs should be. Actually they grew like Topsy, because I was there all the time and it was easy for Father to tell someone to 'ask Anna to do that,' or to look over at me and say, 'Sis,* you handle that.' So 'Topsy' quickly grew into a full-time job.

* Sis was his private name for her, and the origin of my own sister's nickname.

*On the facing page:* The president, with his wife and daughter, greeting the residents of the village of Hyde Park on election night, 1944.
*Wide World*

FDR greets General Charles de Gaulle at the White House, July 6, 1944. Anna stands behind her father. *Franklin D. Roosevelt Library*

"It soon became apparent to me that I couldn't write fast enough to take accurate notes on some of the things Father would ask me to do. Complete accuracy was of the greatest importance. So I taught myself shorthand at night, when the day's work was done.

"It was immaterial to me whether my job was helping to plan the 1944 campaign, pouring tea for General de Gaulle or filling Father's empty cigarette case. All that mattered was relieving a greatly overburdened man of a few details of work and trying to make his life as pleasant as possible when a few moments opened up for relaxation."

Anna was conscious that she helped fill for her father an important emotional need, yet she also knew, and did not wish to exacerbate, her mother's distress at Franklin's easier companionship with less serious and demanding women. "I pray," she confided to John in April, 1944, "I don't get caught in a crossfire between those two! Human nature is so damn ticklish to deal with!"

As one sensitive observer said at the time, "A woman of great and incessant conscience, Mrs. Roosevelt couldn't see Franklin without urging something upon him. . . . Eleanor Roosevelt has many virtues but she is not a restful person." My mother put her own position succinctly: "He knew that there was no axe to grind." However careful Anna was to respect Eleanor's sensitivity, my mother had become a kind of special protector to her father—as her own description so clearly portrays—and her patience was sorely taxed on some occasions. Although her mother knew "the doctors had said he should have half an hour of relaxation, no business, just sitting around, maybe a drink, she would come in more and more frequently with an enormous bundle of letters which she wanted to discuss with him immediately and have a decision." At one such time, "Father blew his top. He took the bundle of letters and pushed it over to me. 'Sis, you handle this.' And here I was striving to be neutral. What she wanted was o.k. but for him it was one more thing at the end of a tough day."

Lash is no doubt right in saying that Anna's relationship with her father at this time "was shaped by the president—his needs, his weariness, his desire to be shielded from the one person [Eleanor] who knew him beyond all masquerade and stratagem." But it is no less true that my mother—for the first and only time in her life—was acting out her most vivid childhood dream: to be her father's companion and helpmate, even his lifeline.

As for Eleanor, if there was sometimes more pointed stress again in her relationship with her daughter—another recurrence of an early theme—my grandmother was, on the whole, acquiescent. Lash writes: "More and more frequently Eleanor was heard to say, 'Anna is the only one who would know about that'; 'I'll have to ask Anna'; 'We'll have to get Anna to ask the President.'" Whatever anger or resentment there may have been, it was mostly hidden beneath Eleanor's extraordinary self-control, her love for her daughter, and her recognition that Anna was in fact fulfilling a need which she would and could not. "Anna's presence," my grandmother wrote in her memoirs, "was the greatest possible help to my husband. . . . She saw and talked to people whom Franklin was too busy to see and then gave him a digest of the conversations. She also took over the supervision of his food. . . . In fact, she helped Franklin in innumerable ways. Everything she did was done capably, and she brought to all her contacts a gaiety and buoyance that made everybody feel just a little happier because she was around."

One of those who visited the White House during this period—in Eleanor's absence—was Lucy Mercer Rutherfurd, whom my mother had not seen since she was ten or eleven. But her memory—the memory of being told as an adolescent of her father's affair and of the feelings then evoked—was vivid. When the fact of her father's relationship with Lucy became publicly known in the mid-1960s, Anna was angry at the play it received in the press. She believed the stories of clandestine and illicit romance were exaggerated, and served to misguide public awareness of the significance and accomplishments of her father as president. And she believed them to be disrespectful to him and to a woman whom she had come to admire and with whom it was natural for her in some measure to identify.

My mother was strongly tempted to compose an article placing the subject in more balanced perspective, but she distrusted her ability to write, wished not to feed further anyone's hunger for more attention to the relationship, and perhaps found that she could not write such a piece without revealing more of her own feelings than she wished. She did begin a draft, and it is worthy of quotation not for any further light shed on Franklin's and Lucy's relationship, but for its confirmation of the essential spirit in which my mother experienced her father.

"I remember [as a child] feeling happy and admiring when I was greeted one morning at home by Miss Lucy Mercer. I knew that she sat at a desk and wrote on cards; and I knew that I liked her warm and friendly manner and smile. . . . Some 28 years later I was to see Mrs. Winthrop Rutherfurd* as one of several guests of my father's at the White House—once or twice for dinner and a couple of times for tea when she was accompanied by her daughter and one or two of her step-children. Never was there anything clandestine about these occasions. On the contrary they were occasions which I welcomed for my father because they were light-hearted and gay, affording a few hours of much needed relaxation for a loved father and world leader in a time of crises. This period was from early 1944 to early 1945 when I accompanied Father to the Yalta Conference.

"Never was I aware of anything self-conscious in Father's attitude, with me, about Mrs. Rutherfurd. In fact, I remember sitting alone with Father on the deck of the cruiser, which took us as far as Malta on the way to Yalta, as we steamed past Virginia shores in the distance and having him discourse on the bird life of these shores, interpose suddenly and casually that 'over there is where Lucy grew up.' As for me, I still found Mrs. Rutherfurd to be a most attractive, stately but warm and friendly person. She certainly had an innate dignity and poise which commanded respect."

It may be natural to wonder whether Anna's renewed closeness to her father at this time, and her central place in the working White House, elicited any jealousy on John's part. If so, there is no indication of it in his diaries or in their exchanges of letters during several brief separations in 1944 and 1945. While there are occasional indications of boredom with administrative routine, John seemed to

* Lucy had married Winthrop Rutherfurd in February, 1920. Her husband died in 1944.

find satisfaction in his work on General Hilldring's staff at the War Department. He made one more trip overseas—a month-long inspection of military government headquarters in England, France, and Italy in late 1944—and was promoted to lieutenant colonel on the day of his return. On the third of June, 1945—just a few days before we left Washington for our home in Seattle—my mother and I watched General Hilldring present a second Legion of Merit to my father: for outstanding service in "formulating and implementing basic policies of civil affairs and military government in Europe."

Neither are there indications, in the diaries or letters, of a recurrence of John's "spells" of the winter of 1942–1943, nor of the general depressiveness and periods of temper that had begun to make themselves felt in their relationship earlier in Seattle. The year between early 1944 and early 1945 seemed, in fact, to be a period of renewed stability and satisfaction for them both. It was the end of the first decade of their marriage, and their expressions of confidence in that marriage and joy in being reunited suggest the image of a second honeymoon. Their birthday and anniversary notes, and the language of their letters generally—when one or the other was on a short trip—is strikingly like the language of their earliest years. Anna wrote on March 25, 1944:

> My Forever Beloved John:
>
> This is a very specially precious birthday of yours because, since your last one, *US* has gone through so much "fire" and come out stronger and more securely *One* than ever before.
>
> There'll undoubtedly be more "fire" to go thru before the end of this war (and may our special Fates make it as little as possible!) but our combined confidence in US will see us thru anything and everything!
>
> . . .
>
> . . . Your other 1/2

Without doubt the climactic event in my mother's wartime relationship with her father, and one of the most memorable experiences of her lifetime, was her journey with him to the Yalta Conference in early 1945. She had wished deeply, as had John, to

*ı the facing page, top to bottom:* Anna and her father on the U.S.S. *Quincy* route to the Yalta Conference, February 2, 1945.

)R receives King Farouk of Egypt aboard the U.S.S. *Quincy,* at Great Bitter ıke, Egypt, February 13, 1945. Anna stands at her father's left.

*anklin D. Roosevelt Library photos*

eanor and Anna at FDR's funeral in the rose garden of the Hyde Park estate, April 15, 45. *UPI-Acme*

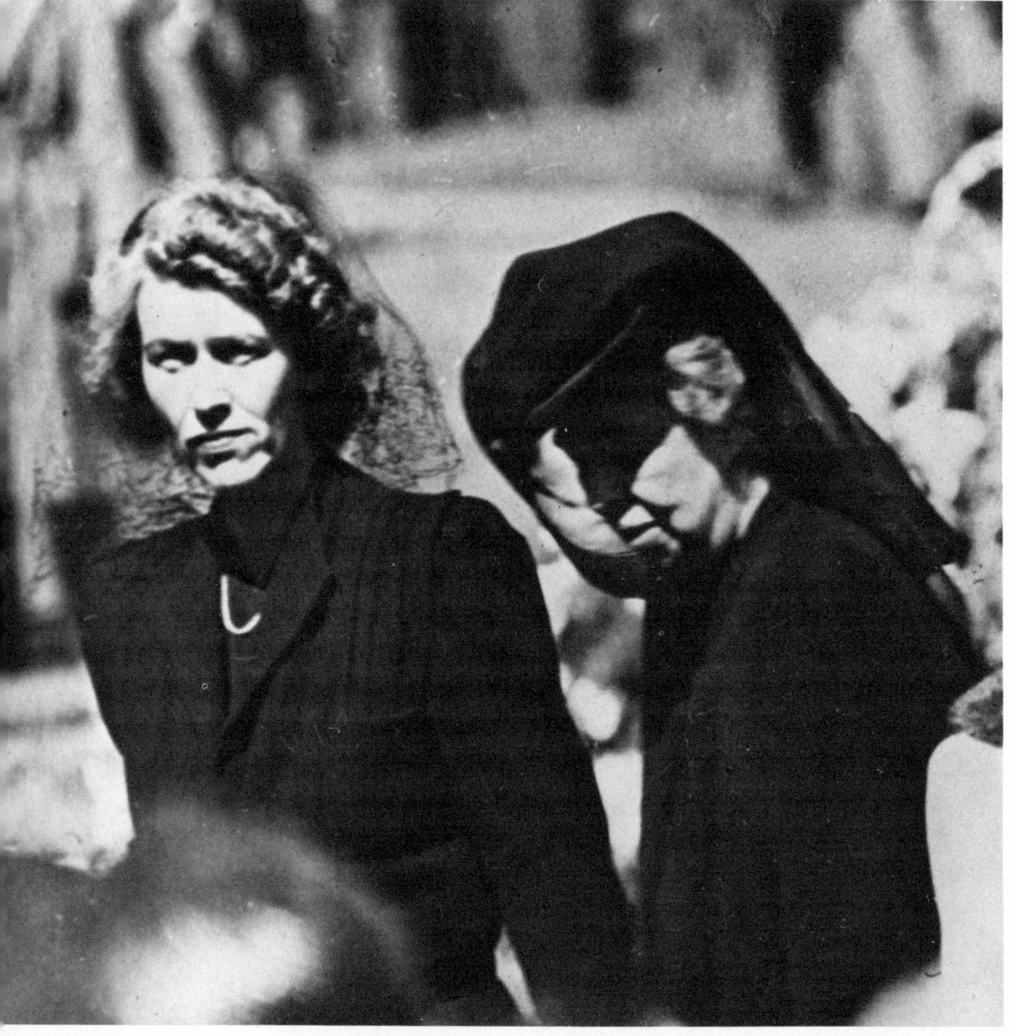

accompany him on earlier such trips, and in January, 1945, had still not wholly lost her gall at being the only member of her family excluded from the great events of the war. Given the progress of battle in Europe and the Far East, it seemed clear that this would be the last and most significant of those dramatic wartime conferences of the Allied heads of state. She was desperately anxious to go, she recalled, and enormously excited as she left Washington with the presidential party on January 22. She wrote John that she wished they were both going, but she clearly relished the opportunity finally to have an adventure of her own.

During the strenuous days of his meetings with Churchill and Stalin, Anna took particular—and, when necessary, insistent—care to see that her father had sufficient rest. She watched him sometimes tire suddenly, and worried, as she wrote John, about those occasions when "he gets all wound up, seems to thoroughly enjoy it all, but wants too many people around, and then won't go to bed early enough. The result is that he doesn't sleep well." She feared that his heart was vulnerable, and must have been distressed to see the gauntness of his face.

Anna returned to the White House—and to a grateful husband—at the end of February. About to turn six, I had been sick intermittently since my mother had left, and had been an obstreperous handful at other times. Both parents agreed, plausibly, that my anxiety at my mother's long absence might well have been responsible. But as it turned out I was seriously ill, and was moved from the White House to the naval hospital in Bethesda, Maryland, on April 4. My mother had hoped to take me with her and accompany her father to Warm Springs in late March, but that plan was abandoned as my condition worsened. Despite my grandfather's evident exhaustion as he left for Warm Springs, Eleanor wrote, "most of us were still far more worried about little Johnny than we were about Franklin, who, we felt, would find in Warm Springs the healing it had always brought him in the past."

But in the middle of the afternoon of April 12 Eleanor and Anna learned by telephone that the president had lost consciousness at his desk in Warm Springs and had been carried to his bedroom. My mother had promised to be with me at the hospital that afternoon, and insistently told Admiral Ross McIntire, FDR's personal physician, "I tell you, I've got to go out." She had not been with me more than twenty minutes when someone drew her out of the room and told her a car was waiting to return her to the White House. "Nothing more was said, but I knew the end had come."

My mother did not speak much to us of her experience of those next days: the funeral service in the White House; the painful encounter with her mother's cold anger after Eleanor learned that Lucy had been at Warm Springs when the president died and at the White House on several occasions when Anna acted as hostess; her father's burial in the rose garden at Hyde Park. She wrote to one of her children long afterward: "It was such an unbelievably difficult time in so many different ways!" Some lines in her story about "The Place"—her childhood home—come again to mind: "Then, without warning, fate struck down the man about whom all of the Place revolved, and who loved it as it seemed to love him. In those grief stricken days she was too numbed to take in fully the significance of all the changes this meant. And almost immediately she went away."

Of one time during those days my mother did write, years later. "I'll never forget that train trip to Hyde Park for the burial. The private car that Father had used for so many years was once more the last car on the train. As usual, the Secret Service had assigned staterooms and berths to each individual. I've never known who assigned it to me, but I was given Father's stateroom. All night I sat on the foot of that berth and watched the people who had come to see the train pass by. There were little children, mothers, fathers, grandparents. They were there at eleven at night, at two in the morning, at four—at all hours during that long night."

Among the letters she received at the time of her father's death, there was one which she kept close by her for the rest of her life, showing it only on a few occasions, in privacy, to those for whom she had a special trust and care, and to whom she wished to convey something of herself for which she had no words of her own. Perhaps no one other than Lucy could have confirmed the father-love she so treasured, first and to the end, and the depth of her loss.

Aiken, South Carolina
May 9, 1945

Anna dear—Your telephoning the other night meant much to me. I did not know that it was in me just now to be so glad to hear the sound of any voice—and to hear you laugh—was beyond words, wonderful.

I had not written before for many many reasons—but you were constantly in my thoughts and with very loving and heart torn sympathy and I was following every step of the way. This blow must be crushing to you—to all of you—but I know that you meant more to your Father than anyone and that makes it closer and harder to bear. It must have been an endless comfort to you that you were *able* to be with him so much this past year. Every second of the day you must be conscious of the void and emptiness. Where there has always been—all through your life—the strength of his beloved presence—so filled with loving understanding—so ready to guide and to help.

I love to think of his very great pride in you and can still hear his voice speaking on a different note when he would say "Hello, Girl—how is Johnny". He was so distressed about his little grandson and so concerned about you and your terrible anxiety. He told me so often and with such feeling of all that you had meant of joy and comfort on the trip to Yalta. He said you had been so extraordinary and what a difference it made to have you. He told me of your charm and your tact—and of how *everyone* loved you. He told how capable you were and how you forgot nothing and of the little typewritten chits he would find at his place at the beginning or end of the day, reminding him of all the little or big things that he was to do. I hope he told *you* these things, but sometimes one doesn't. In any case you must have known—words were not needed between you. I have been reading over some very old letters of his and in one he says: "Anna is a dear fine person—I wish so much that you knew her." Well, now we do know one another, and it is a great joy to me, and I think he was happy this past year that it was so. He was so wonderful about all of the others too, and when after this last Inauguration I saw how wonderfully well he had looked—like a flash he said "but didn't you think *James* looked well". He was so thrilled when Elliott's promotion went thru, and so proud that Franklin had his own destroyer to command. He was looking forward so to having a ball for Sistie at the White House, even though she might be a year or so too young to come out. He also talked of the difference it made having your husband there, and how really devoted he was to him and what a help he was in so many many ways. And through it all one hears his ringing laugh and one thinks of all the ridiculous things he used to say—and do—and enjoy. The picture of him sitting, waiting for you that night with the Rabbi's cap on his extraordinarily beautiful head, is still vivid.

The world has lost one of the greatest men that ever lived—to me, the greatest. He towers above them all, effortlessly, and even those who openly opposed him seem shocked into the admission of his greatness. Now he is at peace, but he knew even before the end, that the task was well done.

It is a sad inescapable truth that you will now suffer in the sense and measure of your love which was so great. No one can spare you that. Your husband will be your strength, and your children who need you so, but it must all seem meaningless and unbearable.

Forgive me for writing of things which you know so much better than I, and which are sacred, and should not even be touched on by a stranger. I somehow cannot feel myself to be that, and I feel strongly that you understand.

My love to your husband, and to you, Anna darling, because you are his child and because you are yourself.

I am very devotedly and with heartbroken sympathy

Lucy Rutherfurd

For my parents' marriage, too, the death of FDR marked the end of an era—of that whole first tumultuous, anxious, inspired time in which they had existed so pre-eminently in his living shadow. My mother had known that life all along, though in ways that had changed markedly as her father grew in public stature and power. For John Boettiger that life had been almost wholly new, and his vulnerability to its impact had been very great. Their challenge now, individually and together, was to find their own way without "the Old Man," to live beyond—in one historian's apt phrase—the Age of Roosevelt. It is ironic, perhaps, but hardly unnatural, that Anna proved more successful in that venture than John.

## TWENTY-ONE

# "It Still Seems So Incredible"

A FEW weeks before my mother's death in the autumn of 1975 she had a simple dream that moved her deeply —so much in fact that she asked her family to gather around her bed to hear it. By then she knew that she was dying of cancer. She lay in a tiny, bare room in a large New York hospital. Her window looked out upon the brick walls of another hospital. Surrounded by the paraphernalia with which well-intentioned doctors seek to sustain the life and relieve the pain of their patients, she longed for a different relief beyond the province of medicine. Her dream had restored a momentary vividness to her face, and as she told it her hands moved with characteristic expressiveness. In the dream she was living alone in a small cottage secluded in the woods. Her only companions were the creatures of the forest and the colorful flowers which surrounded the cottage. She felt at peace there.

That brief dream, uniquely expressive of her dying, was perhaps also the last expression of a theme as central as any in her living.

"I'd like to have some small place somewhere, the kind of place we can turn the key and leave without a qualm, but some place we would think of as 'home.' . . . I honestly have nothing definite in mind—its just a huge vague hope that our years together in the future may be fraught with fewer worries and less hecticness; work, yes definitely, and together or at least in similar type of work; and more time to loll as US wants to loll—whether it be on a cruise, or riding the range or getting pie-eyed and dancing too close on a dance floor! And I don't give a damn *where* all this takes place, just so long as it *does* take place!!"

So Anna wrote John of her hopes for their postwar future, shortly after he had left for North Africa and she and the children had returned to Seattle alone in 1943. "The crux of everything," she added a few days later, "is that I want to get to you at the earliest moment, that I want a life with the least possible amount of 'non-essentials', responsibilities, etc."

My mother was aware that her thoughts were "colored by present circumstances": the loneliness of her return to Seattle without my father, her exclusive responsibility for the three children still at home, and her disappointment with her colleagues and work at the *P-I*. But she expressed in those lines a profound hope, deeply reflective of her nature: a hope imbedded in her moments of happiness as a child in the woods and fields of Hyde Park; a hope of escaping the shadow of prominence, of public life and social responsibility, that had so burdened and complicated her adult years. She felt a no less deep-seated loyalty to her father, and to his presidency. It was not that she wished to abandon her identity as Anna Roosevelt, but rather that she hoped to bear that identity—its pleasures and its inevitable stresses, its security and its obligations—more quietly and privately, with more freedom to choose her own companionship and less of the anxiety that public occasions so consistently provoked.

And above all she wanted to find a way for a renewal of her and John's love and life together. It was, of course, a wish they shared—the most prominent and passionate theme in the hundreds of letters they exchanged during the war. They agreed that they had let their professional and public responsibilities crowd in upon them during the increasingly stressful Seattle years, and that the spontaneity and growth of their marriage had suffered. But while John first wrote of his awareness that they had cheated themselves—"US"—during those six and a half years, it was Anna who conveyed more insight into their choices and feelings, and who emerged with a more solidly grounded wish to avoid a repetition of their mistakes.

She had chosen to submerge her fears, to attribute all of their prewar troubles—including my father's "spells" and "inhibitions"—to their harried circumstances, but her worry about him nonetheless emerged in the strenuousness of her hope: "Darling, there's another thing I hope so desperately hard you agree with me about, and that is that neither of us ever want to be 'big shots' in either a big or a little puddle."

My father's wartime letters convey a similar wish. The war had taught him, he said, "that you have but one life to live and you owe it to yourself to live it sanely and wisely and *not* to engage in nerve-wracking, long-houred enterprises. . . . We were such damned fools not to reserve more time for each other and for relaxing." But their visions of a postwar life together were in fact significantly different. Both spoke of the freedom to travel and the need to keep free of too burdensome responsibilities, but my mother's central image was still of "some small place somewhere," while my father was more intrigued by movement and change. He didn't, in fact, look much beyond the immediate end of the war, suggesting the possibility of a year of travel as roving correspondents covering "the immensely interesting and important things that will be going on in foreign places" and getting "into all the hot situations around the globe." Or, he wrote, "You might give thought to the possibility of our staying in the army awhile, doing the reconstruction end of things, but making certain that we can be and work together." He recognized "the problem of the kids, but I've got an idea or two on that subject and I think you will agree it is not insurmountable."

My mother's response to his ideas was cautious—probably in fact more dubious than she was willing, at that time and distance, to say. Still, her query has some edge: "What do you mean by the possibility of 'our' staying in the army after the war, awhile . . . ?" She said the roving correspondent idea "appeals no end," but then added: "anything so we can be TOGETHER." About the children they probably were of fairly similar mind: the two elder would be in boarding school and would, therefore, no longer need continuous care. "That leaves Johnny as a definite responsibility for a good many years to come," my mother wrote, "but I am convinced that Johnny is adaptable and that it really makes no difference *where* he lives just so long as we have him with us most of the time."

My parents and I left Washington, D.C., for our long-neglected home in Seattle on June 8, 1945, picking up Sis and Buzz from their boarding schools on the way. John told an old friend that they wanted to buy a newspaper in Seattle or somewhere in the Pacific Northwest, or perhaps start an advertising agency in the region. They and William Randolph Hearst had agreed to disagree—with FDR's death Hearst wanted to re-establish control of his now profitable newspaper in Seattle—and they were pleased by the financial settlement made with Hearst Publications, Inc.: $40,000 to John, and $15,000 to Anna. Added to their existing savings, it probably gave them a nest egg of something like $100,000, with which they hoped to attract further capital for purchase of an established paper.

They had in fact offered to buy the *P-I*, and anticipated that declining prices and poor management would change Hearst's mind in a year or so. But the next months brought no indication of a reversal in the trend to high profits in the newspaper industry. "Sooner or later," John wrote his brother Bill, "there will be a recession in these profits, and the present owners may then come down to earth. But to purchase any of the existing papers [in the Seattle-Tacoma region] today would mean about the same as buying things at 1929 prices." Through the fall and into the winter of 1945 he and Anna continued to look without success. Prices were too high, and the idea of starting a newspaper from scratch was not an attractive one, as John explained to his brother: "we would not be foolish enough to try to start a new venture—which would require all kinds of capital and involve risks of failure. . . . The problems of starting from scratch—minus good comics, good columnists, the AP, etc.—are pretty severe, and it would take a lot of time and heart breaking effort to make a go of it."

But within another few months he and my mother were to undertake just such a new venture from scratch; and the risks and costs he so accurately anticipated were in fact to prove catastrophic. It is not easy to explain how their minds changed so radically in such a short span of time. At the center of any explanation would very likely be what John referred to at the time as his and Anna's restlessness. It was mostly his own—as one might have guessed from the differences in their wartime images of a postwar life—and restlessness was probably too mild a word.

He had, he wrote Eleanor, "to go back to 1921 for my last time without a flood of work ahead of me constantly." (Momentarily he had forgotten the similarly painful weeks of waiting in North Africa just two years before.) He felt increasingly at a loss without "a specific business responsibility" and a "clear cut program for our old age!" He tried to remain lighthearted, immersed himself in the tasks of restoring the house that had gone considerably to seed in their absence, and expanded the area of their search for newspapers. But he was evidently struggling against a powerful resurgence of those depressive tendencies that had begun to manifest themselves before the war. In origin, no doubt, they were very old tendencies related to the convictions of inferiority which he remembered torturing him as a child, and whose lingering he admittted: feelings for which the "flood of work" and the public recognition of his competence had always served as a tolerable defense.

But in his forties, somehow, those defenses got out of hand, and while he could still perhaps believe otherwise, by late 1945 I think he was running scared. No one knows just what happened, or how, for he did not—could not—speak clearly, even to my mother, of the changes in his mind; and the manner of impressive warmth and charm and competence was still intact. If there was a critical event, it was probably FDR's death, though had my father's last frantic publishing adventure succeeded, he might well have recovered his earlier balance. That balance became precarious in the prewar Seattle years, as he struggled to cope with the enormously seductive prominence of his identity as the president's son-in-law. He experienced himself moving at unaccustomed altitude where, one might fairly say, the air was thin, the company few, and the visibility very high. Whatever the increasingly severe stresses of that life, it was its collapse that precipitated a more severe crisis. He returned to Seattle in 1945, his public identity mostly defined by what he was no longer, mistrusted by the region's political leadership (who suspected him of rivalrous ambitions), with little in the way of supportive friendship that outlasted the years of fair weather, and a distressing need to prove himself a man of as considerable consequence in others' eyes as he had been.

It was that need, attached to his surviving spirit of adventure and his and my mother's enduring wish to be on their own in common enterprise, that precipitated a decision contradicting all of my father's better judgment, and most of the lessons supposedly learned during the war. Late in 1945 he wrote Bill, "we have been invited to start a daily newspaper in a western city. . . . There is no going concern, no plant, no presses—nothing." It is hardly a promising announcement. Six weeks later, the commitment made, his words were more optimistic, but his tone decidedly lacks the buoyant confidence of earlier adventures: "It is a task which is much to our liking, although it will take a great deal of time and effort."

They bought a small shopping news—a free distribution weekly—then occupying a little gray frame house on North First Avenue in Phoenix, Arizona, with the intention of converting it into a daily newspaper. Phoenix was a growing city, but politically conservative and possessed of two established daily newspapers run by the same well-funded organization. It would not be an easy market to enter, and prices—for plant, presses, equipment, newsprint, staff, all the manifold resources needed to start a major newspaper—were still very high. Anna wrote Sis at Reed College in March, 1946: "Right now (or rather up to now) we have financed our newspaper by ourselves. If all goes according to the plans we've laid out, the newspaper will carry itself until we have to build a small plant and buy a press. This will mean borrowing money. And, we cannot expect any personal income from the newspaper for at least a year. . . . All of this means only one thing, and that is that we must all be very careful of every penny we spend."

Anna, for all the soberness of her advice that Sis find a job waiting on tables to pay for her incidental expenses at school, may in fact have been more sanguine about the tasks ahead than John, and found access, within herself, to some of their old adventuresome spirit. She wrote her mother in May, 1946, a few days before the household move from Seattle to Phoenix: "We need all the good luck you sent us. . . . We're certainly up to our eyes in adventures and work. And, there will be plenty of battles, also, because it's quite obvious . . . that new newspapers in Phoenix are not welcomed by present publishers—and that our brand of newspaper will not be welcomed by the 'big guys'! . . . But, it makes it all the more exciting, and imperative to succeed."

They bought a large rambling, Spanish-style house on the outskirts of Phoenix, and went to work, as Anna put it, "like beavers—all hours of the day and night." At first, the frenetic pace of life seemed again, as in Seattle, to obscure and compensate my father's distress. The première issue of the weekly *Arizona Times* was on the newsstands the morning of June 27, 1946, and Anna wrote Marie Donogh that "it's all great fun and everything is going wonderfully well." The new plant was built and in use by early October, the big press erected and at work a month later. The *Times* went twice weekly in October, then three times a week, and on May 1, 1947, began to publish daily evening editions. But earlier that spring it had become clear that the paper, which had already sought and secured additional borrowed money, was again in need. On April 9 Anna, who was visiting her mother in New York, wrote an extraordinary letter to John, an acknowledgment of her awareness of how deeply entangled were the future of their endangered paper and the future of their marriage, and a ringing reaffirmation of her commitment to both.

My darling, you are about to board a plane for Seattle, where you may be requested by one or two of our prospective investors in our Arizona Times, to pledge my future inheritance as additional collatoral. I am only writing this note because I know, from all you've said, that you do not agree with me that we should do this.

On the contrary, I feel this way: You should bargain with the buzzards up to the hilt (or to the limit of their telling "us" to go to hell). After that you must give concessions that you deem necessary. *And*, if those concessions entail of money which I will inherit directly from Father's estate . . . then I *want* to gamble that inheritance in this project of ours. Why? Because I have unbounded confidence in YOU, and in "US" as a team. I fully accept the "dare" to "US" to succeed, and what's more, I love it!

Our children (and Johnny's training will be the same) have been trained to stand on their own feet, and I do not feel that . . . we owe them more than that.

Don't ever forget this trust and confidence I have in YOU! Above all—I LOVE YOU—but I also mean every word I've written above!

*Your* Anna

John and Anna examine a type form at their just purchased *Phoenix Shopping News*, February 25, 1946. *Phoenix Chamber of Commerce*

Buzz, John, Anna, and Sis probably in the summer of 1946.

The additional money thereby secured—without any pledging of my mother's inheritance—served but to delay the demise of the *Arizona Times*. By the autumn of 1947 the paper was losing $30,000 a month, and it seemed evident to Anna and John and to their principal investors that the venture was in grave danger of failing.

For my father the effect was both crushing and bleakly confirming. He had attached to the *Times* his remaining hopes to recoup his loss of confidence and public consequence, as well as his hope of resisting the downward pull of depression. But those hopes were deeply shrouded even in the first moments of his commitment to Phoenix. In that dim light, the failing of the *Times* only confirmed the experience of personal failure whose fatefulness had so long weighed heavily on him. His diffuse anger and his conviction of defeat brought renewed and severe distress to their marriage, as Anna's response to the *Times*'s losses was remarkably different in spirit. She would not write Eleanor of the extent of the strain and conflict between them, but she did share with her mother a vivid portrait of their contrasting moods:

"John has been terribly upset and pessimistic for a long time now, and I know he will be relieved to be out of it. He is not built to enjoy that kind of a risk when it's someone else's money he's gambling with. To me, it is more disappointing than I can tell you. I love a fight against a reactionary monopoly, and I hate to see the latter winning out in so many fields of endeavor in this country today. . . . While most of the public don't know it, they have fewer and fewer newspapers in this country today which they can depend on to be truthful. The whole damn newspaper business has simply become 'big business.' "

It is a response reminiscent of her father's spirited opposition to such "reactionary monopolies," and it was no doubt from his paternity, as well as from her mother's extraordinary capacity to stand alone, that Anna drew her own remarkable strength in that year in which her love, her marriage, her very world, were falling apart around her.

Although my parents were not legally separated until the summer of 1948, and divorced the following year, their marriage was effectively destroyed during the heartbreaking course of 1947. In the spring of that year Anna at least still had a vivid faith in John and in their life and work together. But over the next seven months my father's despair grew markedly, and with it came erratic outbursts of anger and bitter opposition to Anna's continuing efforts to save the paper and seek further refinancing.

In reflecting on the history of their struggle for the *Times*, Anna recognized that John's spirit had never really been in it. She knew, but could hardly bring herself to admit, that his defeatism was not a function of advertising lineage, circulation figures, or the availability of newsprint. In a letter to Buzz at the end of October she referred to "our very dear but gloomy Pops. . . . Just like last spring, last summer, and long before that, he is *sure* the property cannot be made to pay. And, as per usual, we have spent hour after hour arguing and getting nowhere. It's very sad." They argued about the paper—Anna wanting to carry on, to find new ways to extend its life, John profoundly shaken, wanting to close up and get out—but implicitly, with just those words, they were talking about themselves, about the prospects for their marriage and the prospect of life itself. Love and death still struggled in John's romantic soul, but the wish to die was growing stronger.

In his own suffering, the pain and fright he caused Anna was enormous. His desperation, his black moods and angry recriminations and sleeplessness, led Anna to believe that his mental health was deteriorating, and even to fear for her own physical safety. She begged him again to undertake psychiatric treatment, but he refused.

Under the circumstances, she could have little if any expectation of a reversal in his pervasive sense of defeat. Feeling battered by their bitter arguments, Anna held fast to a scrap of hope that the *Times*—their once common venture—might yet survive. And she feared that in his black pessimism John would pull the paper down with him.

Desperate herself by November, she finally prevailed on him to go away: to leave her to care for their home, their young son, and their ailing newspaper, and to find in rest and travel, if he could, some respite from his distress and destructiveness. So on December 1, 1947, my father left our home in Phoenix. While he returned for a few days at Christmas, and briefly the following summer for Sis's wedding, that was in effect the end. The marriage that had begun on such a note of high romance nearly thirteen years before was over.

Such strong and tangled ties, of course, are never cleanly severed, and neither Anna nor John knew that their marriage was finished in the winter of 1947. Indeed, he pleaded with her almost immediately to allow him to return, that he might do his part to redeem their life together. He wrote her from a friend's ranch in Rimrock, Arizona, on December 11: "I have had plenty of time to think since I have been away from you. . . . It has brushed some of the cobwebs away, and out of it all has come a clearer thinking and a firm resolution. . . .

"I can see now, more clearly than before, the mistakes I have made, the unhappiness I have inflicted on you so many times in the past. . . . I'm terribly sorry for every minute of grief and worry I've caused you.

"I want to make it up to you, and I want to do this more than anything I've ever wanted on this earth. . . .

"I was tired, Baby, and worried overlong. I don't want to dwell on this, but it went back to the Hearst days, before the war, and it's been years since I could see a clear light ahead of US. . . .

"You will not again be troubled by a defeatism in me. I have licked it, will lick it if it shows its head again, and helping me to that end will be the fight I want to make for US."

However real his sorrow and his resolution—and she did not doubt that—Anna had lived with him too long, had been too hurt and angered, too scared by the ominous depth and power of his depression, to believe that such protestations and promises bore likelihood of real change. She was too mistrustful to contemplate so soon his again living or working under the same roof with her. And then there was more to suffer. At some point after he left, she was told by one of their *Times* colleagues that John had been seeing another woman during those last excruciating months that they were together. She remembered the words for the rest of her life: "Anna dear, we didn't dare tell you." The hurt of knowing was compounded by the knowledge that others had known and kept it from her. She had told herself twenty-four years before, when Eleanor confided the pain of her experience of Franklin's love affair with Lucy Mercer, "here I was growing up, and probably going to get married and have a family, and was this something that I was going to have to face? . . . I think I was probably putting myself a little fearfully into Mother's shoes."

She threw herself with renewed fervor into a last-ditch effort to save the *Times*, and my father traveled in search of newspaper work elsewhere. In the spring and early summer of 1948 he spent four months in eastern and southern Europe collecting material for a series of news stories and perhaps a book. But he could not find work; his now chronic underlying despair plagued his efforts and subtly conveyed itself to others. In a letter he wrote to Anna on June 1, 1949, but did not mail, he contemplated the time since their separation: "I hated being alive. I had no incentive to make anything of myself. I couldn't work. The wonderful stories I obtained in Europe wouldn't come out of my mind or my typewriter. I knew I had ability, but there are times when incentive is killed, and no driving or forcing can bring it back."

His old comradeship with his brother Bill was renewed during those lonely months. He wrote Bill a year later: "I only wish I could drop in on you once in awhile, as I did so often, and with such comforting results. You will never know quite how low my spirits fell, and you and Grace were there with exactly the right morale medicine for me and I'll always be grateful." Once, probably in 1948, the two brothers took Bill's old Ford up into the mountains above San Diego to spend several days talking about John's prospects and ways of finding work together. They spoke of seeking their fortunes in the Rockies, and Bill even suggested that the two of them might buy and run a gas station; anything, he felt, if it had a chance of raising the curtain of depression that had fallen over his brother. But John was not to be moved. He told Bill that he'd studied various religions during his lonely moments, and that he'd been unable to find comfort in any of them. He even had several conversations with a Catholic priest, evidently to no avail. While his old romanticism and his devotion to Bill lent a wishfulness to thoughts of working together, he felt constrained by his past achievements and prominence. He could contemplate the kind of modest ventures of which they talked, he said, only if he could abandon his name and identity, and thus avoid the shame of recognition. He had come too far, and could not turn around.

When Anna had finally to give up on the *Arizona Times*, and moved to Los Angeles with Buzz and me in the summer of 1948, John continued crisscrossing the country in a fruitless search for newspaper work. He wrote her, with an effort at humor, in early 1949: "I have pursued every clue, every friend (and some pseudo friends) that I could think of in the East, and so far at least I seem to have one huge jinx on me. I'm about to buy a crop of rabbit feet, witches' powders, magic potions and whatnots. I might as well go crazy in that direction, because if I don't settle down soon I'll go crazy anyhow!" Finally in March he found work as a consultant developing a Sunday edition for a newspaper in Lake Charles, Louisiana: "At least for a little while I'll have a roof over my head and a place to hang my hat."

Meanwhile he had begun to press Anna for a divorce. Her attitude toward him through the months since their separation had been sympathetic but cool. The potency of the hurt and mistrust he had provoked in 1947 was very great, and in his condition there was little he could do that was likely to restore her shattered faith. In her own mind she would not rule out the possibility—perhaps even the hope—of reconciliation, but she had withdrawn into something akin to her wartime "alone poise," and would not allow him near enough to hurt her again. So his efforts to renew their relationship had met with what he experienced as humiliating rebuff. And the stage was set for renewed and mutual bitterness as John turned to seek a divorce.

In the wake of a particularly painful discussion with him in the spring of 1949, Anna wrote her daughter: "he is so adamant on the divorce and on money matters. He has now persuaded himself that the entire Arizona experience was my fault and that therefore the

Father and son: our last visit in Los Angeles during the summer of 1949, the year before his death.

debts incurred are mine alone . . . all the next day I went around feeling like a whipped puppy because as I listened and as I thought it over afterwards it was so hard to realize that this was the same guy I was so terrifically in love with and thought I would be with as long as I lived. Of course, I've made many, many mistakes too. But it still seems so incredible that human beings who once loved each other can get to almost hate each other."

The job in Lake Charles was a temporary one, and my father left it after three months to work for the New York public relations firm of Theodor Swanson & Co. Despite his care and respect for those with whom he worked, the world of public relations was not one in which he could be easy, even in better days. He felt "ill adjusted and unable to exert what abilities I possess to real advantage."

Something else, though, must be said of his choice to marry again, just one year before he took his life. His decision to marry Virginia—a beautiful woman whose romantic soul matched his own—may well have been a genuine reach for recovery and renewal. Though their relationship could not have been without stress and pain, it must also have brought him devoted companionship and some surcease of the despair that had so shadowed his life during its last decade. I know that she loved him deeply. But the depth of his melancholy was profound. His failure, and that of his Swanson colleagues, to find clients to sustain the firm, and the prospect of a renewed search for meaningful employment, were too painful, too reminiscent of earlier failures. His resources of hope for himself were exhausted. He had fought for years, "with all I could produce," he wrote my mother, against the decision to die; and he wished that those who cared for him might understand and accept that its time had come. For an eleven-year-old son it was much to ask.

For my mother it was the loss of him—the loss of that love she had known so absorbingly with him—that gave her great pain. His death was the last but not the worst moment in that long act of separation. Like her mother before her, she struggled and survived the loss of her love remarkably. "I decided to accept the fact that a man must be what he is, life must be lived as it is . . . and you cannot live at all if you do not learn to adapt yourself to your life as it happens to be." Those were Eleanor's words, but they might have been her daughter's as well.

In her later years Anna possessed a vivid blend of qualities familiar to those who had known her parents well. The strong, fine features of her face; a characteristic tilt of her head; her bold laugh and spirited, irreverent sense of humor; her attachment to the land, and love of identifying birds and trees on long woods rambles; her graceful diplomacy on social occasions and the many sorts of people with whom she enjoyed an easy informality—all of that, while distinctively her own, was also reminiscent of her extraordinary father. Her staunch dutifulness and lifelong anxiety in speechmaking and other public occasions; the strength and consistency of her commitment to human rights, and to ethical responsibility in government; her fear of anger and vulnerability to hurt by those she loved, and inclination to withdraw in the face of hurt—in these ways she was distinctively Eleanor Roosevelt's daughter. In her political realism and her emotional reticence she was close kin to both her parents. And, of course, there were qualities of her personality that were notably shaped by the unique course of her growth as an adult and not particularly shared with either parent. I think of her wish to live a mostly private, secluded life (always mixed with the attraction and responsibility of the Roosevelt tradition), and of her interest in the subtleties and perplexing changes in personal relationships and individual human lives.

In short, my mother lived on, through and beyond the loss of my father and the love they knew. Indeed, she lived remarkably well for another twenty-five years, and came to possess a mature integrity that was a great gift to those who knew her. But the loss also endured. She once told my wife, on a cold, gray morning in a countryside not far from her beloved Hyde Park, that when John Boettiger left, when their love had died, a part of her own life spirit had died as well.